STYLES IN FICTIONAL STRUCTURE

STYLES
IN FICTIONAL
STRUCTURE

The Art of
Jane Austen
Charlotte Brontë
George Eliot

BY KARL KROEBER

PRINCETON UNIVERSITY PRESS

PRINCETON, NEW JERSEY

1971

Publication of this book has been aided by
The John Simon Guggenheim
Memorial Foundation

This book has been set in Linotype Times Roman
and IBM Composer Press Roman
Printed in the United States of America
by Princeton University Press

*This book is gratefully dedicated
to the many graduate students
in the Department of English
at the University of Wisconsin
who have studied fiction with me*

Acknowledgments

THREE INDIVIDUALS among those to whom this book is dedicated must be singled out for special thanks. Professor Mary Jane Power, now at the University of New Mexico, was a co-originator of the project which gave rise to this book, and both her tireless labor at tedious details and her unflagging ebullience of spirit kept our work going at many critical moments. Professor Martha Vicinus, currently acting editor of *Victorian Studies* at Indiana University, regularly combined accurate analyses with a persistent questioning of the philosophic implications of what we were doing. Professor Richard Pacholski at Wisconsin State University at Whitewater was a tower of sardonic dependability in all practical matters. What I owe most to these friends, and the many other students with whom I was associated while laboring on this book, is the stimulation of their intellectual curiosity and the example of their cheerful enthusiasm in debating ideas and exploring new methods of criticism.

My distinguished colleague Professor G. T. Tanselle assisted me in some early probes into grammatical analysis before seeing the handwriting on the wall and returning to the enduring truths of bibliography. The subtle critical mind of Professor Martin Meisel, now at Columbia University, doubtless shaped many of my ideas about fiction during our conversations walking homeward under the leafless trees of wintry Madison. Jerry Jacobson of the IBM Corporation did his best for us when we attempted electronics, struggling with the recalcitrance of an immature computer and our technological imbecility. To Mrs. Nandita Ghosh, most gaily dressed and merriest of keypunchers, I owe, among other things, my introduction to Bengali cooking.

I am grateful to the United States Office of Education for a grant which made possible an exploration into the possible use of computers in the study of literary style. The negative results of that undertaking doubtless contributed to some positive results in this one. A substantial portion of Chapter Two appeared as "Perils of Quantification: The Exemplary Case of Jane Austen's *Emma*" in *Statistics and Style*, edited by Lubomír Doležel and Richard W. Bailey for the American Elsevier Company (New York, 1969), and I wish to thank both editors and publisher for permission to reprint this material. A fellowship from the John Simon Guggenheim Memorial Foundation made possible the writing of the first draft of this book. Without grant-in-aid and research leave from the Research Committee of the Graduate School of the University of Wisconsin none of my work would have been possible. My former superior, Dean Robert A. Alberty, now Dean of Sciences at the Massachusetts Institute of Technology, encouraged me by the example of his character and mind—as well as by his generosity in releasing me (surely with relief) a year early from a three-year deanship. I'm happy to have this opportunity to salute Dean Eric Rude of the Wisconsin Graduate School, not alone for his humor and efficiency as an administrative colleague, but also for his skill at quietly subverting inconvenient regulations.

For the extra revision of one chapter I have to thank my small daughter Katharine, who destroyed the better part of the original, encouraging authorial *hubris* by showing no ill effects from eating part of it. Her grandmother sacrificed many hours to the unrewarding task of improving her son's style. To my wife I am most grateful for having managed to live through it all without losing either her cool or her figure.

Madison, Wisconsin
November 24, 1969

Contents

STYLES IN FICTIONAL STRUCTURE

CHAPTER I

Introduction

THE origin of this book lies, I believe, in a question I asked seminar students several years ago: How can one prove without reference to evidence outside the novels themselves that George Eliot's fiction was written after Charlotte Brontë's? The question and the unsatisfactory answers it provoked started me thinking about how little we understand—indeed, how seldom we try to understand—the *aesthetic* history of fiction. There are plenty of "histories" of the novel, but the "history" is usually little more than chronological ordering, with the chronology evaluated in terms of the conventions of sociopolitical history.

I have found, furthermore, few attempts to compare and contrast novels by different authors systematically. Most of the best critical studies concentrate upon investigation into the work of a single writer or even into the writing of a single novel. The studies which treat of several authors, or at least several novels, tend to take the form of unconnected analyses, although recently critics such as Donovan and Lodge[1] have endeavored to develop systematically comparative evaluations. A few scholars have done useful work tracing particular traditions, although the traditions are often rather arbitrarily defined. Most arbitrary of all is Dr. F. R. Leavis, who has done more than any other modern critic to stimulate original criticism of fiction. Although I share several of Dr. Leavis' preferences among British novelists, I find his *Great Tradition* a somewhat intellectually ramshackle façade for the exhibition of his often exciting, usually illuminating, prejudices.

The truth is that little attention has been directed to the possibility of building up an objective, cumulatively rewarding discipline of studies in fictional styles. Most criticism of novels

[1] Full reference to and brief comment upon these and other general works will be found in the Bibliographical Appendix.

in the past generation or two has been fundamentally, though not always overtly, polemical. The argumentativeness is understandable, because until recently even such significant innovators as Henry James and James Joyce needed to be defended, and vigorous defense provokes counterattacks. By now, however, the arguments have served their purpose. We should be directing our energies not toward debate but toward the definition of intrinsic processes in the history of fiction.

By "intrinsic processes" I mean the strictly aesthetic systems which give coherence to the development of a particular kind of work of art. No one doubts that the arts, especially fiction, reflect the course of social and cultural history. Yet all the arts (as historians of the fine arts have been quickest to recognize) possess a history of their own, a system of continuity and innovation which is to some degree independent of, often surprisingly resistive to, the influence of social transformations. The Greek potters of antiquity persisted in decorating their wares in a consistent fashion throughout centuries of social and political turmoil. To identify the probable date of manufacture of a Greek vase one must understand the history not of politics but of vase decoration. In a word, one must understand style.

In this book I am concerned with fictional style. Unfortunately, if the investigations into novels and novelists have too often been polemically biased, fictional style has simply been ignored. There are a great many studies of literary style and even a substantial number of studies of prose style, but it is difficult to turn up a single modern work which systematically attacks the special problems of fictional styles— although, because the word is modish, there are a damnable number of essays and books about fiction which employ "style" in their titles.

One reason for this omission is that specialists in literary style (or what is sometimes called stylistics) have plainly been daunted by the bulk of most novels. I can testify that work on fictional style is time-consuming, as well as messy and frustrating. Yet my work has taught me one lesson: although novels are written in prose, fictional prose style is quite different from nonfictional prose style. The methods of investigation as well as the results of one kind of study are only rarely of use to the other. To cite a simple, specific difference: an analysis of fictional style which does not take account of the difference between prose that is part of narrative and prose that is part of dialogue will be of limited value; whereas a distinction between narrative and dialogue is usually unimportant in a study of nonfictional prose.

A larger difference has never been adequately clarified. The investigator of nonfictional prose is primarily interested in defining the style of a person: What is, say, Matthew Arnold's style? The investigator of fictional style is primarily interested in defining the style of a work of art: What is, say, the style of *Tom Jones*? The distinction holds even when, as in this work, all the novels of one or more novelists are being investigated. To an investigator of fictional style, a name, Jane Austen, for example, is a shorthand term for a certain aesthetic unity which relates six particular novels more closely to one another than to other novels;[2] the name itself is of secondary importance. Such an investigator doesn't really care whether or not George Eliot's name was really Mary Ann Evans, or even whether or not George Henry Lewes was the true author and palmed off the novels from *Adam Bede* to *Daniel Deronda* as his wife's.[3]

[2] This means that investigation into the style of a literary art form is entirely different from investigation into a problem of authorship.

[3] Because the point has been so little discussed, it may be worthwhile to provide additional illustration. Even if fewer of the ancient Greek potters were anonymous, the character of stylistic studies of Greek vases would not be significantly changed. Evidence for this is provided by the occasions upon which the identity of an artist has become known, or widely recognized, only after an intense aesthetic coherence between works of art is discerned. Ghiselbertus, for most nonspecialists, is a case in point—although nobody who has visited Autun can doubt that Ghiselbertus is, in the modern phrase, "for real." So is the sixth-century Greek sculptor whose works are now prominently displayed in the Acropolis Museum in Athens. It seems to me that the desire to find a name, that is, some kind of human identity, to attach to admirable works of art is thoroughly understandable, and interest in the personalities of artists is certainly legitimate. For the student of styles of an art form, however, the artist is subordinate to his work.

5

In fine, I have found few guides or models to assist my efforts at understanding fictional style. Lack of such help, however, has encouraged me to innovate. The chapters which follow represent tentative (and, without doubt, sometimes ill-directed) experiments not only in defining more usefully the fictional styles of three novelists but also in establishing techniques through which it may be possible to create a viable and accumulatively significant humanistic subdiscipline: the history of fictional styles.

Because such a discipline does not now exist, I am able to do no more than propose and test certain methods, indicate the apparent inapplicability of others, and suggest possible results which might be produced by refinements and extensions of my procedures. It is not possible at this time to write a history of fictional style even for the first seventy-five years of the nineteenth century in Britain. As I implied above, critics both of the novel and of style have not yet established principles by which one can objectively and systematically compare and contrast the stylistic coherence of different novels. Until we can do this much we cannot hope to describe usefully the intrinsic processes of change and continuity which constitute the aesthetic history of fiction. In this book, therefore, my principal effort is directed toward developing means for making generally applicable stylistic comparisons and contrasts. I concentrate upon the novels of three authors, but the final value of this concentration will depend on whether or not it opens the way to analogous, but more precise and more penetrating, studies of many other novelists.

Because my area of specialization is the nineteenth century, I originally intended to examine the fiction of Walter Scott, Charles Dickens, and Henry James. But the bulk of these novelists' fiction made the undertaking appear impossible as a beginning study. The bulk of Jane Austen's, Charlotte Bronté's, and George Eliot's fiction is not so large and is contained within a briefer span of time. If Austen, Bronté, and Eliot are not as important as my original trio, the fact that they are women I reckon as appropriate. It is only with the emergence of fiction that women begin to contribute significantly to literary history. The history of poetry or drama would be little affected if all female writers were disregarded, but the history of fiction would be devastated.

More important, Austen, Brontë, and Eliot form a convenient sequence. Their works do not overlap. Each of the latter novelists read in the fiction of her predecessors, so we can assume some influence of the earlier novelists upon the later.[4] The trio is also attractive for other reasons. The work of all three has been subjected to considerable critical scrutiny. Austen and Eliot, in particular, have attracted excellent criticism and scholarship. I feel free, therefore, to concentrate on stylistic congruences and divergencies.

By including Charlotte Brontë's work I am able to touch upon the possible distinction between "novel" and "romance." This distinction as a tool of modern criticism was popularized by Northrop Frye's *Anatomy of Criticism* and Richard Chase's *The American Novel and Its Traditions*, both published in 1957. Chase used the distinction as a means of defining what he felt to be the characteristic difference between the main stream of American fiction and the main stream of British fiction. Whether the distinction is truly useful for finer discriminations remains to some degree doubtful. Frye observes that the best reason for discriminating between novels and romances is to encourage recognition of the integrity of a larger classification, "fiction," which subsumes both. Later critics have subdivided both the novel and the romance to the point where the multiplication of categories tends to obscure the clarification introduced by the original distinction. Nonetheless, some discrimination between the novel and the romance may be helpful to an understanding of fictional styles. Interest in the romance has in recent years permitted critics to give attention to writers who had previously been dismissed as minor. The total span of British fiction suggests an oscilla-

[4] "Influence" in a study of style is often most interesting "negatively." Where a point of contrast occurs between the work of an earlier writer and the work of a later writer known to have been acquainted with the earlier writer's art, we have the possibility of deliberate rejection. The "originality" of a writer is in large measure the pattern of his rejections of tradition and conventions.

tion between a tendency toward the romance and a tendency toward the novel. One may justifiably assume that a factor which distinguishes Charlotte Brontë's art from that of Jane Austen and George Eliot is her preference for romance. Although such an abstract distinction is neither the starting point nor the goal of my work, I hope that some of my analyses may contribute to a clarification of this potentially valuable division between basic forms of fiction.

I begin in the following chapter at the opposite pole from such a fundamental contrast with some limited and detailed analyses of vocabulary. Through these I try to illustrate the discouraging, perhaps insuperable, difficulties which attend not merely statistical but also all "objective" studies of fictional style. In Chapters Three and Four, however, I point up inadequacies in prevailing assumptions about "character" and "point of view," two of the principal subjects of "subjective" fictional criticism. The next two chapters return to matters of language. In Chapter Five consideration of Jane Austen's language is oriented toward illustration of the fact that a first-rate novelist evolves: study of a novelist's style ought to be regarded as examination of a changing, rather than a static, phenomenon. Although I recur to this point in Chapter Six, my central purpose there is to elucidate some aspects of fictional imagery which are usually overlooked. In Chapter Seven I deal briefly with the romance-novel distinction, both as a summary of earlier chapters and as a prelude to the final five, which describe my efforts to overcome, simultaneously, some of the obstacles to "objective" analyses discussed in Chapter Two and the inadequacies, for stylistic definitions, of presently available critical methods discussed in Chapters Three through Six. In Chapter Eight I try to validate my hypothesis that the form of any segment of a novel is to a significant degree determined by the total design of the novel as a whole. In Chapter Nine I describe some attempts at systematic analyses of "total designs." Results of these analyses are used in Chapter Ten as the basis for an examination of the stylistic features of limited, arbitrarily selected passages from three novels. In Chapter Eleven I pursue the examination down to the level of sentence-form, focusing on the importance of the structure of narrative-dialogue interaction. The four chapters Eight through Eleven should serve to substantiate a central thesis of my study: in a work of fiction, the most meaningful systematic stylistic comparisons and contrasts are those focused on the patterns of coherence between structural elements on different levels. In the final chapter I summarize my judgments of the three novelists' styles and of the potential rewards to be gained from further systematized studies of fictional structures.

The book will probably appear too long to anyone who reads it all. Even so, I am conscious of much I have omitted. To cite but one small example: my disregard of theories of fiction expounded and debated during the first seventy-five years of the nineteenth century, theories which indubitably influenced novel writing, limits the relevance of some of my observations.[5] As compensation I hope that, all hypotheses and methodologies aside, I convey some of the pleasure I have gained through intensive reading in the novels of Jane Austen, Charlotte Brontë, and George Eliot. Whatever my limitations as a critic may be, I am certain that no analysis can ever exhaust the richness of their art.

[5] It is necessary also to omit consideration of work in nonfictional forms, narrative poems, plays, and so forth, even when these were composed by one of my three authors. With Eliot at least this may be a serious omission. Her narrative poems, particularly *The Spanish Gypsy*, although virtually disregarded by critics, are important to her development as a novelist. Her play *Armgart* is most illuminating of some essential themes and image patterns in *Daniel Deronda*. And the long short stories *The Lifted Veil* and *Jacob's Brother* deserve careful critical attention. I have largely ignored Charlotte Brontë's juvenilia, in part because any discussion of it would involve me in considering the interrelations between her literary work and that of her sisters—a fascinating but intricate subject. Because I do not concern myself with Emily and Anne, in this study "Brontë" without an identifying Christian name refers to Charlotte.

CHAPTER II

Words in Fiction

To ANYONE seeking systematic and relatively objective methods for evaluating intrinsic relationships between works of fiction, the attraction of vocabulary analysis is strong. Words appear to be irreducible units which can be counted accurately and whose organizational patterns can be defined objectively. Unfortunately, there is no *necessary* relation between the frequency with which a specific word is used and its aesthetic significance. Prepositions, which are useful if one is trying to solve a problem of attribution, occur with great frequency in all novels; but study of "in" or "of" or "to" does not provide much insight into their artistic design. A word used only once may be very significant, or it may be exceedingly trivial.[1] The aesthetic significance of word choice depends upon a patterning of qualities which is not readily identifiable through the discrimination and classification of words as quantities.

If raw frequencies of vocabulary (such as the lists provided by a concordance) are not as helpful as one could wish, it would nevertheless seem possible that preferences for specific groups of words are identifiable and important. But how does one decide upon the proper grouping? The vocabulary of any given piece of writing is largely determined by its subject matter. One wouldn't look for words related to automobiles in nineteenth-century novels, as one might in twentieth-century novels.

Because novels always have characters, it seemed to me a useful cluster would be one of words referring to parts of the

---

[1] Sometimes it is difficult to decide whether usage is casual or subtle. Jane Austen seldom uses color words. Early in *Pride and Prejudice*, however, the Bennet girls are lightly mocked when, by peeking out of an upstairs window at Mr. Bingley, they discover only that "he wore a blue coat and rode a black horse." Much later in the novel Lydia displays her moral idiocy by reporting her concern as to whether or not Wickham would be married to her in his "blue coat."

body and to bodily movements. I therefore scanned some novels for nouns referring to parts of the body and verbs descriptive of bodily movements. Because there are few concordances or wordlists for novels and novelists, I used a sampling system, analyzing brief passages from different novels. It is not at all improbable, of course, that ten pages from a novel will have special vocabulary characteristics not typical of the novel as a whole (or of the novelist's predominant usage), but a series of such samples should have some validity. Figures so derived will be found in Tables II-1 through II-6 in the Tabulations Appendix. Because I want to do full justice to the possible contrasts and similarities such tabulations may reveal, I include in these tables some material from Dickens' novels, even though his fiction is not within the scope of this study.

Although there is considerable variation between samples from different novels by the same author, the general pattern of Table II-1 is clear: *relatively* Jane Austen uses fewer substantives referring to parts of the body than do Eliot, Dickens, or Brontë, and the latter two use relatively more than does Eliot. Verbs follow the same pattern, suggesting that in this case syntactic preferences are of minor importance. That the four novelists together may be part of a larger "nineteenth-century" configuration—part, that is, of a persistent tendency in British fiction—is suggested by analogous figures (Table II-2) derived from two eighteenth-century and two twentieth-century novels.

Although the counting technique might be used for discovery, these figures verify rather than reveal. Most readers recognize that Jane Austen devotes little attention to physical description or to the narration of physical actions. My figures provide not absolute frequency (obtainable only by analysis of all the works of each novelist, that is, by creation of complete concordances) but relative frequency, that is, one novelist's preference for one word cluster vis-à-vis another's. Such relative frequency becomes more and more valuable as more word clusters are tested.

A refinement of this method is illustrated by Tables II-3

through II-6. The vocabulary of each sample is first divided according to conventional parts of speech. Then some high-frequency words are eliminated from each part-of-speech group. Then a further, arbitrary classification is made: descriptive adjectives of "measure," or verbs denoting "psychic action," and adverbs answering the question "how?" and ending in "-ly" are singled out. These subclusters are further screened by the elimination of words which never appear more than once in a single sample and words which, however frequently they may appear in one or two samples, do not occur in at least fifty percent of the samples tested. The purpose of the latter screening is to reduce the vocabulary resulting solely from a particular subject concentration. The purpose of the first screening is to highlight idiosyncratic vocabulary somewhat emphasized by repetition. I do not specially commend this technique; it is meant merely to illustrate the kind of operation which may be helpful in discovering characteristics of word choice.

One should remember that the figures do not show which words of the particular group are used most often by each of the novelists but indicate only relative emphasis. Nonetheless, some statistical balance has to be kept. Results from a sample of 100,000 words from one novelist are not strictly comparable with a sample of 1,000 words from another. In Table II-3, then, we can most properly compare Eliot to Austen and, less effectively, Dickens to Brontë. It is worth noting, however, that reductions of the Austen, Eliot, and Dickens samples to bring their total number of nouns down to the Brontë total of 1,300 would leave a substantially longer list of nouns for each of the three.

Although Dickens' "pool" of nouns is larger than Brontë's, the noun "love" does not pass through the screens for his samples as it does for Brontë's (and Austen's and Eliot's). The point deserves attention because Dickens favors the *verb* "love." Here, for whatever reason, a distinction between parts of speech points up a difference in usage.

Austen apparently operates with a smaller "abstract" noun

vocabulary than Eliot, but she repeats her favored abstract nouns more frequently than Eliot does. The leading nouns for both refer to complex psychophysical conditions involving rationality as well as emotion. But for Austen these occur in a context of specifically social actions and interactions: "visit," "journey," "manners," "attention." Eliot's nouns point toward the more modern concern with "consciousness" of personal "experience."

The relative sombreness of Dickens' list, especially in contrast to Austen's, may be due to the rather "dark" nature of the five novels sampled. But the two words which top his list ("manner" and "look") make one recall his relatively high proportion of nouns referring to bodily parts. Dickens undoubtedly emphasizes "manner" in contrast to Austen's stress on "manners."

Results of the same kind of test for verbs representing "psychic" action I present in a slightly different form, since in this case I work from a common base of approximately 350 words from five samples for each novelist. In Table II-4 the number before the slash indicates the number of samples in which the word occurs, and the number after the slash indicates the total number of occurrences. The most striking feature of this table is the small number of occurrences of a small list of words. With the exception of Dickens' "love" and Eliot's "like" there is no verb which appears frequently enough to be outstanding. Although Austen has only five words which pass through the screens, these five account for nearly twenty percent of her total pool of 350. Eliot's five words account for only about ten percent of her pool. Again we observe Austen repeating more than Eliot. Again, too, we notice Austen's predilection for "common" words: all her words on this list are shared with at least one other novelist sampled. While I would be loathe to base any interpretation on such figures, they do point up Jane Austen's manipulation of a small, unspecialized vocabulary to clarify subtle shadings of meaning within conventionalized, often generalized, terms. One notices, too, that Dickens and Brontë use verbs that are not as characteristic of the other two novelists:[2] the five words unique to Brontë seem remarkably close to the special kind of action she favors in her fiction.

With neither adjectives nor adverbs is it worthwhile to establish consistent pools of words. In the descriptive adjective table (II-5), for example, the figures for Austen are drawn from a total pool of more than twice the size of either Brontë's or Dickens', yet for Austen (as for Eliot) only six words pass through the screens, whereas for Brontë ten and for Dickens eighteen pass through.

The lists for Dickens and Brontë would be longer if derived from pools as large as that used for Austen, but the difference in the kind of adjective would be only slightly accentuated since it is already impressive. As contrasted to Austen, Dickens and Brontë prefer to repeat less frequently a greater number of adjectives, yet, leaving aside the difference in the meanings of the adjectives favored, Dickens is distinguishable from Brontë. Her ten adjectives passing through the screens account for about eight percent of her pool—close to Austen's seven percent for six adjectives. Dickens' eighteen adjectives account for thirteen percent of his pool. (Eliot's preference for nonrepetition of adjectives is highlighted, incidentally, by the fact that her six words account for only some three percent of her pool.)

In Table II-5, as in the others, one observes a patterning which associates Dickens and Brontë as opposed to Eliot and Austen. This patterning may be trivial, but it is at least conceivable that it reflects some differences in larger form, perhaps a difference, as suggested in Chapter Seven, between "novels" and "romances." At any rate, the adverbs (Table II-6) reinforce the patterning, even though, in terms of the

[2] The observation may be important if one thinks of Brontë and Dickens as linked not alone by chronology but also by the form of their fiction—"romances" as opposed to the "novels" of Austen and Eliot. It is one of my purposes in this book to elucidate the difficulties in establishing connections between the "total form" of a work of fiction and the minute details of its articulation, but it is another of my purposes to show that only through study of such connections can we systematically develop meaningful comparisons and contrasts between diverse works of fiction.

14

number of words passing through the screens, the adverb figures reverse the proportions of the adjective table.

Although a larger pool would presumably lengthen the Brontë and Dickens' lists, it would be unlikely to bring them anywhere near the length of Austen's, because in the tests for Table II-6 multiple occurrences were not required—only the second screen was applied. Table II-6 alone is enough to suggest that for Austen the adverb plays a special role. Whereas repetition of modifiers in Dickens and Brontë is found more among adjectives than among adverbs, Austen's tendency is in the opposite direction, Eliot being nearly balanced. Among her repeated adverbs, which are not colorless, Austen favors cheerful ones such as "happily," "heartily," "comfortably," "easily," "warmly," and it is worth remembering the appearance of "happy" on her adjective list and "happiness" on her noun list.

I have been trying to point up the potential rewards of quantitative analyses of fictional vocabularies. The techniques I have used are not in themselves particularly valuable: they only suggest that more sophisticated methods of measurement might help us to understand better the aesthetic characteristics of fiction. But there appear to me to be severe limitations to the effectiveness of any such quantitative analysis. Such analysis tends to obscure precisely what is most significant in a novelist's selection and disposition of words. The point may be clarified by studying the opening paragraph of chapter 3 of *Emma*, a fair sample of Jane Austen's mature prose.

Mr. Woodhouse was fond of society in his own way. He liked very much to have his friends come and see him; and from various united causes, from his long residence at Hartfield, and his good nature, from his fortune, his house, and his daughter, he could command the visits of his own little circle, in a great measure as he liked. He had not much intercourse with any families beyond that circle; his horror of late hours and large dinner-parties made him unfit for any acquaintance, but such as would visit him on his own terms. Fortunately for him, Highbury, including Randalls in the same parish, and Donwell Abbey in the parish adjoining, the seat of Mr. Knightley, comprehended many such. Not unfrequently, through Emma's persuasion, he had some of the chosen and the best to dine with him, but evening-parties were what he preferred, and, unless he fancied himself at any time unequal to company, there was scarcely an evening in the week in which Emma could not make up a card-table for him. (*Emma*, 3)[3]

Analysis of this paragraph of apparently straightforward expository narration reveals an astonishing subtlety in its graciously low-toned representation of the tyranny of dependence. The key is provided by the first sentence: "Mr. Woodhouse was fond . . . in his own way." Everything turns on *him*. "He liked . . . his friends . . . see him . . . his long residence . . . his good nature . . . his fortune, his house, and his daughter, he could command . . . his own circle . . . he liked . . . his horror . . . made him unfit . . . visit him on his own terms . . . he preferred . . . he fancied . . . a card-table for him." Jane Austen likes to use proper names. By my count, one out of five of her nouns is a proper one, a proportion greater than that of any other novelist I have studied. But in this paragraph she uses pronouns exclusively after the opening sentence. The pronoun enables her to maintain a subterranean emphasis on Mr. Woodhouse's egocentrism. The pronouns permit unobtrusive repetition because the different cases of the third person differ in form. In this paragraph all three forms occur frequently, highlighting the fact that subject, object, and possessor are only different aspects of one all-encompassing ego.

[3] As I point out in Chapter Nine, the textual problems involved in a detailed study of fictional style are numerous and frustrating. Because most readers, however, are not concerned with these problems, all quotations and references are to chapters in inexpensive, easily available editions listed in the Bibliographical Appendix. Often modern paperback editions provide as good a text as can be found anywhere. In some cases, however, before analyzing passages I re-edited them to make them consistent with R. W. Chapman's Oxford edition of Jane Austen, the Shakespeare Head edition for Charlotte Brontë, and the Cabinet Edition for George Eliot. The Shakespeare Head is not a satisfactory text and, as Gordon Haight has pointed out, the Cabinet Edition is not always the best text for Eliot. But I wanted a determinate, library-available reference base.

Embodied in the paragraph, moreover, is one of the essential motifs of the novel, tyranny, the exploitation of one human being by another in the guise of love, affection, and so forth. Mr. Woodhouse exploits his dependence upon Emma so as to tyrannize her. He determines her life in much the same way that an infant determines its mother's life, as in fact the children of Emma's sister Isabella determine her life. Emma's befriending of Harriet Smith is virtually a compensatory exploitation and tyranny, Miss Taylor having escaped her loving control. In a different fashion Frank Churchill exploits both Emma and Jane Fairfax, and he is tyrannized by Mrs. Churchill. One need not pursue the point further, except to observe that because Jane Austen represents this exploitation in subtle forms, her apparently simple and straightforward manner of writing is appropriate. What she describes are not crude or overt exploitations. Today we would call Mr. Woodhouse's and Emma's tyrannies "unconscious." They are that, of course, but they are also the unconscious behavior of very civilized people. To put it another way, the unconscious motivations run counter to conscious motivations that are every bit as real and strong. Mr. Woodhouse *is* fond of Emma, who genuinely *does* befriend Harriet. Jane Austen does not oversimplify: Mr. Woodhouse is a gentle, kindly, lovable monster.

Just as Mr. Woodhouse's egocentricity is "concealed" beneath the easy lucidness and conventional exposition, even the formal "correctness," of the paragraph, so that which Jane Austen commends to us as properly civilized relations between human beings depends upon recognition of the inevitability of such discrepancies. For Jane Austen civility means exploiting others as little as possible but graciously submitting to some tyranny by others less rational and imaginatively sympathetic than oneself. Mr. Knightley criticizes Emma for not submitting to the tyranny of Miss Bates' foolishness, and it is noteworthy that she, recognizing the justice of his criticism, tries to soothe her conscience by determining not to fail in her duty to her father. This is no subterfuge: Emma's loyal kindness to the father who victimizes her is one of her most redeeming traits.

17

I doubt that any quantitative analysis of vocabulary could point up what is essential to the form and meaning of the paragraph discussed, because analysis begins by destroying the relation between "macroscopic" and "microscopic" elements in the novel. Fictional style is that relation. Analysis presupposes that the part analyzed is somehow in itself significant. In a work of fiction parts have virtually no significance except insofar as they contribute to the whole. I suspect that many of the "quantities" in fiction, words for example, are in fact qualities. Hence the limited usefulness of even such handy tools as concordances, which take apart what the artist has put together. It is the togetherness that makes the art.

When we speak of a novelist's choice of words we are referring to something different from mere language, just as when we speak of language we refer to something different from mere sound. And just as language is made out of sounds, so literature is made out of language, but to reduce the "higher" system to elements of the "lower" material of which it is composed is to obscure the difference which we wish to define. Quantitative analysis tends to make this fatal reduction; by discriminating parts it blurs the qualitative relation of part to whole which in fact defines the essential nature of the part. Useful analysis of literary works requires methods which might be called those of qualitative dissection. These would discriminate elements (and their interrelations) defined by the forms which build up the design of the work as a whole. The elements would not be defined by the materials, the mere language, out of which the work of literature is made.

The paragraph is both too indefinite and too arbitrary a unit to be treated as a significant form. But since I have used a paragraph from *Emma* to illustrate some aspects of word choice, I shall use paragraphs as a means of illustrating how the aesthetic function of vocabulary in fiction must be defined in terms of its relation to the design of the novel as a whole, how, in other words, even individual words in a novel are less units of language than they are units of form in fiction.

The opening paragraph of each of the early chapters in *Emma* is functionally analogous to the chapter opening I have already discussed. The first, one-sentence paragraph of the novel, for example, pivots on the colorless word "seemed," which suggests unobtrusively a potential discrepancy between the superficial reality of Emma's situation and another reality beneath it, a discrepancy from which will arise the circumstances which "distress" and "vex" her. The initial paragraph of chapter 2, an exposition of Mr. Weston's history, centers on his "independence"—which is presented in terms of his "active cheerful mind and social temper" engaged with and obligated to the demands of both "gentility" in general and a "respectable family" in particular. By chapter 4 we have entered into the immediate action with which the novel is concerned, and Emma's tyranny over her friend is explicitly portrayed: Harriet is "useful" to Emma; although Emma's designs for Harriet are "kind," "*a* Harriet Smith" is "a valuable addition to her privileges." Mr. Knightley's observation to Mrs. Weston at the opening of chapter 5 is a direct moral judgment of this relation. Both the basis and the accuracy of his condemnation are conveyed in the opening of chapter 6, where, moving more deeply into the realm of subjective impression, we find that the manipulation of Harriet and Mr. Elton is "agreeable" to Emma; she is without "scruple"; she enjoys the "gratitude" of Harriet's "young vanity"; she is "confident," "without a doubt" about her control of people. One must again stress the complex balance that is essential to Jane Austen's art: Mr. Knightley will finally admit, without condoning Emma's earlier practices, that she would have chosen better for Mr. Elton than he chooses for himself.

All these chapter openings are directed toward problems of dependence and independence, although in all of them the problem slips in unobtrusively. Austen's art consists of subtle complexities (which give her novels their abiding interest) presented in a simple, lucid, even conventionalized manner. All these chapters, except the fifth where dialogue momentarily delays the appearance of Mr. Knightley's name, open with the name of a character. The very names seem common-place; they do not at first strike one as containing special connotations.[4]

If we turn to the paragraphs which open the final chapters of *Emma*, however, we encounter interesting differences. The focus is now on feelings rather than independence or dependence. There is no longer much discrepancy between the lucid, formalized surface and the complex depths. The first paragraph of chapter 50 (or III, 14) stresses Emma's "happiness" in contrast to her preceding hope for mere "respite from suffering." The beginning of the next chapter tells how Frank's letter makes "its way to Emma's feelings," despite her "determination" to think harshly of Frank: "though it

---

[4] Although I do not want to impede my discussion with a digression on the significance of names in fiction, particularly since there have been several studies of the matter already published, I do want to suggest that literary critics' analyses would be enriched if critics would attend more closely to linguists's efforts to define the nature and function of names, which they recognize as very peculiar words. For my purposes at this point, the central fact about Jane Austen's names is the apparent care with which they are chosen to *minimize* overt symbolic connotations. I know of no major novelist who uses so many names with an almost "zero-degree" of connotation. "Knightley" and even "Went-worth" are exceptional. In their colorlessness "Elizabeth Bennet," "Emma Woodhouse," "Anne Elliot," "Edmund Bertram," "Mary Crawford," and so forth are exceptional in the history of fiction. Such colorlessness, indeed, must be to an important degree deliberate and functional (as is obvious, for example, in the case of Fielding's "Tom Jones"). The obvious symbolism in names such as Charlotte Brontë's "Jane Eyre" and "Lucy Snowe" (let alone Joyce's "Stephen Dedalus") may in fact be the sign of a more superficial functionalism of names. Much second-rate fiction employs names with blatant connotations. That the functionalism of Charlotte Brontë's names is not superficial, however, is demonstrated by the consistent incongruity between the two parts of each of her protagonists' names: the christian name is commonplace and conventional and the surname symbolic. The more complex kind of symbolism used by George Eliot in naming her characters is congruent with the kind of figurative language she favors (discussed in Chapter Six below). Suffice it to say here that in her fiction the symbolic import of a character's name is not independent of other characters' names (as is the case with Brontë's names): the full meaning of "Arthur Donnithorne" is established only through its relationship to "Hetty Sorrel" and "Adam Bede," for example.

was impossible not to feel that he had been wrong, yet . . . he had suffered and was very sorry . . . so grateful . . . so much in love . . . and she was so happy . . . there was no being severe."[5] In chapter 52 (or III, 16) we are first told of Emma's "relief" at escaping a "painful" meeting with Harriet, and in chapter 53 (or III, 17) of the general happiness at Mrs. Weston's "safety." The penultimate chapter begins with possibilities of "an alarming change" and events "to agitate and grieve" Emma, although with Mr. Knightley's entrance "distressing thoughts" are succeeded by "pleasure," the succession foreshadowing the effect of his news about Harriet. The first paragraph of the novel's last chapter moves from Emma's "anxious feelings" to her becoming "perfectly satisfied."

In the second set of opening paragraphs, then, we find uneasy or conflicting emotions being resolved happily. The resolutions reflect the design of the novel as a whole, in which the anxieties of misunderstanding and unawareness are transformed into the pleasures of self-understanding and consciousness of the respect due others.

One way to understand the working-out of this design (which includes the gradual adjusting of the original "discrepancies" into harmonies) is to recognize its involvement with the novel's time structure. In the first chapters a past "outside" the novel's plot becomes the "present," which in its development forms the main body of the book. In the last chapters this present shades off into a future outside the novel, a future which must be at least relatively doubtful and conditional, as the past is certain.[6] This temporal evolution is certainly not unusual in fiction; indeed, it is conventional. By manipulating the conventions of her form Jane Austen attains

[5] The underlying consistency of Jane Austen's style and perhaps Miss Bates' fundamental goodness is dramatized by this mode of citation: by the introduction of ellipses at the proper places one can make many of Emma's speeches sound like Miss Bates'.

[6] This explains in part why the verbs in the two sets of paragraphs discussed differ so strikingly, those in the first set tending to be simple, active, and declarative, those in the second tending to be more complicated and conditional.

the special excellence of her particular fictional design, just as by manipulating the language of her conventionalized description of Mr. Woodhouse she dramatizes the tyranny he exercised through his dependence. The final chapters of *Emma*—conventionally—resolve complications initiated in the first chapters, but the resolutions are more complicated than the original difficulties. In the opening chapters, for example, simple Harriet is merely "useful" to Emma. At the close of the novel Emma does not wish to "use" Harriet, one reason being that Emma has come to recognize Harriet's simplicity as "unaccountable." One thing Emma learns is that to sophistication naïveté is, if not unintelligible, at least difficult to understand and judge. The "lesson" contributes to the emphasis on "pleasure," "satisfaction," and "happiness" in the second set of paragraphs. These are founded upon Emma's deepened awareness of both the hazards and the rewards of the intensified self-understanding which accompanies true charity of thought and feeling toward others.

The resolutions of *Emma* are not the simplifications which conclude second-rate fictions. Instead, the resolutions extend a central meaning of the novel, the revelation of how apparently trivial matters of ordinary life are in fact intricate, difficult, and significant. The conventional happy ending of *Emma* satisfies aesthetically because it symbolizes a profound truth gradually unfolded in the course of the novel: happy relationships are good. They are good because they depend upon a balance between our need for (necessarily selfish) pleasures and our need to recognize the claims and necessities of others. Each of the first set of paragraphs I have discussed describes or implies an individual's denial, in a more-or-less public context, of the "claims" of others. Each of the second set of paragraphs depicts an individual's charitable awareness of others in a moment of private satisfaction and pleasure. So it is no accident that only in the last of the first set of paragraphs is the point of view Emma's, while all of the final set are at least partially (four paragraphs totally) organized around her point of view. A gradually emerging theme, the virtue of overcoming selfishness and self-centeredness, is counterpointed by a structural movement into more and more intensive representation of the internal processes of the mind.

Emma establishes the principle that happy relations are good. At the very first Emma is presented with no relations: she is handsome, clever, and rich. The novel shows us how morally meaningless these attributes are in isolation, and how dangerous they may be if misused. All of Jane Austen's novels follow the pattern of movement from isolation to involvement through the misuse or frustration of the primary characters' attractive attributes. Right and wrong are inseparable from human interactions, those which produce happiness being good, those which produce vexation and distress being bad. The conventionality of her subject matter validates this "morality." Not in unusual and special circumstances are happy relations good but under ordinary and usual conditions. Were the characters in *Emma*, for example, special or spectacular instead of "normal," a central meaning of the novel would be blurred. So the conventional patterning of *Emma*—a "middle-class" love story the comic misunderstandings of which lead to a happy ending—is appropriate to Austen's thematic design, although the conventional patterning does not fully define that design. Without denying the uniqueness of *Emma*, I would propose that these characteristics point up a central feature of fictional form.

The form of a tragedy such as *King Lear* or *Oedipus* is to some degree overt. The spectators' consciousness of a design in the action is part of their aesthetic satisfaction in the experience of the tragedy. Even in comedy, overtness of form contributes to the spectators' appreciation of the drama. The novel, read alone and silently and usually not at one sitting, requires a different *kind* of structuring. One element of this structuring is manifested in the tendency of novels to be "realistic," that is, to represent commonplace and mundane events, to present the objects and circumstances of familiar daily life, and to narrate original, that is, nonmythic and non-legendary, stories. In short, an overtness of form characteristic of drama is replaced in fiction by a concealment of form.

A characteristic of much fiction is apparent formlessness.

It is plain that the illusion of formlessness (which is a factor whenever fiction is "realistic")[7] will effect details of language manipulation. Stylistic analyses of fiction must aim at elucidation of these hidden manipulations. For this reason syntactic or vocabulary analyses founded upon ordinary definitions of sentences and words are likely to fail. Stylistic

---

[7] This is most obvious in epistolary novels, such as *Clarissa*, where each letter is supposedly directed to a particular correspondent and is concerned only with "immediate" events. The point to be emphasized, however, is that all significant fiction, whether apparently "life-like" and "realistic" or elaborately formalized, contains a "concealed" form. The elaborate formality of *Tom Jones*, for example, is in a fashion deceptive because it is superimposed on another kind of form in the novel, evidence for this being provided by the curious fact that there is frequently an inverse ratio between the length of chapters and the amount of significant action which occurs in the chapters.

I should perhaps make clear here that I would not really insist that every word in every novel is absolutely functional, as my argument implies. I deliberately overstate my position to clarify a valid distinction between fictional and nonfictional language which has been disregarded. It would doubtless be more accurate to say that *a great many* words, sentences, and so on that appear in a novel are actually different from what appear to be identical words, sentences and so on appearing in a nonfictional context. But I wish to present my view emphatically (among other reasons) because it modifies a very widespread critical assumption, whose origin can probably be traced back to I. A. Richards. The assumption is that one reads a novel in a different fashion from the way in which one reads nonfictional, or nonartistic, prose. I think this is true, but not because as he begins the reader *sets* his mind in a particular way, subconsciously orienting himself toward "emotional" rather than "logical" truth. I don't believe, in other words, that the "willing suspension of disbelief" is a *precondition* of adequate response—among other reasons because I have occasionally begun fictional works under the illusion that they were not fictional (and vice-versa) and have noticed no difference in my responses. I argue, in these terms, that the "willing suspension of disbelief" is produced by the fictional language itself. *In the process* of reading, the "concealed" functions of fictional language subconsciously orient us toward the "proper" response. I maintain that the conscious awareness of artistic illusion is less operative in reading a novel than in attending a play, and for that reason a kind of subconscious awareness is more important in novel-reading. The above was written, I should add, before I had read Professor Norman Holland's intriguing book *The Dynamics of Literary Response* (New York, 1968), in chapter 3 of which he proposes a most sophisticated psychoanalytic refinement and elaboration of Coleridge's remark on the "willing suspension of disbelief."

analysis of fiction has to begin with redefinitions of "the sentence" and "the word." A sentence in a work of fiction looks like a "nonfictional" sentence but in reality is significantly different, because its function is different. The same is true of words. One must begin a stylistic analysis of fiction with some characterization of the total form of the novel being studied, because it is that form which determines the functions of subordinate parts.

Camus has observed that a remarkable fact about fiction is the capacity of an unfamiliar narrative about trivial people and actions to hold attention. A better illustration of the point than *Emma* might be hard to find, not only because of the obviously "trivial" nature of the novel's *events*, but also because the truly significant *design* of the novel is, as I have tried to show, so adroitly disguised by the simplicity and conventionality of its superficial form.

The use of conventional form to conceal true form is no mere trick.[8] The conventional form orients us and provides a bridge between separate readings. The conventional form gives us a sense of knowing the whole novel even when we have read only a fraction of it. Simultaneously, its superficiality is unsatisfying, urging us to probe more deeply. We are, as Forster says, curious—but we want to know not so much what happens next as how it will happen. A large part of our curiosity is provoked by a developing awareness of the systematic discrepancy between superficial and concealed design. I have pointed out how Jane Austen's simple, lucid, even formally "correct" language can overlie a deeper complexity of meaning contained within it. I have tried to make clear that the existence of both surface and depth are essential to the aesthetic significance of *Emma*, which, among other things, teaches us that trivialities of ordinary life are important because the "simple" facts of commonplace existence are in

---

[8] As it may appear to be in intricate fictions of commentary such as *Tristram Shandy* and *Pale Fire*, parodies such as *Joseph Andrews* and Hemingway's *Torrents of Spring*, and elaborately "recessive" narratives such as *Don Quixote* and *Wuthering Heights*. In all these the common principle of formal structure is concealment.

reality complex. The nature and function of Austen's language, even in its smallest details, reflect the form of her novel as an aesthetic whole.

I do not claim that all fiction has exactly the same form as *Emma*, but I do propose that most novels have an equivalent form. Basically, all novelists face the same problem that Jane Austen faced, how to make an unfamiliar story interesting, how to reveal the significance of commonplace events to a quiet, solitary reader who is unlikely to peruse an entire volume at one sitting. In most novels some kind of discrepancy between "surface" and "depth" is used as a partial solution to this problem. What words are used and what these words "mean" is usually determined predominantly by their role in establishing an evolving discrepancy between surface and depth which defines the basic form of the novel as an aesthetic unity.

If the language of fiction possesses this primary function, there will be serious drawbacks to any criticism derived from quantitative analyses based on systematizations derived from studies of nonfictional language.[9] Irritating as this hypothesis will be to those who want to reduce literary studies to a mere

[9] As illustration I may cite the two sets of paragraphs from *Emma* discussed above, because they contain approximately the same number of words and sentences and so lend themselves to statistical comparison. The differences, such as the fact that the first set contains twice as many preposed descriptive adjectives as the second, and the likenesses, each set contains approximately the same number of the conjunction "and" (although there are notably more occurrences of "but" in the first set), do not point unequivocally to the different functions of the language in the two parts of the novel. While it is probably true that in the first set of paragraphs the chief weight of meaning is carried by substantives and modifiers (there are proportionately more adverbs as well as adjectives in the first set) and that in the second set relatively complex verb structures are emphasized, these distinctions, even when correlated with the "semantic" emphasis on emotions—particularly happy ones—in the second set, suggest only the conventionalized nature of the opening and conclusion of *Emma* without alerting one to the dynamic complexity of Austen's language manipulation. On the relation of the "symbolic" beginning and ending of *Emma* one may consult Joseph Wiesenfarth's chapter on the novel in his intelligent *The Errand of Form: An Assay of Jane Austen's Art* (New York, 1967), esp. p. 138.

26

subdepartment of linguistics, it should cheer literary scholars. And it does not exclude the possibility that quantitative analyses might be founded on definitions of the aesthetic functions of the language of fiction. But to realize this possibility we shall have to improve our methods of defining the larger structural systems of fiction, as I shall try to make clear in the following chapters.

CHAPTER III

Forms of Characterization

"CHARACTERS" are the commonest focus for discussions of novels. There is good reason for this, but here I want to suggest that the criticism of characters has often failed to be illuminating because of its disregard for the "form of characterization." Rather than listing the shortcomings of other critics, I shall try to make my point positively by illustrating how Austen's, Brontë's, and Eliot's forms of characterization contrast.

The description of Mr. Yorke which opens the fourth chapter of *Shirley*, Charlotte Brontë's only mature novel without a first-person narrator-protagonist, provides vivid contrast for the description of Mr. Woodhouse discussed in my previous chapter. The contrast illustrates how the language of fiction is determined by larger structural forms, in this instance by the form of characterization.

A Yorkshire gentleman he was, par excellence, in every point. About fifty-five years old, but looking at first sight still older, for his hair was silver white. His forehead was broad, not high; his face fresh and hale; the harshness of the north was seen in his features, as it was heard in his voice; every trait was thoroughly English, not a Norman line anywhere; it was an inelegant, unclassic, unaristocratic mould of visage. Fine people would perhaps have called it vulgar; sensible people would have termed it characteristic; shrewd people would have delighted in it for the pith, sagacity, intelligence—the rude, yet real originality marked in every lineament, latent in every furrow. But it was an indocile, a scornful, and a sarcastic face; the face of a man difficult to lead, and impossible to drive. His stature was rather tall, and he was well-made and wiry, and had a stately integrity of port; there was not a suspicion of the clown about him anywhere.

I did not find it easy to sketch Mr. Yorke's person, but it is more difficult to indicate his mind. If you expect to be treated to a Perfection, reader, or even to a benevolent, philanthropic old gentleman in him, you are mistaken. He has spoken with some sense, and with some good feeling, to Mr. Moore; but you are not thence to conclude that he always spoke and thought justly and kindly.

Mr. Yorke, in the first place, was without the organ of Veneration—a great want, and which throws a man wrong on every point where veneration is required. Secondly, he was without the organ of Comparison—a deficiency which strips a man of sympathy; and, thirdly, he had too little of the organs of Benevolence and Ideality, which took the glory and softness from his nature, and for him diminished those divine qualities throughout the universe. (*Shirley*, 4)

Compared to Mr. Woodhouse, Mr. Yorke is autonomous in the extreme. Emma's father exists only through others; Mr. Yorke is an independent being. The mere fact that he is characterized by physical description is one testimony to his autonomy. What Mr. Woodhouse looks like is unimportant, because the essence of what he is lies in his relations with others. The essence of Mr. Yorke lies in what separates and differentiates him from others. The difference between the two men is representative of the difference between all of Charlotte Brontë's and Jane Austen's characterizations. The fashion in which Jane Austen imagines her characters makes their physical appearance in large measure irrelevant. She conceives of her characters' existence in terms of their social interrelations. Charlotte Brontë gives physical descriptions of her characters because she conceives of them as existing, to a considerable degree, only through their antagonism to others and their resistance to external circumstances.

Hence Brontë frequently uses "negative" language whereas Austen seldom does. In the first paragraph quoted above one notices the cluster "inelegant, unclassic, unaristocratic." The second and third paragraphs, moreover, tell us more of what Mr. Yorke is not than of what he is; there is even a confession of the author's difficulty in portraying her creation. Charlotte Brontë characterizes by deprivation, in much the same way that a sculptor creates a figure out of a block of marble. The

29

figure is what remains after a great deal has been taken away. But there is nothing statuesque about Mr. Yorke, in whom we recognize a violent assertion of originality and individuality. Most Brontë characters are "difficult to lead, impossible to drive." We are told how Mr. Yorke would impress "fine people," "vulgar people," and "shrewd people," but not how he responds to them, except insofar as that response is implied by an "indocile, a scornful, and a sarcastic face."[1]

The passage from *Shirley* is remarkably abstract for portraiture rich in adjectives, particularly in contrast to the paragraph about Mr. Woodhouse (which is specific about his relations). Mr. Yorke's features show "the harshness of the north," every one of his traits is "English . . . not Norman." In the second paragraph we are told he is not "a Perfection." The third paragraph utilizes phrenology—that is, an abstract system of character definition—and phrenology defines inherent, not socially formed, tendencies of personality. The contrast between concrete physicality and such abstractness might be termed Charlotte Brontë's equivalent for the discrepancy between surface and depth noted in Austen's presentation and for the temporal contrasts we shall notice in George Eliot's characterizations.

Like many of Brontë's characters, Mr. Yorke is "odd." He is made up of incongruent and contradictory qualities, even hereditarily, for he is a French Yorkshireman, but he is not an ambiguous personality. Like a tree on a windy moor, the strange shape of his personality above all else expresses a self-persisting inner vitality. His contradictoriness is primarily evidence of his self-assertiveness. Although difficult to describe, requiring in fact a combination of concrete and abstract delineation, Mr. Yorke is in no sense a dubious or doubtful figure.[2]

[1] Such characterization necessarily has implications for plot. A narrative with agents characterized as is Mr. Yorke must take a different form from one involving agents characterized as is Mr. Woodhouse.

[2] An interesting early example of Charlotte Brontë's concern with the self-contradictoriness of character occurs in *The Spell*, where the heroine is tortured by the fact that she cannot distinguish physically between her husband and his brother although their personalities are

Ambiguity, however, looms large in George Eliot's first presentation of Godfrey Cass in *Silas Marner*.

But it would be a thousand pities if Mr. Godfrey, the eldest, a fine, open-faced, good-natured young man, who was to come into the land some day, should take to going along the same road as his brother, as he had seemed to do of late. If he went on in that way, he would lose Miss Nancy Lammeter; for it was well known that she had looked very shyly on him ever since last Whitsuntide twelvemonth, when there was so much talk about his being away from home days and days together. There was something wrong, more than common—that was quite clear; for Mr. Godfrey didn't look half so fresh-coloured and open as he used to do. At one time everybody was saying what a handsome couple he and Miss Nancy Lammeter would make! and if she could come to be mistress at the Red House, there would be a fine change, for the Lammeters had been brought up in that way, that they never suffered a pinch of salt to be wasted, and yet everybody in their household had of the best, according to his place. Such a daughter-in-law would be a saving to the old Squire, if she never brought a penny to her fortune; for it was to be feared that, notwithstanding his incomings, there were more holes in his pocket than the one where he put his own hand in. But if Mr. Godfrey didn't turn over a new leaf, he might say "Good-by" to Miss Nancy Lammeter. (*Silas Marner*, 3)

Godfrey, unlike Mr. Woodhouse and Mr. Yorke, is a protagonist, and the passage above genuinely introduces him. Mr. Woodhouse and Mr. Yorke appear before they are formally described, the former briefly and casually, the latter

---

antagonistic. The "spell" (from which the story derives its title) cast on the brothers is that if they ever come together they will die. This ingenious conception is of more than casual significance. The Duke of Zamorna (who, like many of the characters in *Villette*, appears under several different names), the chief figure throughout Charlotte Brontë's juvenilia, begins as an idealized hero but rapidly turns into a Byronic villain-hero, sometimes admirable, sometimes despicable. In the last of the juvenilia, however, he becomes merely a demonic scoundrel, and Charlotte Brontë loses interest in him. For her the vitality of character depends on the existence of antagonistic traits. For her the resolution of contrarieties means the end of life—and art.

significantly and at length. Charlotte Brontë is fond of introducing characters without explanation in the midst of dramatic action and of pausing later to describe and analyze them. The procedure seems appropriate to her focus on the assertive independence of her characters. Eliot characteristically slides into her introduction of Godfrey. What is quoted above, in fact, is only the last half of a paragraph which begins with authorial comment on the effect of the death of the Squire's wife upon his home, moves to local opinion of Dunstan Cass, and finally presents Godfrey as he appears to the people of Raveloe. The indirect presentation of a character through the opinion and judgment of a relatively detached public (but a specific one, not the generalized "intelligent people" in Brontë's description of Mr. Yorke) distinguishes Eliot's technique. On one hand, for instance, her adjectives of physical description—"fine, open-faced, good-natured"—are fewer and more generic than Charlotte Brontë's. On the other hand, Raveloe society is idiosyncratic: a different social group would judge Godfrey's generic characteristics differently, and Godfrey would appear as something other than what he appears here if his social context were different. In short, we are introduced to Godfrey through his mask.

Godfrey conceals a desperate secret. It is astonishing how many of Eliot's characters possess such secrets: Arthur Donnithorne, Hetty Sorrel, Tito Melema, Mrs. Transome, Bulstrode, Gwendolen Harleth—to mention only the most obvious. And Godfrey is not unusual in Eliot's fiction in being defined in terms of his awareness of the discrepancy between his inner being and his public situation. His individuality, in fact, is the special relation between his inward and outward selves. Godfrey's ambiguity is not fully comprehended by the disjunction between these "selves." There is an important temporal feature in his characterization. Godfrey's present appearance and psychic condition are contrasted with his previous appearance and psychic condition, with particular emphasis on his relation to Nancy Lammeter. The contrast renders Godfrey's future uncertain.

32

Time, the past's relation to the present, is of overwhelming importance in *Silas Marner*. In Eliot's other novels time is only slightly less important, although it plays no role in Austen's characterizations and only a minor role in Brontë's. For Eliot, characterization is temporal. Even her minor, consistent, or "flat" characters (such as Mrs. Poyser) are consistent because they adhere to historically determined attitudes and codes of behavior. And all of Eliot's protagonists have an individualized history both "in" and "outside" the action of their novel. The protagonist's existence is his development in time. The course of history, even personal history, is uncertain. Characters such as Godfrey are ambiguous *both* because they are beings defined by discrepancies between their inner selves and their public roles *and* because they are individualized by their transformation in time.

I have been attempting to distinguish different forms of characterization. It appears to me more useful to define the fashion in which novelists "realize" the agents of their stories than to discriminate the kinds of people the agents are. Of course the two are inseparable. Scott was the first major European novelist to give peasants a serious and significant role in his fiction. To do this he had to invent new forms of characterization, the most obvious sign of which is his use of more than one kind of language and his careful manipulation of the subordinate forms within his major linguistic divisions. One should, ideally, consider both character and modes of characterization together, but it seems to me useful to isolate, however arbitrarily, form of characterization as a subject of inquiry, because too often critics have lost sight of it in discussing characters.

A puzzle about Jane Austen's art is how she is able to *exclude* so much from her characterizations. Her characters' range of behavior, what they do and how they do it, is remarkably restricted. She might have had Elinor Dashwood stick a hatpin into Lucy Steele or might have had Mr. Bennet clout his wife on the ear, but Austen not only avoids such acts, she also severely limits her characters' repertoire of

33

thoughts and feelings. The repertoire is limited because the characters exist solely as participants in a social decorum that is highly patterned and conventionalized. The decorum is a normative one. Its nature is certainly derived from Austen's knowledge of the "real" society in which she lived, but the "real" society is not much help in explaining the "idealized" societies of the novels, which are infinitely more confined than any actual society could possibly be.

The only thing we know about an Austen character is how he interacts with other characters. The Austen character is almost exclusively a special nexus of a system of interpersonal relations. Sometimes we "see" into the mind of a character. What do we see there? Thoughts or feelings about the character's relations to others or about the relations among others. Ideas and emotions are oriented exclusively toward interrelations. The actions in which the characters participate, the events through which their personalities are manifested, are actions of interpersonal relations. This is why there is so much conversation: conversation is the primary means of relating socially. Significantly, however, colloquy is not the preeminent mode of conversation in Austen's novels. The individual personality conceived as a special focus of social relations takes on added depth and complexity as more and more relations are simultaneously in action. So Austen's colloquys most frequently occur within a group, and, like her "soliloquys," are usually about characters *other* than the speakers.

To Jane Austen a social group is a tightly patterned system of interpersonal relations. All the relations are of the same kind and all are controlled by the same decorum. The social group is a decorous aggregation of individuals. The entrance or departure of any individual is, therefore, "socially" significant: the individual counts for a lot. This is one reason why Austen, except for some satiric passages in *Northanger Abbey*, seldom presents a character as typical. Mrs. Bennet, for instance, may in fact be typical, but Austen represents her as if she were unique. One might summarize Austen's form of characterization as being the depiction of representative figures as unique individuals. This is to oversimplify but may throw into relief some of the peculiar strengths and limitations of Jane Austen's mode of characterizing.

Her characters, for example, do not undergo drastic transformations. We, as well as some of the characters, may not at first know everything about other characters, particularly potential suitors like Wickham and William Elliot, but as our knowledge increases the nature of these "unknowns" does not change: the "villains" to a remarkable degree retain their charm even when exposed. Nor do the protagonists change: they are all really as constant as Anne and Captain Wentworth. Darcy learns to behave differently; he learns to make his personality more effective, but he remains constant. Emma learns, but her learning is the realization of the truth about herself—which has always been ready to hand. In Jane Austen's novels some characters may realize their latent potentials but none truly changes: no character is inherently enigmatic.

This clarity accounts in part for Jane Austen's skill in representing with forceful definiteness minute transformations of feeling and attitude. Because her characters are essentially consistent and unmysterious, nuances in their relations are significant. Unlike most novelists, moreover, Austen can effectively portray vapid and inactive people, such as Lady Bertram and Mrs. Allen. The "reality" of these figures is unaffected by their negativeness, because they are established not by their independent assertions of self but by the simple fact that they are points where relations intersect.

Love in Austen's fictional world is the highest fulfillment of its dominant system, which depends on the individualization of representative figures. The protagonist in love becomes more fully differentiated from the loved one, for the form of personality depends less on the self per se than on the relation between selves. At the climax of each novel, when hero and heroine declare their love, Austen invariably emphasizes the differences between them. Love is constructive because it is affection for one who is appreciated as different: love confirms the worth of social decorousness by demonstrating that it allows the realization of diverse potentialities of individuals— together.

Charlotte Brontë likewise sees social groups as collections of individuals, but for her the individuals conflict rather than interact. Individuality is established not by differentiation but by opposition and confrontation. Brontë's groups change in the course of time but do not embody historical processes.[3] The effect of time is most often signaled simply by loss— characters disappear or die. Transformations in characters tend not so much to modify the group in which they appear as to carry the changed individual into a new group.

The actions through which Brontë's characters manifest themselves of course differ from those found in Austen's novels. There is proportionately less conversation in general, more conversation *à deux*, and far more soliloquy in Brontë's fiction. Jane Austen's characters do little more than sit and walk, but there is considerable bodily action among Brontë's figures. The actions are relatively clear-cut, definable entities, usually occupying specific, identifiable spans of time. Precisely when events occur is sometimes obscure in Austen's novels, and the relation of scene to scene is often temporally fluid. The length of time involved in many actions is not clearly recorded, and no emphasis is placed on the total length of time encompassed by each novel as a whole. Charlotte Brontë's characters exist not in a world dominated by an overarching decorum but in a world in which one becomes an individual by enforcing the significance of one's personality upon a hostile environment. The enforcement of self permits a kind of transformation of personality not available to Jane Austen. The changes that Lucy Snowe undergoes, for example, would simply not be possible in the context of an Austen novel.

[3] This is one reason *Shirley* is not successful as an historical novel despite some vivid reconstructions of scenes of social turmoil. An excellent essay on the novel by a first-rate social historian is Asa Briggs' "Private and Social Themes in *Shirley*," *Brontë Society Transactions*, xiii (1958), 203-19. Jacob Korg in "The Problem of Unity in *Shirley*," *Nineteenth Century Fiction*, xii (1958), 125-36, argues for the work's unity as a "philosophical novel."

Brontë's representation of characters as creative asserters of self involves some opacity: that which is separate and unique must, to a degree, be obscure. Yet ultimately the characters are not enigmatic. Much of Rochester's "mysteriousness" vanishes when we learn who's been laughing in the attic. The lines of the conflicts *within* characters tend to be clearly drawn and the conflicts *between* characters are either resolvable or arrive at a clearly defined impasse, as is the case with Lucy and Madame Beck, for example. As suggested in the discussion of Mr. Yorke, the contradictions in Brontë characters do not produce nor are they the result of ambiguity: the characters are eccentric or original but not dubious. The nature of their interrelations, likewise, is often intense but is not usually problematic.

Charlotte Brontë's colloquies are as a rule conducted by two people alone who discuss only themselves. What we see in the mind of the Brontë character is something more private, more independent of "society" than interpersonal relations—self-analysis, contemplation of personal destiny, a debate between Reason and Hope, or the like. The "intensity" of the relations between characters is the result of their being characterized through their separate, autonomous self-assertions in a world not represented as a decorously patterned system but as a dangerous environment. The environment is dangerous because it is composed of aggressively autonomous forces; it is enigmatic in much the same fashion as Darwin's "entangled bank." So when Brontë characters relate, above all when they love, conflict and struggle are inevitable. Love threatens the structure of the Brontë world. Here love is destructive; at least one of the lovers must be reconstituted, his original being extensively modified. Rochester is mangled physically, Caroline Helstone nearly dies, Lucy Snowe becomes a new woman.

Charlotte Brontë's characters are often not so much different from one another as absolutely unalike. St. John Rivers and Rochester are as different as fire and ice. *Villette* is set in a foreign land, and Paul's and Madame Beck's modes of existence are at first as alien to Lucy as their language and religion. What "common humanity" there is in Charlotte

Brontë's novels is attained only through bitter struggles which transform the strugglers, yet which finally reaffirm an essential autonomy in the major figures. Rochester is a better mate for Jane than St. John because Rochester respects Jane's independence, just as Paul Emanuel learns to respect Lucy's Protestant individualism.

The creative self-assertiveness of Charlotte Brontë's characters works on what I call the subconscious elements of individual life, the appetites and fears which underlie any and all socialization. This is, perhaps, why critics are sometimes drawn to speak of the "primitive" quality of these characters. Paradoxically, George Elliot's characters never strike one as "primitive" in this fashion, although Eliot probes deeper into the psyche than does Brontë.[4] But Eliot's characters give individualized realization to somethng of not much relevance to Charlotte Brontë—sociological forces. Something of Eliot's form of characterization is suggested by Aunt Glegg's support of Maggie Tulliver after her adventure with Stephen Guest in *The Mill on the Floss*. Aunt Glegg's surprising attitude is expressly described not as a change in her view of Maggie or of her principles but as a logical extension of her code, other parts of which have previously made her antipathetic to Maggie. The surprisingness of Mrs. Glegg's action lies more in the peculiar nature of the Dodson mores than in the idiosyncrasies of her personality.

In each of Eliot's novels there are *several* carefully discriminated social groups, and each character is in some meas-

---

[4] The paradox is, in fact, evidence for how "romance" may contribute to the development of "novels," a point discussed in Chapter Seven. The best general studies of Charlotte Brontë's fiction and its significance are Inga-Stina Ewbank, *Their Proper Sphere* (London, 1966), a conscientious examination of the novels of all the Brontë sisters with sensible evaluations based on sound research; and Robert B. Martin, *The Accents of Persuasion: Charlotte Brontë's Novels* (London and New York, 1966), a purely critical work, sensible, illuminating, shrewd. W. A. Craik's *The Brontë Novels* (London, 1968) gives intelligent but less impressive readings. I may perhaps add here that I have found Winifred Gerin's highly publicized biography *Charlotte Brontë: The Evolution of Genius* (Oxford, 1967) somewhat disappointing—Mrs. Gaskell's *Life* of more than a century ago is still in many respects not superseded.

ure a representative of his *particular* group.[5] Hence Eliot's characters are never as autonomous as Brontë's. Silas Marner is isolated in Raveloe because he belongs to the Lantern-Yard from which he has been expelled. At the same time, Eliot's characters are never as purely elements in one fixed, overarching social pattern as are Austen's characters. Eliot's fictional worlds are composed of multiple decorums.

These diversely articulated patterns are regarded by Eliot as historical phenomena, and their interplay makes up the larger system of the novel as a whole. From the influence of his subordinate decorum the individual cannot wholly escape, yet he makes a special contribution to it or, if one prefers, he expresses its pressure in an idiosyncratic fashion. Eliot's form of characterization is in one sense the exact reverse of Austen's: Eliot characterizes by revealing the representativeness of the idiosyncratic. Eliot frequently draws our attention to the typicalness of her characters, though most often the character is representative not of a generalized type but, instead, of a specific pattern of historically determined social circumstances. A portion of her authorial commentary urges us not to see specific behavior as idiosyncratic, and much of her imagery is directed to arousing our imaginative comprehension not merely of why a character exists and acts as he does but also of how his existence and actions are analogous to other existences and actions. Eliot often does what Austen seldom does; she compares characters, either to others in the same novel or to "real" people outside the novel.

Yet representativeness is only half of Eliot's form of characterization. None of her major figures are merely typical. Their representativeness is, so to speak, forged out of personal

[5] This is apparent even in *Adam Bede*, which appears to be a novel concerned with quite a limited social group. But W. J. Harvey in his excellent *The Art of George Eliot* (London, 1961) has demonstrated how plot structure and social differentiations reinforce one another even in this early novel. Probably the best single essay on *Silas Marner* is David Carroll's "*Silas Marner*: Reversing the Oracles of Religion," *Literary Monographs*, I, ed. Thomas K. Dunseath and Eric Rothstein (Madison, Wisconsin, 1967), pp. 165-200. Another valuable essay of Carroll's is "An Image of Disenchantment in the Novels of George Eliot," *Review of English Studies*, XI (1960), 29-41.

idiosyncrasy. We come to recognize Amos Barton, for instance, not merely as an example of ill-educated, dissenting ministers but also as an ill-educated, dissenting minister who undergoes a unique experience of suffering. And Eliot is explicit about Adam Bede's unrepresentativeness. When contrasted to the figures in Charlotte Brontë's fiction, the individualism, the autonomy, of Eliot's figures does seem diminished: Dodson "culture" exists regardless of which Dodsons are on hand, and even Felix Holt might be regarded as typical of one segment of the proletariat. So it is easy to regard Eliot as a determinist. But her sociological determinism is balanced by as strong an antideterminism: Felix Holt, in the final analysis, is as unrepresentative as Adam Bede. For one thing, Eliot sees every social group as transforming itself and being transformed by the influence of other groups. Tom Tulliver is a superb delineation of how, in Riesman's terms, a "decaying" tradition-directed society produces an "inner-directed" man. Moreover, the activities by which the major characters in Eliot's novels are realized are struggles *against* the force exerted by the social group. Eliot's leading figures *recognize* themselves to be creatures of a superpersonal system, but they do not passively submit—they resist, or, like Tito Melema or Arthur Donnithorne, they intensify the system. In either case their awareness prevents them from being passive. This is why there is so often an inconsistency not only between the characters' outward appearance and their inner sense of themselves but also between their "instincts" and their aspirations. It seems logical, therefore, that authorial commentary should play a larger role in Eliot's characterizations than in Austen's or Brontë's. Soliloquies, colloquies, and multiple conversations occur frequently in Eliot's novels, but these are almost always *interspersed among* and *intermingled with* authorial exposition of patterns of thoughts, feelings, and behavior resulting from discrepancies between the expressed and the unexpressed. Authorial "comment," in fact, is a dramatic elucidation of these discrepancies.

Love in Eliot's fiction is not fulfilling as it is in Austen's fiction or destructive as it is in Charlotte Brontë's. Love is both fulfilling and destructive in Eliot's novels because it involves the realization of individual impulses through their accommodation to the necessities imposed by superpersonal forces of social groups. Hence Eliot's protagonists not merely can change—often they must change. Their "reality" is the process of transformation they undergo or refuse to undergo. What Eliot says of Savonarola is true of all her leading characters: "there were great inward modifications accompanying the outward changes."

The *doubleness* of transformation is essential. We are shown both the inner workings of the characters and how they look and behave. Psychologically determining forces are described in detail, and we are also shown the nature of the physical surroundings which channel these forces. For Eliot personality is the private development, manifested in public action, of a combination of personal and more-than-personal potentials.[6] Her characters, therefore, can properly be called *personae,* wearers of masks, who are enigmatic because they are defined by their potential to change and be changed.

Even the nature of the conflicts within Eliot's protagonists may be ambiguous. There is a large role given to self-deception. Typically, a character does not make a simple mistake but, instead, erroneously estimates the relative strength of the conflicting pressures which make up his existence. If instincts are dubious, aspirations are uncertain. Eliot's characters, particularly in contrast to Austen's, have open to them a wide range of possible "careers." Their changeableness concludes in a final realization of only some of their original potential.

[6] Here I touch on problems not merely of Eliot's intellectual opinions but of what may be called her philosophy of life. The most substantial general work on the sources of her thought is Bernard J. Paris, *Experiments in Life: George Eliot's Quest for Values* (Detroit, 1965), although the best brief presentation will be found in the two chapters on Eliot in Basil Willey's fine *Nineteenth Century Studies* (London, 1949). On the matter of "determinism" see the thoughtful essay by George Levine, "Determinism and Responsibility in the Works of George Eliot," *PMLA*, LXXVII (1962), 268-79. Gordon S. Haight's superlative *George Eliot: A Biography* (New York and Oxford, 1968) defines lucidly not alone how much George Eliot owed to the thinking of Lewes but also why, psychologically, she was able to accept his influence.

41

It is not unusual, in consequence, for our sympathy or antipathy toward a character at the end of a novel to differ markedly from our feelings toward him at the beginning.

A final point deserves attention. It can be argued on more than one ground that Jane Austen's novels have no "minor" characters and Charlotte Brontë's very few (see Chapter Nine). In Eliot's novels there is a fairly clear and important distinction between two forms of characterization. The simpler form, producing essentially unambiguous characters, is used for minor figures. Because Jane Austen characterizes by interpersonal relations, her characters tend to be formally alike; and because Charlotte Brontë stresses the autonomy of her figures, her characters tend to be formally alike. Eliot, however, needs representatives of the external sociological forces which press in upon her major characters and against which they struggle. The "choral" characters almost of necessity differ from those central to the themes of the novels. When we speak of a minor character in one of Eliot's novels, we refer not merely to that character's unextended and infrequent "appearances" but also to the form of his characterization. In form as well as in substance the world of Eliot's fiction is far more articulated than is Brontë's or Austen's.

CHAPTER IV

Point of View

POINT OF VIEW in fiction has attracted much attention during the past forty years. The results of this attention, however, are disappointing. Too often discussion of point of view has been polemically oriented, serving merely as an apologia for particular novelists. Few critics have troubled to face up to the complexity of the topic. Seldom is point of view considered in realtion to other "points" of importance in the art of fiction, for example, "point of action" (the character or characters whose activities are being narrated), "point of reaction" (the character or characters who are primarily affected by, and who often make evaluations of, the action), and so forth. The various "points" sometimes coincide and sometimes move apart, and a truly meaningful description of point of view should define its part in these patterns of conjunction and separation. Wayne Booth's *Rhetoric of Fiction*,[1] an extended demonstration of the limitations of earlier point-of-view criticism, perhaps marks the beginning of more thorough, objective, and precise investigations into the subject.

In this chapter I shall consider only one neglected aspect of point of view, its function as an indicator of the novelist's relation, or more exactly, his conception of his relation, to his readers. In the primitive societies where storytelling is a specialized occupation and is conducted on specified occasions and in a socially formalized fashion, the relation between storyteller and audience is an overt expression of aesthetic form. In the sophisticated societies where the novel has flourished, the relation between storyteller and audience is more complex and indirect, yet it is still expressive of aesthetic form. It is by no means unreasonable to define literary "genres" in

[1] Chicago, 1961; see also the Bibliographical Appendix.

terms of the sociological patterning involved in the act of their communication and reception.[2]

A particular point of view in a fictional work indicates, even if only crudely, something about such patterning. Conrad's liking for a narrative in which the action is presented from the limited point of view of a character (or characters) engaged in or associated with the action implies a special kind of relation between Conrad and his readers. Specifically, it implies, if not alienation, at least uncertainty on Conrad's part as to the relation—an uncertainty or problematic quality not characteristic of most earlier novelists. Nabokov in our own day provides an extreme form of this separation of the novelist from his audience. His ingenuity in manipulating point of view in *Pale Fire*, for instance, seems expressive of something close to hostility toward his readers—particularly toward the academic scholars of contemporary literature who have taken to circling closer around his works.

Consideration of this aspect of point of view immediately leads us to recognize the clumsiness of much of our terminology for describing it. For example, although *Moll Flanders* and *Jane Eyre* both employ a "first-person" point of view, it is plain that the functions of the first-person narration in the two works differ, representing different relations between author and readers. My chief concern in this chapter is with an analogous difference between the "omniscience" of Jane Austen and that of George Eliot, a difference which can be illuminated by contrasts with Charlotte Brontë's preference for first-person narration.

When in the final chapter of *Northanger Abbey* Jane Austen observes that "the tell-tale compression of the pages" reveals "that we are all hastening together to perfect felicity," the adverb "together" can be taken almost literally. Throughout her novels Austen speaks with confidence in her readers' understanding and in their fundamental agreement with her as to the proper attitudes of novelist and reader toward fictional subjects. The very conventionality of the form of her novels

[2] If it were unreasonable to define literary genres in terms of sociological patterning, nothing McLuhan says would be of any value.

bespeaks community between author and audience. One can, however, exaggerate the completeness of this community. *Northanger Abbey* is an early, satiric novel, and the directness of communication between author and reader in it is never repeated in later works.[3]

But even the implied "community" of *Northanger Abbey* is not as complete as, say, that implicit in *Tom Jones*. Fielding's brilliant commentary derives its effectiveness from the assured directness with which he addresses his reader. Many of his narrative devices, of which the epic parody is an obvious example, reveal his confidence in participating in a "culture" shared with his readers. This culture is not merely the set of mores and assumptions of a limited class in mid-eighteenth-century England. It is part of the equipment of all civilized men from the time of Homer onward. This assured sense of easy communication within such a super-culture does not belong to Jane Austen.

[3] John K. Mathis in "*Northanger Abbey* and Jane Austen's Conception of the Value of Fiction," *ELH*, XXIV (1957), 138-52, argues for recognition of Jane Austen's educational purposes in her fiction, in effect developing A. C. Bradley's claim for two persistent "strains" in the novels, the moralistic and the humanistic; see his *Essays and Studies* (London, 1911), pp. 7-36. This is a convenient point to indicate a few of the studies to which my readings of Jane Austen's novels are indebted. Howard S. Babb's *Jane Austen's Novels: The Fabric of Dialogue* (Columbus, Ohio, 1962) is excellent on language, not just dialogue; Frank W. Bradbrook in *Jane Austen and her Predecessors* (Cambridge, 1966), does not quite justify the expectations aroused by his title but provides some useful information; A. Walton Litz's *Jane Austen: A Study of Her Artistic Development* (New York, 1965), is possibly the best critical book on Austen (the presentation is so urbane and succinct that it is easy to overlook the careful research which undergirds Litz's critical originality); Marvin Mudrick's famous *Jane Austen: Irony as Defense and Discovery* (Princeton, 1952), strikes me as desperately wrong-headed in conception and simultaneously filled with excellent insights, and is therefore an enormously stimulating work; B. C. Southam in *Jane Austen's Literary Manuscripts* (London, 1964) provides some of the most solidly documented recent criticism; Henrietta Ten Harmsel's *Jane Austen: A Study in Fictional Conventions* (The Hague, 1964) is a somewhat pedestrian treatment of a good subject; Léonie Villard's *Jane Austen, A French Appreciation*, translated by Veronica Lucas (London, 1924), is still of value; Andrew H. Wright's *Jane Austen's Novels: A Study in Structure* (New York, 1953), if never profound, is often illuminating.

Her community is the genteel novel-reading public of her day. The range and significance of her literary references are restricted. Her satire is seldom generalized and is always kept within the traditional scope of light-hearted novelistic comment. She never appeals to her readers except as novel-readers. Even the pervasiveness of her irony may be a sign of her awareness of the limitations of her audience, in that irony tends to disguise complexities of meaning. Moreover, it is plain that a great deal of what Jane Austen must have actually experienced never appears in her fiction. Hers may have been a sheltered and uneventful life, but much of it she chose to exclude from her novels.

Charlotte Brontë's sense of community with her readers is a more uncertain one than Jane Austen's. An interesting feature of the notorious addresses beginning "Dear Reader" or, more imperatively, "Reader" is how often they are not required by the immediate situation. These gratuitous addresses crop up, I believe, because Charlotte Brontë knows that her themes and characterizations run counter to conventional patterns of fiction, and she feels compelled occasionally to *assert* a community between the narrator and his presumable audience.

If Charlotte Brontë sometimes forces a direct communication between narrator and reader, at other times she appears indifferent to her reader's understanding.[4] It is notable that in most of her novels the reader is to some degree misled.

---

[4] The complexity of Brontë's attitudes toward her readers is nothing when compared to the attitudes of Charles Dickens. Not enough serious attention has been given to the paradox that in the course of his career Dickens retained, even extended, his original popularity with the British reading public while progressively intensifying his criticism of British society. The simple cliché that Dickens was merely a "popular" writer becomes meaningless as soon as one takes the trouble to read with an open mind Edgar Johnson's biography of Dickens (or George Ford's study of his reputation)—let alone reviews and comments upon the novels published during Dickens' lifetime. This point is worth making here, because an uncritical assumption that most Victorian novelists had a cozy relation with their readers derives primarily, I suspect, from the simplistic and uninformed opinion that Dickens, the leading Victorian novelist, merely pandered to his readers' most superficial prejudices.

That is, the reader is given after-the-fact narration in which information of moment is deliberately withheld. We never feel Jane Austen's withholding of information to be deceptive because it is always done within the convention of a storyteller's tale. This traditional role is not customarily assumed by Charlotte Brontë. She claims to present us not with "a story" but with truth—and the claim creates a problem of credibility. The problem is perhaps most acute in *Villette*, where she comes close to making a virtue of Lucy's misleadings by rendering her a prototype of the "unreliable" narrator: most of Lucy's deceptions are at least related to self-deceptions.

On the other hand, the frequency and importance of George Eliot's authorial comments testify to how remote she feels her narratives to be from the ready comprehension and sympathy of her audience. Eliot has been accused of being didactic, but the accusers have not always remembered that a teacher-pupil relation is likely to be a remote one. The master of a large class is a distant figure. Whether didactic or not, Eliot assumes again and again that her reader will misunderstand or misjudge her characters and their actions, and she introduces commentary to explain them. Often she feels it necessary to tell "objectively" the "meaning" of events. These explanations arise from Eliot's conviction that she presents the reader with something that is unfamiliar, literally foreign to his experience (such as country life forty years earlier), or, more important, disguised by habits of thought and feeling in contemporary society.

Like Charlotte Brontë, Eliot frequently offers sequences of events which run counter to the conventionalized sequences of light fiction. Unlike Brontë, however, she does not "deceive" her reader and create complicated plots. With important modifications, Eliot plays the role of the traditional storyteller. Her chief modification is her claim to be a teller of "real" tales, tales which expose the actualities hidden from the reader by his ignorance, his superficial familiarity with analogous circumstances, or his unthinking acceptance of cant.

Eliot's explanatory intrusions are not a sign of contempt for her reader; presumably she thinks he is capable of profiting from the explanations. She sees the reader as a victim of what Lewes called "falsism," a faulty view of reality encouraged by the conventions of society. Eliot aims above all else to overthrow socially accepted prejudices: to do this she must work from the inside. She must apear to share a community of attitude with her reader while she is in fact controverting his misconceptions. Many of her characters who do evil are not only socially acceptable but also delighted by the pleasures which come with social approval. Arthur Donnithorne and Tito Melema behave despicably because they wish to be liked. Such characters expose the value systems of their society, which are, when one comes to examine Eliot's presentation of them, remarkably close to the value systems Eliot assumes to be her readers'.

Only if we see the pervasiveness of Eliot's authorial presence not as a sign of coziness in her relation to her audience but as a sign of her shrewdness in subverting it, do we appreciate the difference between the nature and function of her authorial commentaries and the nature and function of Jane Austen's. Consider satire, for satire depends upon a groundwork of assumptions shared by the satirist and his audience. Charlotte Brontë's novels contain little satire. Her protagonists are independent of, excluded from, even hostile to the kind of social intercourse she presumes to be familiar to her readers. Crimsworth, the narrator of *The Professor*, for instance, is both socially and psychologically isolated. Yet his story, like Jane Eyre's and Lucy Snowe's, is told for the sake of the story, that is, to illuminate the narrator, rather than to expose society. The structure of the novel prohibits much satire, even though the preface makes explicit Charlotte Brontë's awareness of the discrepancy between the "realism" which she attempts and her readers' probable preference for the "imaginative and poetical—something more consonant with highly wrought fancy." This awareness would not be inappropriate to the author of *Northanger Abbey*. But Brontë subordinates possibilities for satire to the recounting of individual experiences which call out an empathetic response and which do not make satire's appeal to "common sense."[5]

Northanger Abbey, to bring into contrast Austen's "earliest" novel (which, like *The Professor*, was published only posthumously), communicates hilariously on the level of commonsense. Jane Austen and her readers belong, as it were, to one family and can therefore share the delights not merely of satire but also of burlesque and parody. Yet the satire, burlesque, and parody are predominantly literary. What brings Austen close to her readers is their mutual knowledge of the same fiction, their shared reasons for pleasure in it, and their shared amusement at its foibles. Because the community (expressed by the tone of Austen's "omniscient" comments) is so purely an aesthetic one, Jane Austen's most topical novel retains its charm and vitality. As long as there is silly fiction, *Northanger Abbey* will make readers laugh, even as the details of the actual world and the actual fiction of the late eighteenth century become more remote. The truth which accompanies the laughter is a different kind of truth from that embodied in Charlotte Brontë's more "realistic" narrative. *Northanger Abbey* espouses an ideal, the ideal of rational happiness, by showing that—and how—human beings *learn* to love. Love of hyacinths or Henrys is not instantaneous, instinctual, "natural." It is a civilizing process, a mode of education. So the very theme of *Northanger Abbey* is parodic, an inversion of the basic presupposition upon which light fiction is founded.

If we continue to focus on early works, we find that Eliot's *Amos Barton* provides a good contrast to Brontë's and Austen's early novels. There is plenty of satire in *Amos Barton*, though little of the purely literary kind, but the story doubles back on its beginning to become an antisatire. Ultimately the history of Amos solicits our sympathy for a fellow human being who fails, not spectacularly, but—like most of us—drably. The novel's appeal lies in its pathos, which is effective

---

[5] M. M. Brammer in a useful article "The Manuscript of *The Professor*," *Review of English Studies*, XI (1960), 157-70, demonstrates how in revising Brontë intensified her style.

because it never becomes overly intense. The pathos of *Amos Barton*, like the emotions portrayed by Charlotte Brontë, is dependent upon the representation of specific sufferings, of what may be called passional realism. But whereas Brontë appeals directly to our feelings from the first, Eliot is more indirect. Her indirection is necessary, not gratuitous, for the particularized emotional experience of Amos Barton occurs within and is defined by a particularized social context which is as important as the experience. The context is localized, specific, even idiosyncratic. The basic assumption underlying *Amos Barton* is that readers (blinded probably by the kind of novels which Charlotte Brontë scorns in her preface to *The Professor*) are likely to misunderstand the significance of the social pressures upon Amos and his family. One aim of the story is to enlighten the reader as to the character of these forces, so that he may appreciate the personal pathos of Amos Barton's history.

Eliot's technique is to pretend at first to share her reader's attitudes. While the pretense lasts, satire plays a large role. At first the reader is given the illusion that he and the author share the same view of Milby and that he and the author understand the characters in much the same way. As the novella unfolds, however, the reader discovers a special pathos in the inarticulate (and sociologically "invisible") suffering of the protagonists. The discovery brings him to share the author's real view of Milby and the other persons of the story, a view which is very far from the illusory one on which the earlier, satiric portions of the work are founded.

Eliot uses this technique in all of her fiction. Although it undergoes alterations as she becomes a more sophisticated novelist, even *Daniel Deronda* depends to some degree on the subversion of an original illusion of community between author and reader. Deronda's gradual commitment to his Jewish heritage accompanies a gradual withdrawal by the author from a position that appears to be nearly conventional in its presentation of "Jewishness." I think some objections to Eliot's "omniscient" presence in her novels springs from her readers' vague awareness of having been lured into changing their point of view. Whether or not this is true, it is certain that Eliot is aware that the very sophistication of high civilization tends to devitalize relations between people of different histories, habits, classes, and interests. She strives to overcome this devitalization. Our pains and desires, our sufferings and aspirations should bind us together. It is commitment to commonalty that Eliot wishes to bring us, always with an understanding that it is our habituation to more superficial connections that is the obstacle. It is our superficial knowledge of society which makes us at first indifferent to Amos Barton's grief. It is the author's function to guide us surreptitiously through our superficial sophistication to a profound understanding from which renewed sympathy for our fellows may flow. Eliot espouses the ideal of rational sympathy.

If we turn our attention to differences in authorial irony we must be somewhat more specific. There is a well-known passage in *Sense and Sensibility* which fairly illustrates Jane Austen's irony, although in her later novels the irony becomes subtler.

In the evening, as Marianne was discovered to be musical, she was invited to play. The instrument was unlocked, everybody prepared to be charmed, and Marianne, who sang very well, at their request went through the chief of the songs which Lady Middleton had brought into the family on her marriage, and which perhaps had lain ever since in the same position on the pianoforté; for her ladyship had celebrated that event by giving up music, although by her mother's account she had played extremely well, and by her own was very fond of it.

Marianne's performance was highly applauded. Sir John was loud in his admiration at the end of every song, and as loud in his conversation with the others while every song lasted. Lady Middleton frequently called him to order, wondered how any one's attention could be diverted from music for a moment, and asked Marianne to sing a particular song which Marianne had just finished. Colonel Brandon alone, of all the party, heard her without being in raptures. He paid her only the compliment of attention; and she felt a respect for him on the occasion which the others had reasonably forfeited by their shameless want of taste. His pleasure in music, though it amounted not to that ecstatic delight which alone could sympathise with her own, was estimable when contrasted against the horrible insensibility of the others; and she was reasonable enough to allow that a man of five and thirty might well have outlived all acuteness of feeling and every exquisite power of enjoyment. She was perfectly disposed to make every allowance for the colonel's advanced state of life which humanity required.   (*Sense and Sensibility*, 7)

The entire party at the Middletons' is included in the phrase "everybody prepared to be charmed," but the chief objects of the author's criticism in the opening paragraph are Sir John and his wife. They are exposed not so much as representatives of a class or type but as individuals. We laugh at Sir John and Lady Middleton, not at the aesthetic pretensions of vulgarians. Yet the economy of the passage derives in part from Austen's reliance on her readers' recognition of the typicality of the scene as a whole. Nothing has to be explained, nothing has to be particularized in the first part of the passage—except the Middletons.

With the third sentence of the second paragraph we move away from the Middletons, apparently to Colonel Brandon, who "alone, of all the party, heard her without being in raptures." The pronoun "her," however, slides us into Marianne's viewpoint, the *quality* of which is prepared for by the word "raptures." The tone of this term differs from that of the diction by which the false appreciations of the Middletons are exposed and is like that of the vocabulary through which Marianne's "sensibility" is exposed: "shameless," "ecstatic," "horrible." In the final sentence of the passage Austen drops back into a moderate manner of speech which, by contrast, brings more sharply into focus Marianne's foolishness yet simultaneously gives us grounds for excusing her (the Middletons are provided with no such excuse): Marianne is, after all, only seventeen, an age when thirty-five does indeed appear to be an "advanced state of life."

The passage illustrates Jane Austen's skill at keeping her irony in motion. Not only do we turn from the Middletons to Marianne, but also the ironic form changes. Marianne is exposed in a different fashion from the Middletons, appropriately enough, since her foolishness is of a different kind. In other words, shifts in ironic mode *clarify*, distinguishing among characters and significances. Yet these variations are contained within a consistent style of narration so that our sense of the interrelatedness of the group as a group is maintained. The form of Austen's authorial presence permits individualization through—not in opposition to—interrelationship.

The Sykes' and the curates' visit to Caroline Helstone in *Shirley* might be compared with the scene from *Sense and Sensibility*, though the differences are vast. No part of Brontë's narrative is as economical as Austen's. Brontë's description is slow-paced with none of the sharp discriminations within over-all consistency which distinguish Austen's ironic mode.

When Caroline was going to receive company, her habit was to wring her hands very nervously, to flush a little, and come forward hurriedly yet hesitatingly, wishing herself meantime at Jericho. She was, at such crises, sadly deficient in finished manner, though she had once been at school a year. Accordingly, on this occasion, her small white hands sadly maltreated each other, while she stood up, waiting the entrance of Mrs. Sykes. . . .

In English country ladies there is this point to be remarked. Whether young or old, pretty or plain, dull or sprightly, they all (or almost all) have a certain expression stamped on their features, which seems to say, "I know—I do not boast of it—but I *know* that I am the standard of what is proper; let every one therefore whom I approach, or who approaches me, keep a sharp look-out, for wherein they differ from me—be the same in dress, manner, opinion, principle, or practice—therein they are wrong."

Mrs. and Misses Sykes, far from being exceptions to this observation, were pointed illustrations of its truth. . . .

And now Caroline had to usher them upstairs, to help them to unshawl, smooth their hair, and make themselves smart; to reconduct them to the drawing-room, to distribute amongst them books of engravings, or odd things purchased from the Jew-basket. . . .

It ought perhaps to be explained in passing, for the benefit of those who are not "au fait" with the mysteries of the "Jew-basket" and "Missionary-basket," that these "meubles" are willow-repositories, of the capacity of a good-sized family clothes-basket, dedicated to the purpose of conveying from house to house a monster collection of pincushions, needlebooks, cardracks, workbags, articles of infant wear, etc., etc., etc., made by the willing or reluctant hands of the Christian ladies of a parish, . . .

(Shirley, 7)

It is notable that Charlotte Brontë generalizes as Jane Austen does not. For instance, it is Marianne, not a seventeen-year-old, who pities the aged Colonel, but "Mrs. and Misses Sykes" are "illustrations" of "English country ladies." Also worth observing is the fact that the specific visit of the Sykes is represented as to some degree exemplary: this is indicated by the phrases "when Caroline was going to receive company, her habit was . . ." and "at such crises. . . ." Events and occasions in Jane Austen's novels are almost always presented as unique. At the same time Brontë uses particularized details in a fashion Austen does not, because Brontë introduces some specialized facts about which she must inform her reader—the "Jew-basket," for example. Brontë's irony is coarser than Austen's, in part because it is based upon laboriously presented factual details. In sum, Charlotte Brontë is not comfortable in the role of ironic author, at least partly because her sense of community with her readers is an uncertain one.

George Eliot, on the other hand, uses authorial irony freely and for a variety of purposes. The visit of Mrs. Tulliver's sisters early in *The Mill on the Floss* (chapter 7) illustrates, for example, that George Eliot's irony is sometimes used to supply information about matters with which the reader is presumably unfamiliar. Eliot's presentation, of course, is both more broadly humorous than Brontë's and more dependent upon psychological generalization, as "when grief, which has made all things else a weariness, has itself become weary." Moreover, Mrs. Tulliver's sisters are important characters, whereas the Sykes are really irrelevant to *Shirley*; Charlotte Brontë tends to limit her authorial irony to peripheral figures. Mrs. Glegg and Aunt Pullet are significant to both action and theme of *The Mill on the Floss*: their ridiculousness is inseparable from their seriousness. Willy-nilly, what each of the Tullivers is and does is shaped to some degree by pressure from the Dodsons.

Even in her humorous introduction Eliot is preparing us to understand how oppressive is the Dodson tradition and how difficult it is for those associated with it to reject its influence. Later her point of view shifts us from humorous irony to didactics.

It is a sordid life, you say, this of the Tullivers and Dodsons—irradiated by no sublime principles, no romantic visions, no active, self-renouncing faith—moved by none of those wild, uncontrollable passions which create the dark shadows of misery and crime—without that primitive rough simplicity of wants, that hard submissive ill-paid toil, that childlike spelling-out of what nature has written, which gives its poetry to peasant life. . . . Observing these people narrowly, even when the iron hand of misfortune has shaken them from their unquestioning hold on the world, one sees little trace of religion, still less of a distinctively Christian creed. Their belief in the Unseen, so far as it manifests itself at all, seems to be rather of a pagan kind; their moral notions, though held with strong tenacity, seem to have no standard beyond hereditary custom. You could not live among such people; you are stifled for want of an outlet towards something beautiful, great, or noble; . . .

I share with you this sense of oppressive narrowness; but it is necessary that we should feel it, if we care to understand how it acted on the lives of Tom and Maggie—how it has acted on young natures in many generations, that in the onward tendency of human things have risen above the mental level of the generation before them, to which they have been nevertheless tied by the strongest fibres of their hearts. The suffering, whether of martyr or victim, which belongs to every historical advance of mankind, is represented in this way in every town, and by hundreds of obscure hearths; and we need not shrink from this comparison of small things with great; for does not science tell us that its highest striving is after the ascertainment of a unity which shall bind the smallest things with the greatest?

(*The Mill on the Floss*, 30)

This passage indicates one of Eliot's most persistent interests, her concern with the relations between generations.[6] It also illustrates her remarkable understanding of the core of the scientific method, an understanding which enables her to employ it as a model for art—"the ascertainment of a unity which will bind the smallest things with the greatest." The fusion of the scientific and artistic elucidates the "religious" focus of a specific way of life. For Eliot the religious quality which pervasively shapes individual lives yet remains impalpable and irreducible to definition by simple label is *the* essential feature of any group. Her shifts of point of view in *The Mill on the Floss* are managed so as to delineate for us and to make us empathize with this quality. Having aroused our sense of amused superiority before by treating the Dodsons with ironic humor, Eliot now forces us to take the Dodsons seriously. She then presses on to make us feel the specific peculiarities of their way of life as a kind of challenge to prevailing conceptions of what is right.

> The religion of the Dodsons consisted in revering whatever was customary and respectable: it was necessary to be baptised, else one could not be buried in the churchyard, and to take the sacrament before death as a security against more dimly understood perils; but it was of equal necessity to have the proper pall-bearers and well-cured hams at one's funeral, and to leave an unimpeachable will. . . .
> The Dodsons were a very proud race, and their pride lay in the utter frustration of all desire to tax them with a breach of traditional duty or propriety. A wholesome pride in many respects, since it identified honour with perfect integrity, thoroughness of work, and faithfulness to admitted rules: and society owes some worthy qualities in many of her members to mothers of the Dodson class, who made their butter and their fromenty well, and would have felt disgraced to make it otherwise. To be honest

[6] The pervasiveness of this theme is suggested by two details in *Adam Bede*. In chapter 12, old John, Arthur Donnithorne's groom, "considered a young master as the natural enemy of an old servant, and young people in general as a poor contrivance for carrying on the world." In chapter 15, Hetty, who is not fond of children, also "did not understand how anybody could be very fond of middle-aged people." It is typical of Eliot to characterize through revelation of an individual's attitude toward different age groups.

and poor was never a Dodson motto, still less to seem rich though being poor; rather, the family badge was to be honest and rich; . . . A conspicuous quality in the Dodson character was its gen-uineness: its vices and virtues alike were phases of a proud, honest egoism, which had a hearty dislike to whatever made against its own credit and interest, and would be frankly hard of speech to inconvenient "kin," but would never forsake or ignore them—would not let them want bread, but only require them to eat it with bitter herbs.   (*The Mill on the Floss*, 30)

So dramatized, the Dodson way of life cannot be dismissed, particularly by readers who are inclined to ignore inconvenient kin. We are driven, at the least, to sympathize with the im-portance of the Dodson way of life for Maggie. She may reject it, but she cannot deny its power. Unable to adapt to it, she does not deny its premises: that the present ought not to be cut off from the past, that the commitment of others to oneself must have due respect, in short, that the individual cannot reject his duty to relations which interdict his desires and lay on him a burden of renunciation. Maggie rejects the Dodson way, but she also leaves Stephen and returns to St. Oggs. St. Oggs, of course, consists of more than Dodsons and is close to the presumable society of Eliot's readers, so that the brilliant depiction of *what might have been* followed by *what was* turns the author's irony back upon the reader.

If Miss Tulliver, after a few months of well-chosen travel, had returned as Mrs. Stephen Guest—with a post-marital *trousseau,* and all the advantages possessed even by the most unwelcome wife of an only son, public opinion, which at St. Ogg's, as else-where, always knew what to think, would have judged in strict consistency with those results. Public opinion, in these cases, is always of the feminine gender—not the world, but the world's wife: and she would have seen, that two handsome young people—the gentleman of quite the first family in St. Ogg's—having found themselves in a false position, had been led into a course which, to say the least of it, was highly injudicious, and productive of sad pain and disappointment, especially to that sweet young thing, Miss Deane. Mr. Stephen Guest had certainly not behaved well; but then, young men were liable to those

57

sudden infatuated attachments; and bad as it might seem in Mrs. Stephen Guest to admit the faintest advances from her cousin's lover (indeed it *had* been said that she was actually engaged to young Wakem—old Wakem himself had mentioned it), still she was very young—"and a deformed young man, you know!—and young Guest so very fascinating; and, they say, he positively worships her (to be sure, that can't last!) and he ran away with her in the boat quite against her will—and what could she do? She couldn't come back then: no one would have spoken to her; and how very well that maize-coloured satinette becomes her complexion! . . . Miss Unit declares she will never visit Mr. and Mrs. Stephen Guest—such nonsense! pretending to be better than other people. Society couldn't be carried on if we inquired into private conduct in that way—and Christianity tells us to think no evil—and my belief is, that Miss Unit had no cards sent her."

But the results, we know, were not of a kind to warrant this extenuation of the past. Maggie had returned without a trousseau, without a husband—in that degraded and outcast condition to which error is well known to lead; and the world's wife, with that fine instinct which is given her for the preservation of Society, saw at once that Miss Tulliver's conduct had been of the most aggravated kind. Could anything be more detestable? A girl so much indebted to her friends—whose mother as well as herself had received so much kindness from the Deanes—to lay the design of winning a young man's affections away from her own cousin, who had behaved like a sister to her! . . .

As for poor Mr. Stephen Guest, he was rather pitiable than otherwise: a young man of five-and-twenty is not to be too severely judged in these cases.   (*The Mill on the Floss*, 55)

By presenting the "actual" fictional situation from the perspective of its hypothetical opposite, Eliot compels the reader to recognize and evaluate a multiplicity of implications involving his own attitudes. He has been shown all the narrowness of the Dodsons. Here is the larger world of public opinion as he knows it from his own experience. Is this way of life so much better than that of the Dodsons? Are we, who would act as the world described here might and does act, so much superior to Mrs. Glegg? Any previously established community of attitude between author and reader becomes problematic at this point. The reader is forced by Eliot's technique to re-evaluate his own attitudes, to apply her fiction to his reality.

The Mill on the Floss opens with a personal reminiscence of a vanished way of life, and at first we accept the truth of the novel as that of nostalgic autobiography. Gradually, however, the truth becomes something different. The reader is not allowed to remain a detached observer of someone else's memories; he is engaged by a dramatic narrative. His engagement brings him increasing discomfort, the climax of which is the passage under discussion. At this point it is impossible not to recognize that Eliot's original autobiographical nostalgia is intended to prepare the reader for a criticism of contemporary values and attitudes as searching as that which she applies to the Dodsons.[7]

Fundamental to all of Eliot's novels is the effort to develop in the reader an awareness that his point of view is open to criticism. Such an evolving relation between author and reader is far removed from the static community which links author and reader in Jane Austen's novels. Eliot's omniscience leads the reader to participate in the action of her fiction. Her ironic commentaries force her reader to reassess the powerful intangibles—public opinion, education, tradition—which control his response to the world and to the fiction he reads.

The change from Jane Austen's functionally static omniscience to George Eliot's functionally shifting omniscience is equally a difference in fictional structuring and a difference in the social role assumed by the two novelists. The form of a work of fiction is to an important degree an expression of the relation between the author and his audience. Form is a sociological as well as an aesthetic aspect of fiction. I suspect

[7] Among the several studies of *The Mill on the Floss* which concentrate on aspects of the novel I have slighted, I should like to single out George Levine's "Intelligence as Deception: *The Mill on the Floss*," *PMLA*, LXXX (1965), 402-409; and cite Barbara Hardy's *The Novels of George Eliot: A Study in Form* (London, 1963) as the best critical study of Eliot's fiction with valuable commentaries on each of the novels.

that only when considered as a means for comprehending the sociological as well as the aesthetic form of a novel does point of view begin to contribute significantly to the discrimination of diverse fictional styles.

THE DISCUSSION in this chapter may have created the impression that I regard the development in omniscient point of view from Jane Austen to George Eliot as a simple "improvement" in fictional technique. That impression would be erroneous. In Chapter Seven, I touch upon problems involved in the relation of development to improvement in fictional technique. I suggest there that only on the basis of a rather sophisticated understanding of the nature of evolutionary processes in general (an understanding which I have found only among biologists and cultural historians, men such as Huxley, Waddington, Levi-Strauss, and Teilhard de Chardin) can one hope to solve the problems. It may be worthwhile here (at the cost of some repetition) to exemplify, through a further analysis of Jane Austen's and Charlotte Brontë's irony, my position, which is that no single point of view in fiction is inherently superior to another, but that one can discern an historical rationale for different authors' different preferences among points of view.

I have observed in this chapter, for example, that Charlotte Brontë lays the groundwork for Eliot's form of "omniscient" viewpoint, in that Brontë's fiction gains some of its effect through contravening accepted attitudes. Of course other novelists, notably Dickens and Thackeray, prepare the way for Eliot more directly and significantly. Yet it is important that Charlotte Brontë was uncomfortable with "omniscience." She prefers to conceal her "antagonism" to what she assumes to be her readers' values by embodying it in the nature and circumstances of a dramatic character. Her irony, therefore, flows into language which narratively articulates hidden themes in her fiction.

A representative scene from *Jane Eyre*, such as the drive to Millcote (chapter 24), shows Brontë's tendency to channel irony into images which function prefiguratively (or "post-figuratively") as elements of plot. Rochester's stories to Adele are themselves pictorializations of the magical transformation he works in Jane's life. They support the persistent imagery of the moon, under whose aegis Jane's special destiny of passionate chastity is worked out. Rochester is, as Adele observes, *"un vrai menteur."* On the return from Millcote Jane and Rochester become involved in a verbal skirmish over the suggestion that Jane is worth a whole "seraglio." Jane remarks that it is Rochester's metaphor, "the eastern allusion," which "bit me." She refuses to be the object of "slave purchases" and tells him to go to "Stamboul" if that is what he wants. While he is there she will be "preparing myself to go out as a missionary to preach liberty to them that are enslaved." In the light of St. John Rivers' plans for Jane later on, the image is ironically prophetic. Like many images in *Jane Eyre*, this one is *verbal* preparation for subsequent *actions*. At the same time it is a formulation of one of the novel's main themes, the dependent human being's duty to pursue the attainment of a meaningful personal identity.[8] This attainment is not for selfish ends. Jane *is* a "good fairy" to Rochester, but the identity she establishes is the only sound one for their relation, different as they are in sex, class, wealth, education, and temperament.

Brontë's irony is narratively oriented. It represents a step toward the changing author-audience relations we see produced by Eliot's shifting, structurally-oriented irony and a step beyond the simpler, localized, character irony employed by Jane Austen. The simplicity of Austen's irony, however, is often its strength. In *Pride and Prejudice*, for example, she summarizes local reaction to Lydia's elopement with Wickham.

The good news quickly spread through the house; and with proportionate speed through the neighbourhood. It was borne in the latter with decent philosophy. To be sure it would have

---

[8] Because Eliot's themes are more complex (although not necessarily more profound than Brontë's) they can not be so neatly formulated in single images as Brontë can. Eliot's themes are formulated through more complex *patterns* of interrelated images.

been more for the advantage of conversation, had Miss Lydia Bennet come upon the town; or, as the happiest alternative, been secluded from the world, in some distant farm house. But there was much to be talked of, in marrying her; and the good-natured wishes for her well-doing, which had proceeded before, from all the spiteful old ladies in Meryton, lost but little of their spirit in this change of circumstances, because with such an husband, her misery was considered certain. (*Pride and Prejudice*, 50; or III, 8)

The paragraph is devastating in its humorous economy. We need not know who the "old ladies" are or the specific manner in which they express their disappointment and pleasure, because our attitude can only be that of the author, whose judgments (expressed in terms such as "spiteful" and "*advantage* of conversation") are presented not for our acceptance but as our view. Possibly only on our second or third reading does the significance of the passage register in our consciousness. These "spiteful old ladies" in fact embody the moral vacuity—peculiarly dangerous because so eminently "respectable"—which surrounds the marriage choices of the Bennet girls. It is Jane Austen's formal simplicity in presenting moral complexities which makes her novels so unusually re-readable.

Near the end of *Emma*, for a subtler example, Mrs. Elton is discomposed at the plans for Emma's marriage to Mr. Knightley.

Poor Knightley! poor fellow!—sad business for him.—She was extremely concerned; for, though very eccentric, he had a thousand good qualities.—How could he be so taken in?—Did not think him at all in love—not in the least.—Poor Knightley!— There would be an end of all pleasant intercourse with him.— How happy he had been to come and dine with them whenever they asked him! But that would be all over now.—Poor fellow!— No more exploring parties to Donwell made for *her*. Oh! no; there would be a Mrs. Knightley to throw cold water on everything.— Extremely disagreeable! But she was not at all sorry that she had abused the housekeeper the other day—Shocking plan, living together. It would never do. She knew a family near Maple Grove who had tried it, and been obliged to separate before the end of the first quarter. (*Emma*, 53; or III, 17)

In this passage overt authorial irony is transposed into the speech of a character, a speech which dramatizes the values and attitudes and understanding surrounding the union of the protagonists, the context of their love, and which defines the moral rightness of Emma's and Mr. Knightley's action. Mrs. Elton is probably the most contemptible character in the novel. She is given the next-to-last word to emphasize a simple but decisive fact: the fineness, the preciousness, of the union of Emma and Mr. Knightley is something that no other characters in the novel are capable of fully appreciating. Jane Austen's adoption of a fixed, shared community of values with her audience does not imply her blind submission to it. She *chooses* her role of genteel, comic storyteller. Her choice enables her to direct her irony (without oversimplifying the actualities of social life), to clarify the tangled complexity of interpersonal relations, and, above all to lead her reader to recognize the most civilized forms of social intercourse as morally the best.[9]

Different points of view are appropriate to different purposes, to the revelation of different kinds of truth, and to different kinds of author-audience relations. No one point of view is intrinsically "superior" to another, yet one can discover reasons why one author prefers one and another author another. The reasons, however, involve one in considering matters other than point of view alone.

[9] Jane Austen's view that the most civilized forms of social intercourse are morally the best goes far to account for the violent hostility she arouses in some readers—Charlotte Brontë and Mark Twain being the most famous of these "over-reactors." But one should recognize that Jane Austen's severest censure falls on those who pretend to be civilized, who understand only the letter and not the spirit of civilized intercourse. A considerable proportion of the criticism praising Jane Austen has been written by the spiritual heirs of Mrs. Elton and the Reverend Mr. Collins.

CHAPTER V

Style and Change: Jane Austen

A DRAWBACK to the method employed in this study is its tendency to obscure changes in a novelist's career. One tends to speak of a particular kind of representation as illustrative of *the* manner of the writer, but good writers improve. The manner of their earliest work is related to but different from that of their latest. In this chapter I want to illustrate how important such changes can be by tracing one line of development through the course of Jane Austen's fiction. In so doing I can perhaps also illuminate certain characteristics of her language which have hitherto escaped notice.

In each of Jane Austen's novels is to be found at least one "scene" in which the heroine believes that she has lost the chance of marrying the man whom she loves and to whom she will, in fact, finally be betrothed. The situation lends itself to metaphoric writing: in similar scenes, as we shall see later, Charlotte Brontë uses metaphors. Jane Austen does not. If, however, we examine representative scenes from each of her six novels, we find changes which look toward metaphoric writing. Each of the "scenes" is quite different from the others, just as each of the novels is a self-sufficient work of art. Nonetheless, a focus on "disappointed-lover" scenes reveals a consistent development from rational to passional presentation.

Catherine Morland's experience of disappointment in love in *Northanger Abbey* is brief, belated, and superficial. After her sudden expulsion from General Tilney's house she undergoes some depression which is described succinctly and objectively.

The hope of meeting again in the course of a few years could only put into Catherine's head what might happen within that time to make a meeting dreadful to her. She could never forget Henry Tilney, or think of him with less tenderness than she did at that moment; but he might forget her; and in that case to meet!—Her eyes filled with tears as she pictured her acquaintance so renewed; . . . She could neither sit still, nor employ herself for ten minutes together, . . . Her loss of spirits was a yet greater alteration. In her rambling and her idleness she might only be a caricature of herself; but in her silence and sadness she was the very reverse of all that she had been before.

(*Northanger Abbey*, 30; or II, 15)

There is in such "rational" passages no self-analysis. In fact, there is little tension of any kind—for example, Catherine has no rival to meditate upon—and the language is lucid and uncomplicated.

In *Sense and Sensibility* Marianne is jilted. Her suffering is extreme. The only point I wish to make about the physical anguish produced by her emotional suffering—scribbling her desperate letter with tears streaming down her face, stretching out on her bed almost screaming with agony, sinking into frigid indifference—is that Jane Austen's descriptions are convincing. The portrayal of Marianne is in itself sufficient to prove that when Austen wished to represent violent emotions she could do so expertly and effectively. But she did not often wish to. Therefore, I want to concentrate attention upon her representation of Elinor's disappointment, for Elinor is closer to the central line of Austen's development. Elinor considers the possibility (which does not appear in *Northanger Abbey*) that the man she loves has jilted her—and rejects it.

Had Edward been intentionally deceiving her? Had he feigned a regard for her which he did not feel? Was his engagement to Lucy an engagement of the heart? No; whatever it might once have been, she could not believe it such at present. His affection was all her own. She could not be deceived in that. Her mother, sisters, Fanny, all had been conscious of his regard for her at Norland; it was not an illusion of her own vanity. He certainly loved her. . . . He had been blameable, highly blameable in remaining at Norland after he first felt her influence over him to be more than it ought to be. . . . but if he had injured her, how much more had he injured himself! If her case were pitiable, his was hopeless. His imprudence had made her miserable for a while; but it seemed to have deprived himself of all chance of ever being otherwise. (*Sense and Sensibility*, 23; or II, 1)

In this passage we enter into Elinor's mind, as we do not enter into Catherine's, and there find real complexity of thought and feeling. Elinor has to disentangle reality from the "illusion of her own vanity": her "persuasion" of Edward's love can "tempt her to forgive." Furthermore, her disappointment includes (and *must* include because her feeling for Edward is a more mature emotion than Catherine's for Henry Tilney) concern for Edward and concern for her mother and sisters.

. . . she wept for him more than for herself. Supported by the conviction of having done nothing to merit her present unhappiness, and consoled by the belief that Edward had done nothing to forfeit her esteem, she thought she could even now, under the first smart of the heavy blow, command herself enough to guard every suspicion of the truth from her mother and sisters. And so well was she able to answer her own expectations, that when she joined them at dinner only two hours after she had first suffered the extinction of all her dearest hopes, no one would have supposed from the appearance of the sisters, that Elinor was mourning in secret over obstacles which must divide her for ever from the object of her love, . . . (*Sense and Sensibility*, 23; or II, 1)

Elinor's concealment of her feelings is, of course, in part self-protection. But it is more than that. It is protection of Edward and even of Lucy and the complicated truth of Elinor's and Edward's relation, which would be distorted by the oversimplifications of Marianne's and Mrs. Dashwood's uncontrolled emotionality. The "climax" of personal anguish lies in its control by a sense of social decorum. The value of this control is difficult for modern readers to appreciate, and we tend to regard Elinor (rather as we do Fanny Price) as priggish.

You do not suppose that I have ever felt much. For four months, Marianne, I have had all this hanging on my mind, without being at liberty to speak of it to a single creature; knowing that it would make you and my mother most unhappy whenever it were explained to you, yet unable to prepare you for it in the least. . . . I have known myself to be divided from Edward for ever, without hearing one circumstance that could make me less desire the connection. Nothing has proved him unworthy; nor has anything declared him indifferent to me. I have had to contend against the unkindness of his sister, and the insolence of his mother, and have suffered the punishment of an attachment without enjoying its advantages. And all this has been going on at a time when, as you too well know, it has not been my only unhappiness. If you can think me capable of ever feeling—surely you may suppose that I have suffered *now*. The composure of mind with which I have brought myself at present to consider the matter, the consolation that I have been willing to admit, have been the effect of constant and painful exertion; they did not spring up of themselves; . . . (*Sense and Sensibility*, 37; or III, 1)

If there is priggishness in Elinor's speech, it springs in part from the fact that she is *explaining* the history of her complex feelings and the variety of motives which induced her to conceal them. One might argue that the complexity of Elinor's sentences reflects the complexity of her conflicting emotions and that the formality of her language is a sign of her ability to master, rather than to be mastered by, her feelings. But the principal feature of Elinor's explanation, to my mind, is its implicit insistence through both form and substance on the necessary relation of propriety to personal emotion. Mere impulse is not sufficient cause, is not "justification," for behavior. Today we tend to think of this as a stilted and repressive attitude. Jane Austen believes that unless "impulse" is controlled the full potential of personality cannot be realized. But control of feeling does not mean denial of feeling. In Elinor's final "disappointment" scene, the first two paragraphs of chapter 48 (or III, 12), there is no lack of emotional stress. The language in this passage is still formal and rational: "she condemned her heart for the lurking flattery which so much heightened the pain of intelligence." But in the third paragraph, describing Elinor's imaginative vision, brilliantly etched as to Lucy, hopelessly blank as to Edward, we find something that serves as a substitute for metaphoric language —a picture that concretely embodies the turmoil of Elinor's feelings. Immediate intensity is not, however, the primary effect for which Jane Austen aims in portraying Elinor's response to the news of Edward's "marriage." She aims, instead, for clarification of the relations among her thoughts and emotions, even those that are "muddled." This clarification is necessary because Elinor, remaining true to herself, realizes her being through interpersonal relations controlled by a rigid system of decorum.

In *Pride and Prejudice* Elizabeth's "disappointment" comes as a shock. Only when she tells Darcy the news of Lydia's elopement does Elizabeth clearly "understand her own wishes."

> Darcy made no answer. He seemed scarcely to hear her, and was walking up and down the room in earnest meditation; his brow contracted, his air gloomy. Elizabeth soon observed, and instantly understood it. Her power was sinking; every thing *must* sink under such a proof of family weakness, such an assurance of the deepest disgrace. She could neither wonder nor condemn, but the belief of his self-conquest brought nothing consolatory to her bosom, afforded no palliation of her distress. It was, on the contrary, exactly calculated to make her understand her own wishes; and never had she so honestly felt that she could have loved him, as now, when all love must be vain.
>
> But self, though it would intrude, could not engross her.
>
> (*Pride and Prejudice*, 46; or III, 4)

Unlike Elinor's, Elizabeth's awareness of her sentiments is precipitated by a sudden crisis, a crisis, moreover, of which there appears to be no possible concealment. The crisis is not a personal one, except that Elizabeth is affected by her family's behavior. Yet the representation of Elizabeth's disappointment probes more deeply into the nature of her feelings than does that of Elinor's. With Elinor we are shown her response to the apparent necessity of giving up the man she loves. Her love, however, is not represented: it is a *donnée*. With Elizabeth we are shown the emergence of love: "never had she so honestly felt that she could have loved him as now. . . ." The phrase is astonishing in its precision. "Now"—at this instant "when all love must be vain"—Elizabeth does not *know* she loves Darcy; instead she "honestly" *feels* she "*could* have loved him." Nobody, so far as I am aware, has satisfactorily explained in what "love" between man and woman consists, but in *Pride and Prejudice* Jane Austen depicts one form of its genesis. Shortly after the passage quoted above she comments:

> If gratitude and esteem are good foundations of affection, Elizabeth's change of sentiment will be neither improbable nor faulty. But if otherwise, if the regard springing from such sources is unreasonable or unnatural, in comparison of what is so often described as arising on a first interview with its object, and even before two words have been exchanged, nothing can be said in her defense, except that she had given somewhat of a trial to the latter method, in her partiality for Wickham, and that its ill-success might perhaps authorise her to seek the other less interesting mode of attachment. (*Pride and Prejudice*, 46; or III, 4)

Because "gratitude and esteem" precede the love Elizabeth comes to feel for Darcy, it is accurate for Jane Austen to represent Elizabeth in the earlier passage as experiencing an authentic sentiment that she *could* love Darcy, implying, of course, that she very soon *will* love Darcy.

Elizabeth's position is more dramatic than Elinor's. Elizabeth's potential affection is frustrated by a sudden crisis which produces her awareness of that affection (a pattern which is to some degree repeated in *Emma*). This drama makes Austen's presentation in *Pride and Prejudice* seem less formalized than that in *Sense and Sensibility*, although it might be difficult to prove that either the vocabulary or syntax in the passages from the later novel differ significantly from those in the earlier. The action of the disappointment scene in *Pride and Prejudice* is immediate, even violent, and involves dynamic interpenetration of emotion and perception. Elinor, on the other hand, reflects alone or explains her *past* feelings, thereby removing to the distance emotions which are in the forefront with Elizabeth. In both novels the relevance of social context to personal anguish is essential. It is, after all, "family weakness," the threat of public "disgrace" arising from Lydia's indecorous behavior, which seems to deny Darcy to Elizabeth. And, like Elinor's, Elizabeth's "self, though it would intrude, could not engross her." Still the personal and interpersonal interactions are more subtle and more complex, and so more meaningful, in *Pride and Prejudice*. When Lydia's marriage has been arranged and Elizabeth is still ignorant of Darcy's role in the arrangements, she regrets Darcy's knowledge of the truth.

> Not, however, from any fear of disadvantage from it, individually to herself; for at any rate, there seemed a gulf impassable between them. Had Lydia's marriage been concluded on the most honourable terms, it was not to be supposed that Mr. Darcy would connect himself with a family, where to every other objection would now be added, an alliance and relationship of the nearest kind with the man whom he so justly scorned.
>
> From such a connection she could not wonder that he should shrink. The wish of procuring her regard, which she had assured herself of his feeling in Derbyshire, could not in rational expectation survive such a blow as this. She was humbled, she was grieved; she repented, though she hardly knew of what.
>
> (*Pride and Prejudice*, 50; or III, 8)

Elizabeth has no "fear of disadvantage" from Darcy's knowledge "individually to herself," although Lydia's marriage to Wickham appears to deny her the "advantage" of marrying Darcy. It is perhaps more significant than it first appears to be that, whereas Elinor spends more time contemplating and analyzing the past, Elizabeth's thoughts turn more persistently to the present and future.

> She began now to comprehend that he was exactly the man, who, in disposition and talents, would most suit her. His understanding and temper, though unlike her own, would have answered all her wishes. It was an union that must have been to the advantage of both; by her ease and liveliness, his mind might have been softened, his manners improved, and from his judg-

ment, information, and knowledge of the world she must have received benefit of greater importance.

(*Pride and Prejudice*, 50; or III, 8)

The advantages to both are "personal," yet the union seems impossible because of the importance of "connection," "alliance," and "relationship," all social considerations. For Elizabeth, as for all of Jane Austen's heroines, personal fulfillment is possible only within the social sanction of a "good" marriage; this makes for Elizabeth's distress. The "best" marriage of which she can conceive is made impossible by the very code which defines it as a "good" one. Elizabeth is no slave to the mores of her society, but her strong emotions are balanced by her judicious "rational expectation." She recognizes that if she wishes to be treated as a "lady" and as the daughter of a "gentleman" according to the definitions of her society, she would be childish to object when the same rules prevent a gentleman from marrying her.

Of course the rules don't prevent Darcy from finally marrying her. Such rule-breaking doesn't occur in the earlier novels: the dynamics of personal fulfillment through successful social relations are more complex in *Pride and Prejudice*. One notes in Elizabeth's reflections that "she repented, though she hardly knew of what." It is appropriate for Elizabeth to be uncertain about why she regrets both having told Darcy about Lydia and having rejected his proposal. The latter act is inseparable from the *form* of Darcy's proposal—it was ungentlemanly. This accusation tortures him; its justice he not only admits but finally insists upon. In one sense Elizabeth should not, and in fact she does not, regret rejecting an ungentlemanly proposal, even though she comes to regret losing the gentleman. Neither Henry Tilney nor Edward Ferrars is ungentlemanly. Neither, for that matter, are the later heroes. Jane Austen's development is not simply in the direction of increasingly "mixed" protagonists, rather it is in the direction of increasingly profound insight into the intricacies of the interplay between personal and social relationships. Elizabeth wins Darcy by sticking to the rules. Her steadfastness in

71

playing the role of a lady provokes Darcy into a self-examination which produces recognition of the superficiality of the "gentlemanliness" upon which he prides himself. He reforms, becomes a true gentleman, and Elizabeth makes the best marriage in the novel, its public quality being evidenced by her mother's "extraordinary" reaction to the news of it: "on first hearing it, Mrs. Bennet sat quite still, and unable to utter a syllable." It is also the "best" marriage from Elizabeth's private, personal point of view—"individually for herself." In the earlier novels both the personalities of the protagonists and the system of the society in which they exist are fixed. In *Pride and Prejudice* both elements (and their interactions) become dynamic. Individuality is still conceived of as a nexus of interplay with others, the individual is still defined by the pattern of his interpersonal relations, but interplay and pattern have become more fluid, hence more complex and meaningful.[1]

This development, however, is not altogether conducive to the introduction of metaphor. Rational clarification as a primary aim becomes more, not less, important. Intensity in the representation of emotions recedes in importance as an artistic virtue. As the emotions which form the subject of Jane Austen's art begin to mature, become both stronger and more complicated, her representation of their activity at first becomes cooler, more rationally articulated, ever more logically lucid.

The movement is visible in *Mansfield Park*, first of all in the nature of the heroine. It is a critical commonplace that Mary Crawford is more nearly the equivalent of Elizabeth Bennet

[1] Reuben A. Brower's deservedly famous essay, "Light and Bright and Sparkling: Irony and Fiction in *Pride and Prejudice*," is now available in the Galaxy Book edition of his *The Fields of Light* (New York, 1962), pp. 164-81. Samuel Kliger in "Jane Austen's *Pride and Prejudice* in the Eighteenth-century Mode," *University of Toronto Quarterly*, XVI (1947), 357-70, argues that the governing theme of the novel is an antithesis between nature and art. While it is obvious I do not agree with Kliger, I think his essay deserves more serious attention than it usually receives. Another essay whose value is sometimes overlooked and which has bearing on *Pride and Prejudice* is Donald J. Greene's "Jane Austen and the Peerage," *PMLA*, LXVIII (1954), 1017-31.

than is Fanny Price.[2] Yet Fanny's moral standards are clear and consistent, and she musters the strength to stand by her principles in critical moments; but, more important, without being an emotionalist like Marianne, she is much more a creature of feeling than the earlier heroines.[3] Her debility, which offends modern taste, is nevertheless an apt expression of the vulnerability of one who lives by and through feeling. *Mansfield Park* may not be a complete success, but it testifies to Jane Austen's steadily deepening concern with personal emotion. Fanny's "disappointment" scene, for example, reveals a new tendency toward the representation of emotional processes in action.

She was one of his two dearest—that must support her. But the other!—the first! She had never heard him speak so openly before, and though it told her no more than what she had long perceived, it was a stab; . . . He would marry Miss Crawford. It was a stab, in spite of every long-standing expectation; and she was obliged to repeat again and again that she was one of his two dearest, before the words gave her any sensation. Could she believe Miss Crawford to deserve him, it would be—Oh! how different would it be—how far more tolerable! But he was deceived in her; . . .

It was her intention, as she felt it to be her duty, to try to overcome all that was excessive, all that bordered on selfishness in her affection for Edmund. To call or to fancy it a loss, a disappointment, would be a presumption; for which she had not words strong enough to satisfy her own humility. To think of him as Miss Crawford might be justified in thinking, would in her be insanity. To her he could be nothing under any circumstances—

[2] The commonplace, however, is only partially true. The "illusion of reality" created by the characterization of Fanny (however unpleasant she may be) seems to me stronger than that created by the characterization of Mary Crawford (however pleasant she may be). All of Jane Austen's protagonists are more fully realized than the secondary figures.

[3] With some justice Fanny might be described as the first psychoneurotic heroine in British fiction, if one accepts a typical dictionary definition of "psychoneurosis" as an ". . . emotional disorder in which feelings of anxiety, obsessional thoughts . . . and physical complaints without objective evidence of disease . . . dominate the personality" (*The American College Dictionary*).

nothing dearer than a friend. Why did such an idea occur to her even enough to be reprobated and forbidden? It ought not to have touched on the confines of her imagination. She would endeavour to be rational, . . . she seized the scrap of paper on which Edmund had begun writing to her, as a treasure beyond all her hopes, and reading with the tenderest emotion these words, "My very dear Fanny, you must do me the favour to accept"—locked it up with the chain, as the dearest part of the gift. It was the only thing approaching to a letter which she had ever received from him; she might never receive another; it was impossible that she should receive another so perfectly gratifying in the occasion and the style. Two lines more prized had never fallen from the pen of the most distinguished author—never more completely blessed the researches of the fondest biographer.

(Mansfield Park, 27; or II, 9)

Although there is irony and formality in this passage, it represents the surge of emotion: the long sentences interrupted by short ones are not placed merely for rhetorical effect but to convey something of the ebb and flow of Fanny's feelings. The passage contains and obvious metaphor, the repeated "it was a stab."[4] At the same time there is comedy in the presentation of Fanny's feelings that is not found in the depictions of Elizabeth's and Elinor's disappointments. The comedy is partly verbal, as when Fanny strives for words "strong enough" to satisfy "humility," but partly it is tonal, as when Fanny's attitude to Edmund's scrap of writing is portrayed. The comic irony here is appropriate because Jane Austen shows Fanny *in the process* of making the "endeavor to be rational." Rationally considered, Fanny's behavior is incongruous, and may be made fun of—which is also a way of distancing the emotion. That Jane Austen here feels the need for distancing is significant. Fanny's situation as contrasted to that of Elinor and Elizabeth is genuinely private. Relative to the earlier novels, public and social influences are in the

---

[4] A number of Jane Austen's overt metaphors used to portray emotion involve an image of penetration—see, for example, the passage from *Emma* cited later in this chapter.

background, coming to the fore only in the generalizations which support the ironies of the final paragraph.[5]

When we turn to *Emma*, we find that the heroine's disappointment can not be illustrated by a single, brief quotation.

A few minutes were sufficient for making her acquainted with her own heart. A mind like her's, once opening to suspicion, made rapid progress. She touched—she admitted—she acknowledged the whole truth. Why was it so much worse that Harriet should be in love with Mr. Knightley, than with Frank Churchill? Why was the evil so dreadfully increased by Harriet's having some hope of a return? It darted through her, with the speed of an arrow, that Mr. Knightley must marry no one but herself!

(*Emma*, 47; or iii, 11)

This passage is only introductory. Emma's recognition that Mr. Knightley might be in love with Harriet is an authentic revelation, but the revelation is not, as the disappointment scenes in the earlier novels are in essence, a mere incident. Emma's revelation is the central action of the novel and articulates its major issues. This alone testifies to how much more "internalized" is the subject matter of *Emma*. It is appropriate, therefore, that Emma's meditations occupy a considerable length of time and are imaged by restless, unsatisfying bodily movement.

It is notable that in *Emma* the social and the interpersonal are presented in terms of individual attitude and response, and that the particular representation of Emma's revelation reflects the limitations of the novel's society as a whole. In the following passage, for example, "general opinion" is dramatized by "smiles" and "sneers," both individual expressions, and Emma sees herself as individually responsible for her friend's "elevation" and Mr. Knightley's "debasement."

[5] Two particularly valuable critiques of *Mansfield Park* are Thomas R. Edwards, Jr.'s "The Difficult Beauty of *Mansfield Park*," *Nineteenth Century Fiction*, xx (1965), 51-67, seeing the novel as "a prediction of what fiction was to be for the masters of the next hundred years," and Avrom Fleishman's *A Reading of Mansfield Park: An Essay in Critical Synthesis* (Minneapolis, 1967), a thorough, original, thought-provoking analysis.

With insufferable vanity had she believed herself in the secret of everybody's feelings; with unpardonable arrogance proposed to arrange everybody's destiny. She was proved to have been universally mistaken; and she had not quite done nothing—for she had done mischief. She had brought evil on Harriet, on herself, and she too much feared, on Mr. Knightley.—Were this most unequal of all connexions to take place, on her must rest all the reproach of having given it a beginning; for his attachment, she must believe to be produced only by a consciousness of Harriet's; —and even were this not the case, he would never have known Harriet at all but for her folly.

Mr. Knightley and Harriet Smith!—It was an union to distance every wonder of the kind. . . . Such an elevation on her side! Such a debasement on his!—It was horrible to Emma to think how it must sink him in the general opinion, to foresee the smiles, the sneers, the merriment it would prompt at his expense; the mortification and disdain of his brother, the thousand inconveniences to himself.—Could it be?—No; it was impossible. And yet it was far, very far, from impossible.—Was it a new circumstance for a man of first-rate abilities to be captivated by very inferior powers? Was it new for one, perhaps too busy to seek, to be the prize of a girl who would seek him?—Was it new for any thing in this world to be unequal, inconsistent, incongruous—or for chance and circumstance (as second causes) to direct the human fate?   (*Emma*, 47; or III, 11)

The vocabulary and syntax of these passages differs from the vocabulary and syntax of those cited from earlier novels. The vocabulary is more violent, "horrible," "evil." The sentence structure is more abrupt and broken, there are many exclamatory and interrogatory phrases, and the "philosophic" generalizations emerge with a personal anguish similar to that of a passionate Shakesperean soliloquy. "Was it new for any thing in this world to be unequal, inconsistent, incongruous . . . for chance and circumstance . . . to direct human fate."

These characteristics need to be cited because there has been a tendency for critics to regard *Emma* as the most "representative" of Jane Austen's novels in its compactness of cast and setting, in the pervasiveness of its ironies, and in its depiction of an extremely rigid system of social decorum. *Emma is* representative, but it is also a product of an evolving art. The very compactness and highly decorous social system of the novel come from Jane Austen's increasing emphasis on the personal side of the personal-social interplay which is her constant subject matter. It is noteworthy, too, that in the climactic scenes irony plays a surprisingly small role. Emphasis is on the direct representation of psychic agitation.

Emma is a more subjective book than its predecessors. We spend much time following the inner workings of Emma's mind and, as critics have stressed, a substantial portion of the action is narrated from her point of view. This explains in part the unusual pervasiveness of irony in *Emma*: it enables Austen to elucidate the complex processes of Emma's sophisticated, if erring, intelligence and her refined, if self-misunderstood, sentiments.[6]

In the passages cited above we are presented with Emma's revelation of the true nature not only of her feelings but also of her conduct. This is a new experience for an Austen heroine. None before Emma can accuse themselves of seriously faulty conduct, as distinct from simple error. In *Emma*, problems of self-knowledge and social behavior, heretofore distinct, are unified; feeling and conduct are inseparable, whereas in the earlier novels the action consisted of their conflict; the dramatic center of Austen's fiction shifts slightly, but significantly. Social relations are now represented in terms of individual psychic activity, e.g., the possibility of Knightley's social "debasement" lies in his possible "consciousness" of Harriet's affection for him. Not only has Emma raised Harriet's social position but also, simultaneously, she has "educated" her "humility" into "self-consequence." This im-

---

[6] I would cite as especially perceptive studies of *Emma*, a novel which has attracted much fine criticism: G. Armour Craig's "Jane Austen's *Emma*: The Truths and Disguises of Human Disclosure," *In Defense of Reading: A Reader's Approach to Literary Criticism*, ed. Reuben Brower and W. R. Poirer (New York, 1962), pp. 235-55; W. J. Harvey's "The Plot of *Emma*," *Essays in Criticism*, XVII (1967), 48-63; Edgar F. Shannon, Jr.'s "*Emma*: Character and Construction," *PMLA*, LXXI (1956), 637-50; and Lionel Trilling's remarkable introduction to the Riverside edition of *Emma* (Boston, 1957).

plies a subtler and more profound extension of the "revolution" initiated by Darcy's determination to marry Elizabeth despite her "connections." Throughout *Emma* there is emphasis (particularly by Emma herself) on the "superior" and the "inferior." The possibility of Harriet's marrying Mr. Knightley threatens the social embodiment of that hierarchical order. It is far more important, however, that Emma's awareness of this possibility accompanies her realization that she is personally responsible for the threat. Emma's relation to Harriet, incredible as it first appears to be, can be regarded as analogous to that of Frankenstein to his monster, but the meaning of Emma's sudden understanding of her responsibility for creating a threat to her own ordering of values is worked out with a precise profundity far beyond Mary Shelley's artistic abilities. Emma's realization of her responsibility is inseparable from her recognition of the true nature of her "heart," her feelings. What we see in the moment of Emma's crisis is *not* the overthrow of the hierarchy of "superior" and "inferior" but, instead, the re-affirmation of this hierarchy on a different basis. Emma's fault has been to treat superiority and inferiority superficially. She casually dismisses Robert Martin as Harriet's inferior and as casually makes Harriet Mr. Elton's equal. Harriet's pretensions to Mr. Knightley are, in fact, an extension of Emma's practices. Faced with this, Emma realizes that superiority and inferiority are tremendously important, not because of their ordering of social relations but because that ordering is an expression of what Keats called "the holiness of the heart's affections." Mr. Knightley "ought" not to marry Harriet because he "must marry no one but herself." This is the truth of personal emotion. It is primary. The social disorientation which would result from Knightley-Smith nuptials is not trivial (as are the results of Darcy's marriage to Elizabeth) because they would represent the failure (through willful self-misunderstanding) of a superior person to exercise her imaginative, intellectual, and emotional superiority to the benefit not merely of herself but also of those upon whom her life impinges. Knightley would be debased by a marriage to Harriet and the benefits to Harriet would be illusory and short-lived. "It was impossible. . . . And yet it was far, very far, from impossible." Incredible social disorder is always possible when people of superior education and sensibility abuse their advantage by denying its source, the individual heart.

Emma is a great novel because it has a profound theme and Jane Austen possesses the art to express it effortlessly. That art, as I have tried to show, develops from her earlier practice, and the development is continued in *Persuasion*. Let me remind the reader, however, that Austen's "progress" is especially interesting because it occurs within such definite limits. All her novels are shaped to a form of rational lucidity. Their organization is essentially logical and their language essentially nonmetaphorical. The individual is defined and distinguished by his social role not by the representation of his sensory perceptions. The chief quality of Austen's language is its transparency: transpicuous itself, it works to clarify the obscure, which often involves the revelation of complexities within apparently simple relationships.

Persuasion comes close to transgressing these limits.[7] It is Jane Austen's only novel with a plot involving considerable temporal complexity. This is a symptom of the nature of the novel's action: the re-creation of personal feeling. In subject and theme *Persuasion* is original: I know of no other major novel so focused on the reanimation of affection. Because *Persuasion* is so concerned with feeling, it is far less ironic than *Emma*. Conduct is not a major issue in *Persuasion*: until the very end, even Mr. Elliot's propriety is impeccable. The irony of *Emma* would be inappropriate in *Persuasion*, for Anne knows her heart perfectly from the first. The problem of the last novel is the destiny of Anne's emotional commitment.

In all of Austen's earlier novels love is presented as a learning process, but Anne is educated. In the other novels the underlying presupposition is that genuine love is the highest

---

[7] Litz's discussion of *Persuasion* in his *Jane Austen,* pp. 150-60, is splendid; and Mark Schorer's celebrated essay "Fiction and the 'Matrix of Analogy,'" *Kenyon Review,* XI (1949), 539-60, skillfully contrasts Jane Austen's last novel with *Wuthering Heights* and *Middlemarch.*

good. That presupposition is tested in *Persuasion* and found to be true. This is why *Persuasion* treats feeling as feeling, not the understanding of feeling. The concentration leads to a considerable change in the social relationships by which individual character is realized. It is no coincidence that *Persuasion* includes Jane Austen's sharpest indictments of rank. And Anne is the first heroine to be, to a significant degree, isolated. There is little community between her and her father and sister. Her relation to Lady Russell is characterized by a detachment not visible, for example, in Emma's relation to Mrs. Weston. One is made conscious of Anne's peculiar isolation through intimacies amongst the Musgroves.

> One of the least agreeable circumstances of her residence there, was her being treated with too much confidence by all parties, and being too much in the secret of the complaints of each house. . . .
> How was Anne to set all these matters to rights? She could do little more than listen patiently, soften every grievance, and excuse each to the other; give them all hints of the forbearance necessary between such near neighbours, . . .   (*Persuasion*, 6)

Jane Austen's appearances as narrator in *Persuasion* differ from her appearances in other novels. In *Persuasion* her function is to enable us to appreciate the subtle personal experiences Anne undergoes. When, for example, Captain Wentworth takes the troublesome child off Anne's back, the emotions precipitated are so immediate and agitating that ironic representation of them could only obscure the principal point of the scene: a simple action can produce bewilderingly powerful emotional effects.

Even as there is relatively little irony in *Persuasion*, so there is no "disappointed-lover" scene equivalent to those in the earlier novels. One important reason is that *Persuasion*'s subject, a resurrection of love, does not allow such a scene. The equivalent situation is an exactly inverted one: Anne realizes that Wentworth is jealous of Mr. Elliot and "for a moment the gratification was exquisite." A few passages which represent the initial phases of Anne's and Wentworth's reacquaintance, beginning with the expository account of Anne's mature judgment on her earlier behavior, merit attention.

> She did not blame Lady Russell, she did not blame herself for having been guided by her; but she felt that were any young person, in similar circumstances, to apply to her for counsel, they would never receive any of such certain immediate wretchedness, such uncertain future good.—She was persuaded that under every disadvantage of disapprobation at home, and every anxiety attending his profession, all their probable fears, delays and disappointments, she should yet have been a happier woman in maintaining the engagement, than she had been in the sacrifice of it; and this, she fully believed, had the usual share, had even more than a usual share of all such solicitudes and suspense been theirs, without reference to the actual results of their case, which, as it happened, would have bestowed earlier prosperity than could be reasonably calculated on.   (*Persuasion*, 4)

This sentence structure is more complex than is usual in the earlier novels, the complexity reflecting the extreme fineness of the discriminations contained in the passage. Unusual, too, is the temporal perspective: here we are given a later attitude toward former behavior, but, notably, the attitude is not ironic. Still later when Anne learns of Captain Wentworth's remark on her appearance we find a passage equally unironic but tonally distinct from that just quoted.

> "Captain Wentworth is not very gallant by you, Anne, though he was so attentive to me. Henrietta asked him what he thought of you, when they went away; and he said, 'You were so altered he should not have known you again. . . .' "
>
> "Altered beyond his knowledge!" Anne fully submitted, in silent, deep mortification. Doubtless it was so; and she could take no revenge, for he was not altered, or not for the worse. She had already acknowledged it to herself, and she could not think differently, let him think of her as he would. No; the years which had destroyed her youth and bloom had only given him a more glowing, manly, open look, in no respect lessening his personal advantages. She had seen the same Frederick Wentworth.
>
> "So altered that he should not have known her again!" These were words which could not but dwell with her. Yet she soon

began to rejoice that she had heard them. They were of sobering tendency, they allayed agitation; they composed, and consequently must make her happier. (*Persuasion*, 7)

This concern with specific physical appearance is a new element in Austen's fiction, and once more a temporal perspective is central to the presentation. These elements recur when Wentworth's "ceremonious grace" to Anne gives her acute pain, in part because she believes he sees in her "altered features . . . the ruins of a face which had once charmed him." The writing here is, at the least, close to metaphoric. In the passage quoted above one can observe a phrase for which I know of no counterpart in the earlier novels: "These were words which could not but *dwell* with her." These "new" stylistic features seem to me to derive from Austen's probing deeper into the intricacies of personal relations, intricacies resulting from her recognition of the often paradoxical interplay of feelings—e.g., "mortification" operating so as "to make her happier"—especially when a sense for the temporal life of sentiments, above all their persistence, is taken into account.

In the eavesdropping scene, Wentworth's speech is given focus by the hazelnut he picks. Once more, there is no real prototype for this. Wentworth uses the hazelnut as a metaphor for the constancy of character which he commends and in fact exhibits. Even more interesting, perhaps, is the description of Anne's reaction when the others have moved off.

The sounds were retreating, and Anne distinguished no more. Her own emotions still kept her fixed. She had much to recover from, before she could move. . . . She saw how her own character was considered by Captain Wentworth; and there had been just that degree of feeling and curiosity about her in his manner, which must give her extreme agitation. . . . Her spirits wanted the solitude and silence which only numbers could give.

(*Persuasion*, 10)

Anne is agitated by her perception of "just that degree of feeling and curiosity about her in his manner." But Wentworth's *manner* is scarcely perceptible to the reader in his two questions, "Do you mean that she [Anne] refused him [Charles]?" and "When did that happen?" Austen's emphasis is shifting to those nuances expressing affective relationship which are scarcely representable in her earlier style. She still aims for lucidity, but now she seeks to make clear that which is inexpressible through logic, through rationality, through intellectualized irony, but requires, instead, something akin to metaphoric prose. The extent of Austen's development is suggested by the last sentence of the passage. This is, I believe, the first time that she presents a social grouping not as a means for the expression and realization of individual thought and feeling but as refuge within which the individual can nurture and explore purely private emotion. In *Persuasion* for the first time Austen probes deeply into the sentiments which defy the resources of rational, discursive language, and this is why we find there her first "symbolic use of natural setting" and the autumnal imagery which has attracted the comment of many critics.

These qualities accompany another new but less noticed element in Jane Austen's language, a shift toward the representation of reiterated experience. *Persuasion*, like many of Wordsworth's poems, is concerned primarily with recurrence, with the processes of emotions as defined by experiential repetitions. Like Wordsworth, Austen becomes interested in the relation of feeling *now* to feeling *then*, of the novel to the familiar. The comparison to Wordsworth is not arbitrary. It helps to explain why, in moving away from logical, ironic representation, Jane Austen did not move farther in the direction of the pictorial and metaphoric. Probing more deeply into the sources, persistence, and significance of personal emotion, she sought not that which separates the private from the rest of the world but different, more fundamental, bonds between the individual and his surroundings. Even more important than "romantic" description in *Persuasion* is Austen's delineation of the qualities of her heroine's sensibility which make her so appropriate a character both to respond to the immediacy of sensory impressions and to dramatize constancy of affection. In the following passage I italicize those phrases which most clearly structure the description as an affirmation of what might be called the preciousness of familiarity. In her last novel Jane Austen begins to represent the values of perceptiveness and affection which emerge only when perceptions and feelings are regarded in a temporal context.[8]

> . . . *a very strange stranger* it must be who does not see charms in the immediate environs of Lyme, to make him *wish to know it better*. The scenes in its neighbourhood, Charmouth, with its high grounds and extensive sweeps of country, and still more its sweet retired bay, backed by dark cliffs, where fragments of low rock among the sands make it the happiest spot for watching *the flow of the tide*, for *sitting in unwearied contemplation*;—the woody varieties of the cheerful village of Up Lyme, and, above all, Pinny, with its green chasms between romantic rocks, where the scattered forest trees and *orchards of luxuriant growth declare that many a generation must have passed away* since the partial falling of the cliff prepared the ground for such a state, where a scene so wonderful and so lovely is exhibited, as may more than equal any of the resembling scenes of the far-famed Isle of Wight: these places must be visited, *and visited again*, to make the *worth* of Lyme understood.   (*Persuasion*, 11)

[8] Several of the statistical measures reported in Chapter Nine below point to *Persuasion*'s difference from Austen's earlier novels. One notices, in particular, that *Persuasion* contains relatively little dialogue, a kind of action which is essentially "a-temporal."

CHAPTER VI

Image and Metaphor

IT IS obvious that Charlotte Brontë prefers the first-person narrative form whereas Jane Austen does not. What is not so obvious is the connection between a total narrative form such as the first-person point of view and the sentence structures and word choices which embody the form. Yet the difference between two novels with the same total narrative form lies in this connection. Because the art of a first-rate novelist changes, even in different novels by the same author the connections are likely to differ. In the preceding chapter I tried to illustrate, however, that in some novelists at least there is a persistent direction of change. Where this is the case (and it is always the case if my hypothesis that style *is* consistency of development is correct) one can hope to find patterns of connection between total form and sentence structures and word choices.

Now if, for example, one were to strike out of *Emma* all the recurrent images, Jane Austen's novel would remain largely intact. If, however, one were to strike out of *Middlemarch* all the recurrent images, George Eliot's novel would be a shambles. Furthermore, if one looks through British fiction before Austen one does not find significant use of the *kind* of recurrent imagery employed by Eliot, though it is commonplace after her time. Between Jane Austen and George Eliot there occurred a radical change in the fashion in which the "omniscient" point of view was embodied in the language of fiction. One can identify fairly easily some of the leading contributors to the change. Walter Scott is one. *The Heart of Midlothian* might be cited as the first important British novel in which a place, the prison, is treated as a metaphor (as well as a location) essential to the structure of the narrative. And it is difficult to find a British novelist before Dickens who organizes his fiction so pervasively and significantly by means of recurrent imagery.

The problem of *why* these changes occur remains. A thorough history of British fiction, which would be a very long work indeed, would provide some answers. My more modest aim here is to point up some specific differences between three novelists so as to make clear how study of the connection between the large and small structures of fiction is necessary to establish even rudimentary contrasts between novels. These contrasts are the necessary starting points for the development of a history of style in fiction.

Thus one can usefully juxtapose one of Brontë's "disappointed lover" scenes with the pattern of such scenes in Austen's novels, the pattern traced in the preceding chapter. Jane Eyre's "disappointment" (the final few paragraphs of chapter 16) involves more self-mortification than do the disappointments of any of Jane Austen's heroines. The major portion of the passage is controlled by the metaphor of bringing the heart to trial. There are also subordinate metaphors, such as the internal landscape, "imagination's boundless and trackless waste" with its "miry wilds."[1] At least as striking, however, is the sentence of judgment requiring the "actual" painting of portraits which serve (both Jane and the reader) as physical symbols of the difference between the "real" Jane Eyre and the "imagined" Blanche Ingram. In all Brontë's novels, paintings are used as symbols of psychological attitudes. In *Jane Eyre*, in which art plays an unusually impressive role, the function of both the symbolic pictures and the metaphoric language is to concretize the central conflict of the novel: Jane's striving to control her imagination with her sense of reality without killing imagination, and the accompanying struggle to keep her passion honest without killing it.

Jane lacks the support for her "realism" and honesty that

[1] This is perhaps most noteworthy because it so plainly prefigures the actual landscape Jane encounters when she runs away from Thornfield, even to the light of Moor Cottage, which is a kind of *ignis-fatuus*. An important study of imagery in *Jane Eyre*, upon which both Ewbank and Martin, in the books cited earlier, rely, is Robert B. Heilman's "Charlotte Brontë, Reason and the Moon," *Nineteenth Century Fiction*, XIV (1960), 283-302.

Austen's heroines derive from the standards of their society. Even Anne Elliot is true to herself by sustaining ideals implicit in her society's strict decorum. Jane Eyre controls her passion, does what she calls her "duty," but she consistently flouts the conventional proprieties. The reviewers who deplored *Jane Eyre* when it was published and regarded its popularity as an ominous sign of the decay of accepted standards had read the book perceptively. No proper child would give Mrs. Reed a tongue-lashing, nor would a proper young girl so violently condemn Mr. Brocklehurst. Such examples could be multiplied. At no point in the novel does Jane applaud her conduct (or anybody else's, for that matter) because it adheres to traditional standards of propriety.

Jane never even implies that Rochester's attempt to commit bigamy is socially reprehensible, that it is, in the usual sense, a crime. She refuses to become his mistress because to do so would be to destroy the basis of personal respect upon which the mutuality of their love is founded. Almost nowhere does Jane pay any attention to what others think she *should* do— except to scorn them. Jane acts in accord with her private judgment of right and wrong. The first-person form of *Jane Eyre*, therefore, is an appropriate one, and a pictorial, personifying language gives force to the "independence" that the form expresses.

Insofar as Jane is realized through her resistance to the conventions and decorums of her society, a language of representation is needed which will give concrete or, as it were, objectified reality to Jane's subjective energy of resistance. The functionalism of Brontë's language can be illustrated by contrasting Jane's reflections on Rochester's relation with Blanche (*Jane Eyre*, 18) to Fanny Price's reflections on the relation of Edmund to Mary Crawford in *Mansfield Park* (see Chapter Five above).

Fanny and Mary are more nearly social equals than Jane and Blanche, but the crucial point is that Fanny could never find Mary, as Jane finds Blanche, "beneath jealousy." Edmund is genuinely fond of Mary as Rochester is not of Blanche.

Moreover, Fanny's role is relatively passive as compared to Jane's. This is not merely the result of different temperaments. Fanny's superiority over Mary is predominantly moral. Jane is superior to Blanche not only in morals but also in perception and passion. These qualities are expressed by the metaphors which enliven the relatively cool, prevailingly explanatory passage (including a direct address to the reader) in which Jane "exposes" Blanche.

The drama of Jane's feelings is like Fanny's drama in being hidden: Jane, too, observes rather than acts. But it would not be possible for Fanny even to think of her condition as "one vital struggle with two tigers—jealousy and despair," or to conceive of her "heart torn out and devoured." Such imagery would falsify not only Fanny's timidity and tenderness but also the relations which constitute the essential structure of her personality, relations which are in fact the basis of the morality in which she surpasses Mary. Fanny is "better" than Mary not because she is prettier or emotionally livelier, not even because she is intellectually keener, but simply because she understands better, and is willing to sacrifice more for, the mutuality of regard upon which useful and worthy relations must depend in her society. Even retiring Fanny's existence is essentially social: her being consists in her interacting with others according to the accepted social decorum. Jane's existence, on the contrary, depends upon an inner integrity, a self-consistency which cannot really be affected by social relations. Jane is defined by her independence, by her difference from others, by her essential isolation. To a degree even the reader, let alone other characters in the novel, cannot know the inner, private reality that is Jane Eyre. We can only "guess" at it, that is, interpret her figurative language, to comprehend the "ceaseless excitation and ruthless restraint" which constitutes the interior dynamics of her personality. We must, in other words, judge what she says in the light of how she says it.

The true dramatic action of *Jane Eyre* is expressed only indirectly in its "sensational" events, which serve, indeed, as "narrative metaphors" for psychological events in Jane's mind. These psychic events constitute the important action of the novel. Because they can find only partial expression in social relations, they must be represented figuratively. Despite the the necessarily pervasive figurativeness of language in *Jane Eyre*, even the passages I have referred to make it clear that the nature and function of the metaphors are limited. Charlotte Brontë's pictorializing language is embedded in a context of writing that is logical, even expository. Analogously, the design of the novel as a whole is simple, linear, chronologically "regular"—rationally lucid.

Whereas *Jane Eyre* is a relatively early work, *Villette* is Charlotte Brontë's last novel. Although it lacks something of the force which *Jane Eyre* attains through its very simplicity, *Villette* exploits and extends many of the characteristics of the earlier work. Both works are written from the first-person point of view, but *Villette* is a more intimate account (of a more reserved narrator) in which the *form* of presentation is more overtly the central feature of the novel's action. There are in *Villette* no events separable from the gradual liberation of Lucy's intellectual and emotional capacities. Mere chronology and "literal" spatial relations exercise less control over the narrative than they do in *Jane Eyre*.

Lucy is poorer, homelier, less talented, and both more inhibited and more isolated than Jane Eyre. From her first appearance Jane displays vigor, an ability to bite. Lucy begins as frigid in every way. The "action" of her story is the gradual thawing of her mental, emotional, and sensual frigidities. There are, significantly, two "disappointed-lover" scenes in *Villette*. In the first Lucy "gives up" Graham Bretton. The parallels between this scene and the passage from chapter 16 of *Jane Eyre* are striking—there is, for example, personification to dramatize an inner debate—but the differences are more impressive. In *Villette*, "Reason" is not finally rejected, but "Imagination" is exalted above her, which does not happen in *Jane Eyre*. In Brontë's last novel the "waste" landscape is the realm of reason. Not surprisingly, we find in *Villette* not metaphors scattered through a logical and rationalized presentation, but a tissue of metaphors in sentences which twist and invert the order of conventional syntax.

This hag, this Reason, would not let me look up, or smile, or hope: she could not rest unless I were altogether crushed, cowed, broken-in, and broken-down. According to her, I was born only to work for a piece of bread, to await the pains of death, and steadily through all life to despond. . . . Reason is vindictive as a devil: . . . Long ago I should have died of her ill-usage: her stint, her chill, her barren board, her icy bed, her savage, ceaseless blows; but for that kinder Power who holds my secret and sworn allegiance. . . . looking up, have I seen in the sky a head amidst circling stars, of which the midmost and the brightest lent a ray sympathetic and attent. A spirit, softer and better than Human Reason, has descended with quiet flight to the waste—bringing all round her a sphere of air borrowed of eternal summer; bringing perfume of flowers which cannot fade—fragrance of trees whose fruit is life; bringing breezes pure from a world whose day needs no sun to lighten it. . . .
This daughter of Heaven remembered me to-night; she saw me weep, and she came with comfort: "Sleep," she said, "Sleep, sweetly—I gild thy dreams!"   (*Villette*, 21)

This passage scarcely requires comment except for the observation that the personifications and metaphors are not embellishments but embodiments, embodiments of the interior processes whose irregular evolution is the essential action of the novel. Plot and point of view coincide in *Villette*. Thus, the next morning, wakened by "the peevish cry" of a rainy wind, Lucy represses her imagination, and the representation of that repression appears in a form equivalent to that of its previous exaltation: "Reason relieved the guard." In *Jane Eyre* the metaphors of landscape are relatively scattered; in *Villette* they are more pervasively recurrent and more directly expressive of the spiralling currents in Lucy's psychic development. Similarly, the plot structure of the later novel is more irregular, more dependent on the coherence of intensifying personal feelings than upon the coherence of causal sequences of events.

The more significant "disappointment" in *Villette* is a climax of the novel. Lucy mistakenly believes that Paul Emanuel loves his ward. The mistake is deeply ironic, for it results from Lucy's expanded consciousness and developed emotionality: as Lucy says, her Fancy has become "generous and creative."

I might have waited and watched longer that love scene under the trees, that sylvan courtship. Had there been nothing of love in the demonstration, my Fancy in this hour was so generous, so creative, she could have modelled for it the most salient lineaments, and given it the deepest life and highest colour of passion. But I *would* not look; I had fixed my resolve, but I would not violate my nature. And then—something tore me so cruelly under my shawl, something so dug into my side, a vulture so strong in beak and talon, I must be alone to grapple with it. I think I never felt jealousy till now. . . . This was an outrage. The love born of beauty was not mine: I had nothing in common with it: I could not dare to meddle with it, but another love, venturing diffidently into life after long acquaintance, furnace-tried by pain, stamped by constancy, consolidated by affection's pure and durable alloy, submitted by intellect to intellect's own tests, and finally wrought up, by his own process, to his own unflawed completeness, this Love that laughed at Passion, his fast frenzies and his hot and hurried extinction, in *this* Love I had a vested interest; and for whatever tended either to its culture or its destruction I could not view impassibly. (*Villette*, 39)

In this passage separate metaphors play a small role; an intense impulse toward figurization characterizes the texture of Lucy's developed perceptiveness and consciousness. There is still personification in the broadest sense, the transformation of thoughts and feelings into objects and agents, but now the *personifier* participates angrily in the metaphoric reality she creates, and it is the *process of participation* which holds our interest: "in *this* Love I had a vested interest." The commercialism of the last phrase is specially appropriate, for Lucy's love, unlike Jane Eyre's, is not only self-created but also inseparable from her hard-won and jealously hoarded financial and psychological independence—not an unexpected legacy or the reward of mere consistency.

Lucy's mistake, her "outrage," is in fact proof that she has won "Freedom" and "Renovation." Her mistake is testimony that she can now be "warm, jealous, haughty." She is mistaken because she is sexually alive. Returning from the sight of Paul and his ward, Lucy finds in her bed the "nun," whose illusoriness is then explained. She tears this theatrical prop to pieces, destroying the nun *in* herself. Although the nun motif in *Villette* is not faultlessly handled, it is an advance on the ironic manipulation of Gothic motifs in *Jane Eyre*. The theatrical fake Gothicism of the nun represents a true impulse in Lucy, whose temptation is to become cloistered (chapter 15) but whose destiny is self-dramatization, creation of self. For Lucy to become cloistered would be evil, partly because Charlotte Brontë disliked Catholicism, but more importantly, because cloistering represents for Lucy a tempting denial of her true potential. Paul-Emanuel, who sees her potential and nurtures it, is a good Catholic who nevertheless comes to wish Lucy to remain Protestant—in all senses. Lucy's danger is not that she will become a Catholic nun but that she will give way to an inclination toward self-sacrifice.

The appearances of the nun coincide with sexual crises in Lucy's life, but the nature of the crises changes. They change, broadly speaking, as Lucy's bitter recognition of the incompatibility between her earth-transcending dreams and her perception of reality changes, becoming transformed into a growing belief in the possibility and the worthwhileness of what may be called a temporary paradise. Lucy learns to accept the reality of both her imagination and the mundane facts of ordinary existence, an acceptance foreshadowed in her compromise of playing a man's role in the school play while retaining her female dress.[2] She learns that the factual "truth"

[2] Transvestitism is recurrent in Charlotte Brontë's fiction, appearing even in her juvenilia. The heroine of *Caroline Vernon*, for example, disguises herself as a boy in order to find her way to the man she loves. The motif is attractive to Brontë because she challenges the "conventional" roles assigned to men and women in her society.

must accommodate itself to the reality of both subconscious impulse and more-than-rational aspiration.

These lessons are not part of Jane Eyre's education; Jane, indeed, changes very little. The language which represents her history is relatively simple and fixed in its figurativeness. The figurativeness of *Villette* is more profound and more flexible. One can instructively contrast the imagery which introduces Rochester (*Jane Eyre*, 12) with that with which Miss Marchmont describes the crucial event of her life. Jane's fancy of Gytrash endows Rochester with a spurious preternaturalism and ominousness which serve primarily as contrast for his solid, even homely reality: the "spirit" ends by slipping on ice and spraining his ankle. Jane dismisses her own fancy as "rubbish," so that only a superficial, as it were, purely verbal, echo lingers in the reader's mind to reinforce the sense of mystery which later envelopes the upper floors of Thornfield. Subsequent events in Thornfield repeat the pattern of Rochester's introduction: unusual appearances—Rochester as a gypsy, Bertha in Jane's "dreams," etc.—are resolved into rationally comprehensible circumstances. To say this is not to condemn Brontë's art, which by exploding the fancies of romantic fiction uncovers the passional realities concealed by the superficial and incomplete rationalism of the ordinary social intercourse celebrated in much polite fiction of her day. But the same purpose is realized more subtly and significantly in *Villette* when Miss Marchmont describes to Lucy how thirty years earlier "one happy Christmas Eve I dressed and decorated myself, expecting my lover. . . ."

"Would he for once fail me? No—not even for once; and now he was coming—and coming fast—to atone for lost time. 'Frank! you furious rider,' I said inwardly, listening gladly, yet anxiously, to his approaching gallop, 'you shall be rebuked for this: I will tell you it is *my* neck you are putting in peril; for whatever is yours is, in a dearer and tenderer sense, mine.' There he was: I saw him; but I think tears were in my eyes, my sight was so confused. I saw the horse; I heard it stamp—I saw at least a mass; I heard a clamour. *Was* it a horse? or what heavy, dragging thing was it, crossing, strangely dark, the lawn? How could I name that

thing in the moonlight before me? or how could I utter the
feeling which rose in my soul?" (*Villette*, 4)

There is no "fancy," no metaphor, in this beautifully written
passage, in which we hear the sound of hooves (though it is
not mentioned) through the representation of the narrator's
impatience, and in which we feel the pull of the body
through the unusual positioning of the modifiers in the phrase
"what heavy, dragging thing was it, crossing, strangely dark,
the lawn?" Jane thinks of a name, "Gytrash"; Miss Marchmont asks "*Was* it a horse?" . . . "How could I name that
thing in the moonlight. . . ?" The scene from *Jane Eyre*
introduces the hero of the novel; the function of Miss Marchmont's account is subtler. It prefigures, of course, Lucy's loss
of Paul (notice the "Would he for *once* fail me?"). But in
introducing Miss Marchmont's judgment of herself in the
paragraph immediately following that quoted above, the story
also prefigures Lucy's successful struggle to avoid becoming
a "woe-struck and selfish woman" who finds "salvation" not in
thinking more of her Creator than of her lover but in recognizing the impress of her Creator upon her lover.

It is no accident that there is little metaphor in Miss Marchmont's account, which *as a whole* is a significant metaphor of
Lucy's evolving destiny. Just as the plot and point of view
more nearly coincide in *Villette* than in *Jane Eyre*, in the later
work incident becomes image. All the "theatricalness" of the
novel relates to Lucy's self-dramatization, that is, her creation
of her own identity. Imagery in *Villette* is more narratively
functional than in *Jane Eyre*. The process of making images,
the process of Lucy's imagination, *is* the main story of *Villette*.

It remains true, nonetheless, that the source of Charlotte
Brontë's figurative language in both works is predominantly
the phenomena of the natural world and that her metaphors
usually have but a single reference. She never employs extended multireferent comparisons which depend on scien-
tifically intellectual abstraction, as George Eliot does, for example, in the following passage from *Middlemarch*.

An eminent philosopher among my friends, who can dignify even your ugly furniture by lifting it into the serene light of science, has shown me this pregnant little fact. Your pier-glass or extensive surface of polished steel made to be rubbed by a housemaid, will be minutely and multitudinously scratched in all directions; but place now against it a lighted candle as a centre of illumination and lo! the scratches will seem to arrange themselves in a fine series of concentric circles around that little sun. It is demonstrable that the scratches are going everywhere impartially, and it is only your candle which produces the flattering illusion of a concentric arrangement, its light falling, with an exclusive optical selection. These things are a parable. The scratches are events, and the candle is the egoism of any person now absent—of Miss Vincy, for example.   (*Middlemarch*, 27)

This "parable" is presented in the form of an illustrative diagram suitable for a scientific demonstration. It is the tone of such a passage which defines George Eliot's special characteristics as omniscient narrator of *Middlemarch*. But to describe such a passage as "intrusive," as an interruption of the novel's "story," appears to me misleading. The scientific parable of the scratched mirror is an integral part of *Middlemarch*'s narrative structure. It is only one of many "mirroring" metaphors in the novel, and it is related by its form to other "scientific" (as opposed to "naturalistic") metaphors, many of which are also presented extensively, almost as if they were epic similes. Then, too, the metaphor is characteristic in its *abstractness*. Rosamond Vincy is, literally, only one "example" of the "truth" of the scratched mirror. All the leading characters in *Middlemarch* are represented in terms of their conflicting selfish and selfless impulses. No important metaphor in *Middlemarch* is confined to a single character or single event: they all connect. The "story" of *Middlemarch* is not a simple sequence of events, it is several distinguishable sequences. The "narrative" consists in the evolving connections between and contrasts among multiple patterns of events and agents. These connections and contrasts are provided by the omniscient narrator—often through the use of "abstract," that is, multireferent, metaphors. Eliot was conscious of the danger that a novelist's "picture" might turn into a "diagram," because her style emphasizes the "diagrammatic" function of its pictorial elements.

While I do not want to trace the full course of the development of George Eliot's pictorializing language, it may be useful to point out quickly one or two features in that development before I try to define the special character of her mature use of metaphor. It would be rewarding, I believe, to study (even more meticulously than Barbara Hardy has) the fashion in which Eliot's handling of the same images changes throughout the course of her career. In *Adam Bede*, for example, words and phrases referring to water are predominantly "literal": "tears" are tears, the "stream" in which Thais Bede's body is found is simply a stream. But even as early as her next novel, *The Mill on the Floss*, in which "literal" water plays a significant role, words and phrases referring to water take on more than literal connotations. References to water are used to foreshadow the deaths of Maggie and Tom. In two obvious instances of a preternatural power's being associated with rivers, the legend of the Floss and the ruined villages on the Rhone remind us of almost forgotten outbursts of that stream's concealed power. Moreover, "literal" water is itself described figuratively, as when the Floss, at Christmas, "flowed and moaned like an unresting sorrow." Finally, "figurative" water is used to define other things, as when Eliot tells us that Maggie's destiny "is at present hidden and we must wait for it to reveal itself like the course of an unmapped river."

In *Middlemarch*, to skip rapidly ahead, words and phrases referring to "literal" water are subordinate to those which represent water figuratively, particularly as a definition of emotional, intellectual, and spiritual capacities. This is not simply a matter of the writing in *Middlemarch* being more metaphoric than that in *The Mill on the Floss*. It is more metaphoric, but, more important, the nature and function of the metaphors in the later novel are different. In *Middlemarch* the metaphors establish a multidimensional network of parallels and connections. Indeed, it is difficult to illustrate briefly the complexity of the network. I shall cite but a few examples out of literally hundreds of water images in *Middlemarch.*

Rosamond first appears as a young woman vain of her skill in singing "Flow on Thou Shining River," and she sees Lydgate, new to Middlemarch, like a stranger "wretched and clinging to a raft." When Lydgate and Rosamond's marriage is failing, he "continually deferred the final steps . . . like many a man who is in danger of shipwreck." The transformation is marked by many slight water references. At first with Rosamond, Lydgate has "no sense that any new current had set into his life"; he continues to think of his profession as primary; he "had the sea to swim in there." In the early days of the marriage minutes "flowed by them like a small gurgling brook with the kisses of the sunlight upon it." Later Rosamond's voice "trickled like cold water-drops." Lydgate discovers that "the shallowness of a water-nixie's soul may have a charm until she becomes didactic." He becomes "conscious of a new element in his life as noxious to him as an inlet of mud to a creature that has been used to breathe and bathe and dart after its illuminated prey in the clearest of water."

Mud and shallowness are used to display the limitations of Casaubon, Dorothea's partner in a parallel unhappy marriage. "Having once embarked on your marital voyage, it is impossible not to be aware that you make no way and that the sea is not within sight, that, in fact, you are exploring an enclosed basin." Casaubon's soul is described as "fluttering in the swampy ground where it was hatched." Celia sees "Mr. Casaubon's learning as a kind of damp which might in due time saturate a neighboring body." The depth and vigor of Dorothea's spirit are described with a contrasting image: her mind is "a current into which all thought and feeling were apt . . . to flow." After the depressing first weeks of her marriage, "it seemed like fresh water to her thirsty lips to speak without fear." She comforts Rosamond "soothingly as a warm stream over shrinking fears" when they clasp "each other as if they had been in a shipwreck." When Dorothea and Will

Ladislaw embrace, it begins to rain, releasing "the flood of her young passion, . . . the great tears rising and falling in an instant." Many other illustrations could be brought forward,[3] for water imagery is used in relation to virtually all the characters: Mrs. Garth's face is "like a change below the surface of the water which remains smooth," and Bulstrode, literally "immersed" in his past, watches Raffles' sleep, "the sleep which streams deeper and deeper into the gulf of death."

Even with these few citations at least two features of the metaphoric network stand out: its dynamism and its connective function. Whereas almost all of the water references in *The Mill on the Floss* are directly associated with the "river," in *Middlemarch* water references are varied and constantly changing. The imaginative conception is more "abstract" in the later novel, and for this reason, far more effectively than in the earlier novel, "water" can connect disparate people, events, and ideas. To cite an obvious instance: insofar as references to the river in *The Mill on the Floss* foreshadow Tom's and Maggie's doom, the references distinguish these two characters, whereas the references to shallowness and muddiness in *Middlemarch* on one level distinguish but on another level connect the Lydgate-Rosamond and Dorothea-Casaubon "shipwrecks."

What has been said here about water imagery could be illustrated at far greater length and with many other image patterns, such as mirrors, eyes, and windows. But the develop-

---

[3] Many are brought forward by a former student of mine, Miss Patricia Ann Schroeder, in her University of Wisconsin honors thesis, "George Eliot's Song of Man" (1968), to which my discussion is indebted. Barbara Hardy's examination of imagery in *The Novels of George Eliot* is exemplary. Among the multitude of studies of *Middlemarch*, I should like to call attention to Jerome Beaty's *Middlemarch: From Notebook to Novel* (Urbana, Illinois, 1960), a fine volume, reference to which gives me the opportunity to express my gratitude to Professor Beaty for giving me the benefit of his knowledge about textual and editorial problems connected with Eliot's fiction. Neil D. Isaacs, "*Middlemarch*: Crescendo of Obligatory Drama," *Nineteenth Century Fiction*, xviii (1963), 21-34, provides an interesting description of the structural rhythm of the novel. And of course one must pay tribute to the splendid collection of essays in *Middlemarch: Critical Approaches to the Novel*, edited by Barbara Hardy (London, 1967).

ment of Eliot's writing toward a figurative "abstractness" which makes connections with increasing subtlety and flexibility, above all by revealing a concealed system of interrelations between the apparently disparate, can be defined in another fashion:[4] one can examine a type of metaphor which appears only in Eliot's later fiction. For exemplification I shall use the "abstract metaphor" of "acting" in *Daniel Deronda*.

Strictly as a figure of speech "acting" is not too important in *Daniel Deronda*. The figures of the serpent, the horse, the dead face, and the empty horizon, for instance, are more important. Yet even these do not play as dominant a role in the totality of *Daniel Deronda* as do analogous figures in *Middlemarch*. There are no diagrammatic metaphors in *Deronda* equivalent to the mirror in *Middlemarch*, and there are fewer simple metaphors. This diminishment accompanies a decrease in exposition and authorial comment. *Deronda* is more "dramatic" than *Middlemarch*; it is also more "abstract," which is why "acting" pervades it.[5]

[4] The development of Eliot's figurative techniques can also be seen as an increasing realization of the essential nature of metaphor, which demands a simultaneous perception of similarity and dissimilarity. The effectiveness of "men are wolves," as compared to "timber wolves are wolves" (to use the example cited by Colin Turbayne in his intriguing *The Myth of Metaphor*, New Haven, 1962), lies in our recognition that in some respects men are *not* wolves. Eliot's figurative language becomes increasingly complicated (and meaningful) because it increasingly forces us to respond to likenesses within differences and differences within likenesses simultaneously.

[5] I hope that my discussion of "acting" will not obscure the fact that of all the arts music is the most significant in *Daniel Deronda*. This is why Klesmer is so important a figure in the novel; see Gordon S. Haight, "George Eliot's Klesmer," *Imagined Worlds*, ed. Maynard Mack (London, 1968), pp. 205-14. *Deronda* has in recent years attracted much impressive criticism, for example, Maurice Beebe, " 'Visions are Creators': The Unity of *Daniel Deronda*," *Boston University Studies in English*, I (1955), 166-77; David R. Carroll, "The Unity of *Daniel Deronda*," *Essays in Criticism*, IX (1960), 369-80; Albert R. Cirillo, "Salvation in *Daniel Deronda*," *Literary Monographs*, ed. Dunseath and Rothstein, I (1967), 203-43; F. R. Leavis, "George Eliot's Zionist Novel," *Commentary*, XXX (1960), 317-25 (this essay, which somewhat modifies Leavis' judgment in *The Great Tradition*, serves as the introduction to the Harper Torchbook edition

"Acting" is not, of course, an object like a mirror but is rather a type of behavior which encompasses a variety of activities. "Acting" is a kind of abstraction. As such it would not fit the figurative system of Charlotte Brontë's language (which is more amenable to literally theatrical scenes): her metaphors, above all else, serve as tangible embodiments of intangible ideas and feelings. But "acting" is specially suited to Eliot's purposes in her last novel because it is abstract and can function simultaneously on a variety of levels. It reveals hidden relations between disparate events and personalities.

There are professional actors among the characters in *Deronda*, notably Mirah and Deronda's mother. For both, the theatrical experience is, in opposite ways, characterologically decisive. The contrast between them embodies one of the novel's themes, the need to discover and to commit oneself to the most meaningful realities of human experience. When Deronda prevents Mirah's suicide her first question to him is "Were you the singer of Dante's verses?" and her second is "Do you belong to the theatre?" " 'No, I have nothing to do with the theatre,' said Deronda in a decided tone" (chapter 17).[6] Because he has "nothing to do with the theatre," Gwendolen, whose entire existence is "an unconscious kind of acting," can find him a guide toward truth through the maze of artificialities in which she is involved. But before turning to Gwendolen, let us take note of how Mirah's theatrical background is tied both to the "Jewish problem" and to the development of her love for Deronda. When the question of what Mirah should wear at Klesmer's concert is discussed, Mirah wants to wear her black merino.

> "This would be thought a very good stage-dress for me," she said, pleadingly, "in a part where I was to come on as a poor Jewess and sing to fashionable Christians."

---

of *Daniel Deronda*); Robert Preyer, "Beyond the Liberal Imagination: Vision and Unreality in *Daniel Deronda*," *Victorian Studies*, IV (1960), 35-54.

[6] It is noteworthy that the "agitating impression" Mirah makes on Daniel is specifically identified by Eliot as "close to his deepest interest in the fates of women—'perhaps my mother was like this one.' "

"It would be effective," said Hans, with a considering air; "it would stand out well among the fashionable *chiffons*."

"But you ought not to claim all the poverty on your side, Mirah," said Amy. "There are plenty of poor Christians and dreadfully rich Jews and fashionable Jewesses."

"I didn't mean any harm," said Mirah. "Only I have been used to thinking about my dress for parts in plays. And I almost always had a part with a plain dress."

"That makes me think it questionable," said Hans, . . .

"But it is what I am really. . . . It is all real, you know," here she looked at Hans—"even if it seemed theatrical. Poor Berenice sitting on the ruins—any one might say that was theatrical, but I know that is just what she would do."

"I am a scoundrel," said Hans, overcome by this misplaced trust. "That is my invention."[7]   (*Daniel Deronda*, 39)

Mirah is, however, forced to recognize that reality is even more complicated than is implied by Hans' falsification in his too dramatic *Berenice* picture. When Hans suggests that Deronda will marry Gwendolen, Mirah's reaction brings back the experiences of her theatrical life.

Something of the old life had returned. She had been used to remember that she must learn her part, must go to rehearsal, must act and sing in the evening, must hide her feelings from her father; and the more painful her life grew, the more she had been used to hide. The force of her nature had long found its chief action in resolute endurance, and to-day the violence of feeling which had caused the first jet of anger had quickly transformed itself into a steady facing of trouble, the well-known companion of her young years. . . .

"What I have read about and sung about and seen acted, is happening to me—this that I am feeling is the love that makes jealousy":—so impartially Mirah summed up the charge against herself. But. . . . In the Psyche-mould of Mirah's frame there rested a fervid quality of emotion sometimes rashly supposed to require the bulk of a Cleopatra; her impressions had the thoroughness and tenacity that give to the first selection of passionate

---

[7] Hans Meyrick "plays" at being an artist. It is significant that at one point he *mimics* Klesmer, a true artist.

feeling the character of a life-long faithfulness. And now a selection had declared itself, which gave love a cruel heart of jealousy:. . . (*Daniel Deronda*, 61)

The deepest reality of Mirah's love is that it does possess "a cruel heart of jealousy." What Mirah had "read about and sung about and seen acted" as mere theatrical illusions she now experiences. And on the basis of this experience she can challenge Mordecai's interpretation of a story from the *Midrash*.

". . . the story of a Jewish maiden who loved a Gentile king so well, that this was what she did:—She entered into prison and changed clothes with the woman who was beloved by the king, that she might deliver that woman from death by dying in her stead, and leave the king to be happy in his love which was not for her. This is the surpassing love, that loses self in the object of love."

"No, Ezra, no," said Mirah, with low-toned intensity, "that was not it. She wanted the king when she was dead to know what she had done, and feel that she was better than the other. It was her strong self, wanting to conquer, that made her die."

Mordecai was silent a little, and then argued—

"That might be, Mirah. But if she acted so, believing the king would never know?"

"You can make the story so in your mind, Ezra, because you are great, and like to fancy the greatest that could be. But I think it was not really like that. The Jewish girl must have had jealousy in her heart, and she wanted somehow to have the first place in the king's mind. That is what she would die for."

"My sister, thou hast read too many plays, where the writers delight in showing the human passions as indwelling demons, unmixed with the relenting and devout elements of the soul. Thou judgest by the plays, and not by thy own heart, which is like our mother's."

Mirah made no answer. (*Daniel Deronda*, 61)

Without pressing the point further (a temptation because few critics have escaped from their admiration of Eliot's handling of Gwendolen to appreciate the skill with which she develops Mirah's personality), I suggest that this episode is important in marking a limitation to the worth of Mordecai's "visionariness" and thereby illuminating Eliot's treatment of the "Jewish problem." Because he is great, Mordecai can *"fancy* the greatest that could be." But "it was not *really* like that." The irony, though not destructive, is inescapably vivid when Mordecai says to Mirah, the person nearest and dearest to him, "Thou judgest by the plays, and not by thy own heart." An idealism such as Mordecai's is needed, but even so, in Eliot's view, it carries its own special falsifications.

The "reality" of Deronda's mother's experience is the reverse of Mirah's, as she makes clear in explaining to Deronda why she married (chapter 51). Her "make believe" marriage from which there is, of course, no escape recalls the girl who dreams of becoming an actress but who marries a distinguished Englishman. One should not, however, overlook the description of the impact of Alchiarisi's narrative on Deronda. "He had gone through a tragic experience which must forever solemnize his life, and deepen the significance of the acts by which he bound himself to others" (chapter 53). This language is not overtly metaphorical, yet it subtly reinforces the novel's dominant concern, the exploration and explanation of the difficulties of bringing forth the truth of the profoundest realities in a world where, of necessity, we all play roles,[8] roles which tend to separate us from, rather than bind us to, our fellow creatures.

It is in this abstract fashion that "acting" is most important in Gwendolen's part of the novel. The charades and her interview with Klesmer are examples, to be sure, of overt emphasis on the "acting" motif.[9] But throughout most of her appearances in the novel, except in dialogue with Deronda, Gwendolen is portrayed as "acting." This is obvious in scenes

[8] In chapter 35 Daniel remarks, "I wonder whether one oftener learns to love real objects through their representations, or the representations through the real objects."

[9] The tableau from *The Winter's Tale*—in which Klesmer's resounding chord, intended to wake Hermione (a loyal wife unjustly victimized by her husband's jealousy), unexpectedly reveals the hidden picture which terrifies Gwendolen—emblemizes the relation between true art (associated with genuine music) and false role-playing in *Deronda.*

such as her conversation with Mrs. Arrowpoint, but it is even more meaningful in the many episodes in which her self-control is stressed. In the celebrated opening scene in which Deronda watches Gwendolen playing roulette, she is acting, indeed, overacting, a part. She looks around "with a survey too markedly cold and neutral not to have in it a little of that nature which we call art concealing an inward exultation." When Deronda's attention is arrested by Gwendolen's figure, "suddenly the moment became dramatic." This is as close to a metaphor of acting as the language of the scene comes, for it is the *conception* of the moment, an "artificial" moment as the chapter's epigraph points out, which is "theatrical." The scene itself is a pictorialization of the unconscious acting which is the main reality of Gwendolen's life until Deronda impinges upon it. He affects her life merely by watching her, by being a spectator of her acts. He is, however, a devastating spectator because he is not, like the others, dazzled by the artifice of her "presence." His *is* an "evil eye," for he sees that Gwendolen's poised queenliness is an ambiguous if not an incongruous pose. Were she what she wants to appear to be she would not be gambling exultantly. Deronda looks at her with an eye of ironic questioning: "Was she beautiful or was she not?" Once Gwendolen encounters this glance the basis of her power is destroyed, for she is not a queen nor is she really poised. Her dependence upon creating an artificial sensation reveals the self-contradictory nature of her psychology: "Since she was not winning strikingly, the next best thing was to lose strikingly." This is nonsensical, unless life is merely playacting, and much of sophisticated British life as portrayed in *Daniel Deronda* is only glamorous playacting. In Eliot's view, this is its essential fault and the reason for its inferiority to the idealism of Mordecai and Daniel, who seek a society founded on reality rather than role-playing. Deronda's first glance threatens Gwendolen with loss of "glamour," because it forces her to think about her role, to evaluate it.

Once we recognize the pervasive significance of "acting" in *Deronda*, we understand why it need emerge only rarely in overt figures of speech. Klesmer accuses Gwendolen of lack-

ing the disciplined training requisite for acting, yet few fictional characters devote more time and energy to the control
of their feelings and behavior in order to create a desired
effect. If, however, the control of bodily movements and
nuances of tone is an essential of good acting, Grandcourt is
the best actor.[10] The wealthy prospective peer of the greatest
realm on earth is so completely the actor that he has become
his role, become almost literally a zombie. All of his vitality
is drained into his role. This is the source of his power: he
achieves what others struggle for less successfully, oppressed
as they are by some sense of realities other than those of the
parts they play. Grandcourt is especially effective against
Gwendolen. Again and again he subdues her by a simple
reference to "appearances," to her role as his wife, to the
necessity of her playing her part in society.[11] Against this
Gwendolen, having committed herself to the illusoriness of a
"position in society," is helpless. Of course she enters into her
married life with a mind divided and still naive and ignorant.
Her first conversation with Grandcourt (chapter 11) is unique
in Eliot's fiction in the formality of its structure. The form of
the conversation dramatizes Gwendolen's confusion between
her impulse to exploit her power to make an effective appearance and her sense of the inadequacies of appearance, a conflict discernible to Deronda from her artificial queenliness in
the opening scene. This scene, one notices, takes place in time
between Gwendolen's first rejection of Grandcourt and her
later acceptance of him, and she quite literally "accepts"
Grandcourt (the word is stressed in a variety of ways in
chapter 27). She tries not to "choose" Grandcourt, but in
"accepting" him she of course chooses a role in preference
to the reality of individual being. Like Deronda's mother, she
becomes the prisoner of her role, although in a different way.

[10] Notice the first description of Grandcourt: "His complexion had a
faded fairness resembling that of an actress when bare of the artificial
white and red . . ." (chapter 11).

[11] Chapter 44: "Constantly she had to be on the scene as Mrs.
Grandcourt, and to feel herself watched in that part by the exacting
eyes of a husband. . . . And she herself, whatever rebellion might be
going on within her, could not have made up her mind to failure in
her representation."

From the first, Gwendolen is impressed by Grandcourt's knowledge of what to say and how to act, though what he says and does is banal. The banality of power (and the power of banality) revealed by Grandcourt is terrifying because the artificialities of social roles are important: for better or for worse, they are the media of civilized intercourse. Grandcourt, who exists only through them, is totally effective as a role-player. Gwendolen is victimized by her role. Shortly after she has accepted Grandcourt, they prepare for a ride.

> The scene was pleasant on both sides. A cruder lover would have lost the view of her pretty ways and attitudes, and spoiled all by stupid attempts at caresses, utterly destructive of drama. Grandcourt preferred the drama; and Gwendolen, left at ease, found her spirits rising continually as she played at reigning. Perhaps if Klesmer had seen more of her in this unconscious kind of acting, instead of when she was trying to be theatrical, he might have rated her chance higher.   (*Daniel Deronda*, 28)

Perhaps the key word in this passage is "unconscious." Grandcourt is always fully conscious of "acting," which is why everything that happens is boring to him: nothing is spontaneous and genuine, his life is composed of recognized falsifications. Gwendolen gradually becomes conscious of the significance of this "acting," how it destroys all inner spontaneity and genuineness, which together are necessary to individuality and meaningful associations of individuals. Deronda, by breaking through the illusory artificialities of his position, his assigned role in society, achieves another, more purposeful role, one that is "social" yet expressive of the deepest level of his private being and integrity. Because he genuinely "chooses" his own role (the proof that his is "choice" not "acceptance" is that it involves sacrifice), Deronda sets off at the end of the novel for what is, literally and figuratively, a promised land. On the contrary, the climax of Gwendolen's development is a passage which explicitly recalls *Paradise Lost* both in vocabulary and in its definition of hell as a state of chosen unreality. It is this hell from which Daniel helps Gwendolen to escape, Gwendolen whose maiden name suggests a fallen woman and whose married name suggests the elaborated artificialities of the wealthiest aristocratic society in history.

There was a dreamy, sunny stillness over the hedgeless fields stretching to the boundary of poplars; and to Gwendolen the talk within the carriage seemed only to make the dreamland larger with an indistinct region of coal-pits, and a purgatorial Gadsmere which she would never visit; till, at her mother's words, this mingled, dozing view seemed to dissolve and give way to a more wakeful vision of Offendene and Pennicote under their cooler lights. . . . All that brief experience of a quiet home which had once seemed a dulness to be fled from, now came back to her as a restful escape, a station where she found the breath of morning and the unreproaching voice of birds, after following a lure through a long Satanic masquerade, which she had entered on with an intoxicated belief in its disguises, and had seen the end of in shrieking fear lest she herself had become one of the evil spirits who were dropping their human mummery and hissing around her with serpent tongues.   (*Daniel Deronda*, 64)

This is an effective passage because it so sharply focuses an underlying issue of the novel through a complex verbal figurization of its central theme. The theme can be most succinctly defined as an exploration into the ambiguity of the verb "to act." "Acting" can mean "playing a part" or "doing something." In social life the ambiguity is constantly relevant, for doing something often involves performing a duty. Deronda chooses to act in the latter sense. Gwendolen (until the end of the novel) accepts a "part": ironically, Grandcourt drowns because she is unable to act at the crucial moment. In this passage one should notice that the final "image" of the "Satanic masquerade" is only part of the figurization of the whole: the first sentence prepares for the image by representing Gwendolen as a spectator of her own past "acts," her past "role." There is, then, an entire dimension of structural-verbal interaction in *Daniel Deronda* which is not found, or is only found in rudimentary form, in Charlotte Brontë's fiction. If we wish to trace developments in fictional style, we must recognize that merely to describe patterns of images and metaphors is not enough: we must specify their character and function. To do this is to become engaged in defining the particularized systems by which verbal and structural organizations interrelate, which in turn, as I have tried to suggest, necessitates consideration of theme and meaning. Perhaps I can illustrate briefly how, in my view, analysis of "verbal modes" leads to concern with novelists' differing plot arrangements, forms of characterization, and the sociological significance of their themes.

An abstract metaphoric concept such as "acting" is appropriate to a novel with a multiple plot. Novels such as *Deronda* are composed of separate stories which intersect at only a few points. All of Eliot's novels tend toward the multi-plot structure (a form characteristic of mid-nineteenth-century British fiction),[12] and this tendency is connected with that of using "abstract" metaphors. *Deronda* contains at least fifteen distinguishable flashbacks. Such complication of the narrative form is possible because the multireferent metaphors provide a deeper form of aesthetic coherence.

Of necessity, complex narrative structures unified in this way are involved with thematic developments. *Daniel Deronda* condemns British society severely. In this, the only

---

[12] Thackeray was a significant innovator of the multiplot novel with *Vanity Fair*. He is seldom given credit for the impetus he gave this development. The formal clarity of the multiple-plot structure of *Vanity Fair* may account for its influence. At any rate, there are few important novels published before 1846 with such structure and many published during the following thirty years. In the last quarter of the nineteenth century there was a counter-movement toward simplified plot structures. Conrad and James, for example, prefer relatively simple stories: their complexities derive from characterization, point of view, and symbolization. This plot simplification accompanies a shift of focus from temporal sequentiality to temporal simultaneity. *Ulysses* is, among many other things, a climax of this trend. Joyce's literal story, a day in the life of Leopold Bloom, is utterly simple and in itself apparently unstructured (which is why it can so richly and organically, rather than reductively and mechanically, serve as a giant metaphor for an entire mythic narrative). And of course much of the effect of the events, characters, and even the language of *Ulysses* depends upon Joyce's various techniques for breaking down our conventional perception of fiction as the rendering of temporal sequences and compelling us to see reality as a vital mosaic of simultaneities.

one of Eliot's novels which looks seriously toward the future, "Zionism" is used to contrast the shortcomings not of a limited way of life but of the total system of British civilization. In *Jane Eyre* some individuals and some social types are criticized, but the entire social system is not condemned. Society is accepted in Austen's novels. The development from acceptance to condemnation is associated with the increasingly rich and varied potential for individual inner life with which the novelists endow the protagonists of their fiction. The range of possible existences open to Austen's heroines is quite limited: baldly, they can be spinsters or wives. The suffering of Brontë's protagonists is the price they pay for the increased variety of experience open to them. Eliot's protagonists are conceived of as possessing a very wide range of possible experience. Richness of inner potential is less important when the basic systems of society are regarded as satisfactory than when they are felt to be seriously deficient or evil. The reverse is also true: an author's belief that the social order is bad is likely to encourage him to explore individual potential. The connection between the total design of a novel and the language which embodies the design thus expresses the author's understanding of the actual and ideal relation between an individual and his society.

MUCH OF MY COMMENTARY about *Villette* in this chapter should be read in conjunction with the commentaries on its structure in Chapters Ten and Eleven. In particular I want to call attention to my later remarks on the function of the "nun," which is not properly understood except in a context larger than that of the present chapter.[13] I have not dwelt on the image of "the temporary paradise" here, because this, too, can only be fully understood in a larger context, specifically in relation to the symbolic patterns of the "parched wayfarer" and "shivering jailbird" I talk about in Chapter Twelve. Also,

---

[13] An excellent discussion of how the "nun" functions to mark stages in Lucy's growing self-realization will be found in E.D.H. Johnson's "Daring the Dread Glance: Charlotte Brontë's Treatment of the Supernatural in *Villette*," *Nineteenth Century Fiction*, xx (1966), 325-36.

because criticism of particular novels (or segments of novels) in this book is always meant to contribute to the development of improved methods of analyzing and evaluating the history of fictional style, I do not want to burden the reader with details relevant predominantly to one novel in itself and without much relevance to that novel's function in fictional history. One of my aims in this chapter has been to distinguish between the nature and function of images and metaphors in Charlotte Brontë's and George Eliot's fiction. I have concentrated only on material which clarifies the distinction, but one result of this concentration, I am afraid, may be the impression that I do not find recurrent images of importance to the structure of *Villette*.

That impression would be wrong. Imagery and metaphor are important to the structure of Brontë's fiction, above all in *Villette,* but, as opposed to Eliot's imagery and metaphors, they are self-contrastive (built upon the principle of contrariety) and invariably connected with "natural" phenomena. Their *function* is not "abstract" (multireferent), like that of Eliot's imagery and metaphors, but intensely limited. They are, in fact, concretizations of the development of Lucy's psyche. The nature and function of Brontë's imagery, particularly those images which are part of recurrent patterns, have led many critics to regard her fiction, in contrast, say, to Eliot's, as "symbolic." This view seems to me correct, although the terminological difficulties in such a definition are admittedly oppressive, because in one sense *all* fiction is "symbolic," and in an even broader sense all language is symbolic. It may be useful, therefore, to point out quickly how the nature and function of Brontë's imagery tie in with the special symbolic quality of her fiction. For the sake of brevity I shall confine my comments to the "temporary paradise" pattern in *Villette*.

The novel begins and ends in autumn and autumnal references occur at many key passages throughout the book, although the autumnal quality stressed is not that of *Persuasion* or the fulfillment of Keats' poem, but rather a "wildness" closer to the creative-destructiveness in Shelley's *Ode to the*

West Wind, which Brontë's frequent association of autumn and wind brings to mind. Within this "context" of a natural season, Brontë develops a coherent sequence of references built around dramatic contrasts between the temporary and the permanent and between actual and paradisiacal nature, that is, "idealized" nature expressive of spiritual truth. These verbal references are, of course, linked to events and situations in the story. Thus the introduction of the "temporary paradise" motif in the novel's seventh paragraph refers to Lucy's impressions of Mrs. Bretton's home: "My visits to her resembled the sojourn of Christian and Hopeful beside a certain pleasant stream, with 'green trees on each bank, and meadows beautified with lilies all the year round.' " The significance of this first reference can perhaps best be appreciated by juxtaposing it to the last, twenty-four paragraphs from the conclusion of the novel, which follows Paul's full expression of his love.

We walked back to the Rue Fossette by moonlight—such moonlight as fell on Eden—shining through the shades of the Great Garden, and haply gilding a path glorious for a step divine—a Presence nameless. Once in their lives some men and women go back to these first fresh days of our great Sire and Mother—taste that grand morning's dew—bathe in its sunrise. (*Villette*, 41)

Two observations about this paragraph will illustrate the system by which its pattern of references establishes its special symbolic quality. The actual moonlight is the sunlight of Paradise, and in the one chapter after this paragraph we learn that Paul drowned in a November storm before he could return to marry Lucy—"*once* in their lives some men and women go back. . . ."[14] The pattern of references is of course worked out in a variety of ways. Maria Marchmont's lover's last words are "I am dying in paradise"; Lucy's magnificent vision of the continent of Europe while on a rough channel crossing is followed immediately by the realism of "becoming excessively sick" and faltering into the cabin; Lucy's awaken-

[14] It is almost too much that this walk back to the Rue Fossette takes place during the Feast of the Assumption.

ing at La Terrasse after her collapse in an October storm is described in terms which force us to see her as "saved" in more than the literal sense; and the significance of the scene of the fete (discussed in this chapter) turns on the fact that it is a "pasteboard" paradise.

Many other references could of course be cited, but enough has been said to make clear the composition and function of the elements of Brontë's recurrent images—particularly in contrast to George Eliot's. I repeat: the mere fact that imagery is structurally important to a work of fiction is only a starting point. The more significant questions a critic must answer are, Of what does the imagery consist? and How does it contribute to the structural coherence of the novel as a whole? Only by answering these questions can one usefully compare and contrast the art of different novelists. And, as I try to show in subsequent chapters, to answer these questions effectively one should not isolate patterns of images, metaphors, and symbols but, instead, discover their relationship to other structures contributing to the total coherence of the fictional work in which they occur.

I HAVE TRIED to show in this chapter and the preceding one that attention to the fashion in which different novelists make the structural systems of their fiction cohere is more rewarding than debates about simple conceptions of point of view and arguments about the "reality" of characters. What I want to work toward is a better understanding of how and why different novelists compose the various parts of their novels in diverse fashions ("parts" meaning everything from scenes to sentences) and why the novelists choose different actions and different words as means of representation. The difficulty I face is that literary criticism has not as yet developed effective techniques for making reasonably objective investigations into questions of this kind. In subsequent chapters I shall propose an outline for such methods. But before doing that, I want to deal briefly with the potentially significant distinction between what might be called primary types of fiction—the novel and the romance.

CHAPTER VII

Novel and Romance

CHARLOTTE BRONTË's writing belongs to a tradition of romance, whereas Jane Austen's and George Eliot's do not. This means that to compare and contrast the individual literary styles of the three authors one should have some idea of how the romance and novel differ. "Romance" has been variously defined, but the most persuasive definitions share several important characteristics.

Doubtless the main difference between the novel and the romance is in the way in which they view reality. The novel renders reality closely and in comprehensive detail. It takes a group of people and sets them going about the business of life. We come to see these people in their real complexity of temperament and motive. They are in explicable relation to nature, to each other, to their social class, to their own past. Character is more important than action and plot, and probably the tragic or comic actions of the narrative will have the primary purpose of enhancing our knowledge of and feeling for an important character, a group of characters, or a way of life. The events that occur will usually be plausible; . . .

By contrast the romance, following distantly the medieval example, feels free to render reality in less volume and detail. It tends to prefer action to character, and action will be freer in a romance than in a novel, encountering, as it were, less resistance from reality. . . . The romance can flourish without providing much intricacy of relations. The characters, probably rather two-dimensional types, will not be complexly related to each other or to society or to the past. Human beings will on the whole be shown in ideal relation—that is, they will share emotions only after these have become abstract or symbolic. . . . Character itself becomes, then, somewhat abstract and ideal, so much so in some romances that it seems to be merely a function of plot. The plot we may expect to be highly colored. Astonishing events may occur and these are likely to have a symbolic or ideological, rather than a realistic, plausibility. Being less committed to the immediate rendition of reality than the novel, the romance will more freely veer toward mythic, allegorical, and symbolistic forms.[1]

The foregoing definition by Richard Chase parallels the following by Northrop Frye.

The essential difference between novel and romance lies in the conception of characterization. The romancer does not attempt to create "real people" so much as stylized figures which expand into psychological archetypes. It is in the romance that we find Jung's libido, anima, and shadow reflected in the hero, heroine, and villain respectively. That is why the romance so often radiates a glow of subjective intensity that the novel lacks, and why a suggestion of allegory is constantly creeping in around its fringes. Certain elements of character are released in the romance which make it naturally a more revolutionary form than the novel. The novelist deals with personality, with characters wearing their personae or social masks. He needs the framework of a stable society, and many of our best novelists have been conventional to the verge of fussiness. The romancer deals with individuality, with characters in vacuo idealized by revery: and, however conservative he may be, something nihilistic and untamable is likely to keep breaking out of his pages.[2]

The only weakness in these definitions is their tendency to connect the modern romance closely with older forms of the romance. There are, of course, connections, but one difference is decisive. Modern romances, those written in the past two centuries, have been created by writers deeply aware of the novel. The special character of the modern romance is determined by the influence of the novel as an important and developed form, and its resistance to that influence.

Earlier romances, such as the Hellenistic ones, did not have to compete with the novel. One of the first and most influential of the modern romances, Walpole's *Castle of*

[1] Richard Chase, *The American Novel and Its Tradition* (New York, 1957), pp. 12-13.

[2] Northrop Frye, *The Anatomy of Criticism* (Princeton, 1957), pp. 304-305.

Otranto, is described by its author, in his preface to the second edition, as a work which is distinct both from the older romance and the modern novel.

It was an attempt to blend the two kinds of romance, the ancient and the modern. In the former, all was imagination and improbability: in the latter, nature is always intended to be, and sometimes has been, copied with success. Invention has not been wanting; but the great resources of fancy have been dammed up, by a strict adherence to common life. But if, in the latter species, Nature has cramped imagination, she did but take her revenge, having been totally excluded from old romances. The actions, sentiments, and conversations, of the heroes and heroines of ancient days, were as unnatural as the machines employed to put them in motion.

The author of the following pages thought it possible to reconcile the two kinds. Desirous of leaving the powers of fancy at liberty to expatiate through the boundless realms of invention, and thence of creating more interesting situations, he wished to conduct the mortal agents in his drama according to the rules of probability; in short, to make them think, speak, and act, as it might be supposed mere men and women would do in extraordinary positions. He had observed, that, in all inspired writings, the personages under the dispensation of miracles, and witnesses to the most stupendous phenomena, never lose sight of their human character: whereas, in the productions of romantic story, an improbable event never fails to be attended by an absurd dialogue. The actors seem to lose their senses, the moment the laws of nature have lost their tone.[3]

In his "attempt to blend the two kinds of romance, the ancient and the modern," into a new form, a *tertium quid,* Walpole lays the groundwork for the modern romance's special claim to "truth." The modern romance claims to represent realities which have been excluded from the novel by a too narrow verisimilitude; in Walpole's language, "the great resources of fancy have been dammed up." Specifically, the modern romance claims to represent the truth of that which is *abnormal* (in Walpole's terminology, "extraordinary posi-

[3] The quotation is from the text of the second edition printed in *Three Gothic Novels,* ed. E. F. Bleiler (New York, 1966).

115

tions"), asserting that the novel's concentration on the normal prevents it from adequately representing actual experience as fully as is possible in fiction: "Nature has cramped imagination."

The "Gothic" romance introduces supernatural features into fiction. In different fashions, Gothic romancers assert the reality of events and experiences, outside the range of conventionalized normality, which circumscribe the action of novels. As a rule, moreover, the Gothic romancer feels no need to explain away the supernatural features of his story, his task being that of making their actuality impressive. Mrs. Radcliffe, who cautiously provided rationalized explanations for her most preternatural effects, is somewhat unusual, and even in her own day her practice was condemned by many admirers of the romance.[4] Even Mrs. Radcliffe, however, did not "explain away" the violent personalities of her villains, the strange architecture of her buildings, the impressive natural scenery of her countrysides, and the variety of extreme emotions suffered by her protagonists. Most Gothic romancers, Walpole, Lewis, Maturin, and Mary Shelley, for example, explain little. They strive, rather, to make us *feel* (hence the "thrill of terror") the actuality of agents, actions, and scenes remote from the normal experience favored by novelists. The "extravagance" of the romance is not merely a protest against the literal verisimilitude of the novel but is also a positive assertion of the exciting ranges of experience potentially open to man.

For example, a key motif throughout Mrs. Radcliffe's romances—so far as I know without significant precedent in earlier fiction—might be defined as *transport*, travel combined with rapture. Her romances are always about trips; frequently her protagonists undergo sublime rapture while traveling; often her characters move through awesome natural scenes or

[4] For example, by Sir Walter Scott in his prefatory essay to Mrs. Radcliffe's novels in *Ballantyne's Novelists Library*, vol. x (Edinburgh, 1824). Parts of this essay, as it appeared in Scott's *Miscellaneous Prose* (1827), are included in Ioan Williams' useful collection *Sir Walter Scott on Novelists and Fiction* (London, 1968).

through decaying edifices to discover psychological as well as physical "secret passages." The physical movement in the story is sometimes the result of abduction, sometimes the result of a character losing his way, but whatever the plot excuse, the reader is invited to share in a transport, to cross over into a new kind of experience. The heroine of *The Mysteries of Udolpho*, trembling under the gateway of a moldering castle, tempts us to move with her into different modes of sensation and feeling. A lost traveler in the Highlands of *The Castles of Athlin and Dunbayne* literally stumbles forward to carry us into a world of new perceptions. And it is while being hurried off to a strange (and improbable) destiny by her abductors that Ellena in *The Italian* undergoes one of her most ecstatic visions.

Mrs. Radcliffe's "transports" are interesting because they point the way toward new moral and psychological complexity, even as her fictional form, combining poetry and prose contributes (albeit clumsily) to the development of new diversity. Probably her most important successor is Sir Walter Scott, whose "historicism" is an improved fashion of making the past vividly present, whose landscapes often function to define psychological transformations, and whose frequent employment of hypnogogic states serves to dramatize transitions in moral perception. However awkward Mrs. Radcliffe's artistry, one must credit her with some innovation. In centering her stories on movements which embody transitions from one order of experience to another, which cross the invisible division between antinomial psychic modes, she begins—most ineptly, to be sure—the exploration of territory her great predecessors in fiction had left relatively unexamined.

The modern romance, in my view, is best understood as a form competing with but complementary to the novel, not simply an antagonistic one, because the persisting aim of the fiction of the past three hundred years has been the representation of actuality. Modern fiction's claim to our attention has been that it presents things as they really are, that it is truthful to the facts of life on this earth, and that insofar as fiction creates "ideal" worlds these are ideal in the sense of being rearrangements or reorganizations of things as they are, not transmutations of them. The modern romance keeps cropping up as the expression of efforts to expand our sense of what actually exists. It is not escapist literature. It asserts that actuality includes more than is generally recognized, that "reality" is more complicated, peculiar, diverse, and sensational than the existent novel admits.

The history of modern fiction follows roughly this sequence: an outburst of "realistic" novels, succeeded by a flowering of romances, followed by another outburst of realistic novels which incorporate the new dimensions of reality explored by the immediately preceding romances. An essential difference between George Eliot's and Jane Austen's "realism" can be attributed to the flourishing of the romance during the early and middle years of the nineteenth century. Eliot's novels comprehend within their realism matters which would have been too "abnormal" for Austen's realism. These were introduced into fiction by "sensational" romances, including those of Dickens and the Brontës. For example, Romola's mystic journey in a boat and the religious experience represented by Maggie Tulliver's brief enthusiasm for Thomas à Kempis have no prototypes in Austen's fiction but are "prepared for" by the spiritual intensity of several characters and situations in both the major and minor fiction of the period 1820-55, including Charlotte Brontë's. To cite specific sources: Dorothea Brooke's shattering encounter with the Catholic-pagan art of Rome is "anticipated" by Lucy Snowe's experience in the art gallery of Villette, and Herr Klesmer's intense dedication to the discipline of music is adumbrated by the impassioned artistry of Vashti.[5]

Northrop Frye quite justly distinguishes romance from

---

[5] In Eliot's description of Mirah Cohen in chapter 61 of *Daniel Deronda* there is an obvious reference to the Cleopatra of *Villette*, yet Brontë's significant "contribution" to the development of Eliot's art lies not in such specific details but in the opening up of new realms of experience. And of course Charlotte Brontë is neither the only nor the most significant of the "romancers" who flourished between the times of Austen and Eliot—that distinction belongs to Charles Dickens.

novel in terms of psychological characterization. Connecting psychological insight with plot structure, Shelley in his preface to *Frankenstein* cites as a primary virtue of his wife's story its effectiveness in providing means for delineating psychological truths which would be obscured by a more "realistic" plot.[6] Shelley's defense is not unique. The commonest justification for "improbable" occurrences in a romance is the psychic truth such occurrences reveal, truth which is often disturbing because it is outside the limits of accepted logicality. Such truth, the romancer feels, can be dramatized only by "extraordinary" events, although succeeding novelists will absorb his discoveries into the ordinary, "normal" reality of their more conventional fictional worlds. The function of the modern romance is to explore abnormality and illogicality which the novel will then normalize and rationalize.

I believe, therefore, that the Austen-Brontë-Eliot sequence is a representative one. The fact remains, however, that in defining the unities upon which even the details of fictional language depend, one must bear in mind that Charlotte Brontë's works are not strictly comparable to those of Eliot and Austen: they are, so to speak, different species of the same genus. Yet this analogy is misleading. Any effective system of describing developments within fictional art must be able to account for the *interplay* between novel and romance, for that interplay is the salient characteristic of the history of modern fiction.[7]

[6] Shelley's key observation is: "The event on which the interest of the story depends . . . affords a point of view to the imagination for the delineating of human passions more comprehensive and commanding than any which the ordinary relations of existing events can yield." The quotation is from the Everyman edition of *Frankenstein* (London, 1921), p. 1.

[7] I should perhaps make it clear that my term "modern" romance includes much more than "Gothic" romance. For example, to leave aside the more complicated problems posed by "novelists" such as Dickens and Stevenson, I believe that William Godwin's much underrated *Caleb Williams* can usefully be considered as part of a modern-romance development, even though it is not usually classed as Gothic fiction. There are at least three aspects of *Caleb Williams* relevant to the rise of the modern romance which have been unduly neglected. One finds there the first effective structuralization of a concept of

The intrinsic necessity for such interplay can perhaps be stated in this fashion: the forces of development operating in a particular art form tend to modify the means by which it takes shape. C. H. Waddington, in defining the process of evolutionary change, has hit upon two illuminating analogies.

At the beginning of the Industrial Revolution . . . there were many factories capable of producing manufactured products; and the forces of competition between the factories . . . not only brought about an evolution of the factory products . . . into more elaborate and better fabricated articles, but equally brought to pass improvements in the organization of the factories themselves, that is to say, in the mechanisms by which the articles are produced. Again, to take another example, if a group of beginners take up the practice of playing card games with one another, they would not only become more skillful at playing the game they first start on, but are likely to pass on to playing subtler and more complicated games. Thus, this, as it were, two-tier evolution—an evolution of the end-product itself and also an evolution of the mechanism by which the end-product comes into being—is quite a normal sort of happening.[8]

One might argue that nobody plays Jane Austen's "game" as well as she does, but Charlotte Brontë has a place in the

---

personality as a thoroughgoing antagonism between morally good and morally bad aspects. By "structuralization" I mean reinforcing and enriching this concept through the formal arrangements within the fiction, most obviously, I suppose, by having the "split" between good and bad in the leading characters, Falkland and Caleb, reflected and refracted in several of the minor characters, such as Spurrel, Gives, Forester, and Collins. The underlying design of *Caleb Williams* is a prototype for the later detective story in that the purpose of the work is embodied in its presentation of events in reverse of historical or chronological sequence. A detective story begins, as it were, with a corpse and works backward, which is the direction of movement in *Caleb Williams*. This backwardness permits the detective story's emphasis upon the rational, inductive and deductive reasoning. Such emphasis has stylistic implications: broadly speaking, the essential style of the detective story is intellectual rather than sensory, emotional, or evocative. It seems to me that in *Caleb Williams* Godwin rather significantly advanced the intellectual capabilities of English fictional prose.

[8] C. H. Waddington, "The Human Animal," *The Humanist Frame*, ed. Julian Huxley (London, 1961), p. 75.

history of fiction because she contributes to the development of a new kind of game, which Eliot later makes more subtle and complicated. In analogous fashion, Mrs. Radcliffe contributes to the development of a game different from that played by the Augustan masters of fiction, a game which Scott in turn refines, preparing the way for a subtler, more complex realism in later nineteenth-century novels. So it may be argued that one reason we have few worthwhile histories of fiction is that literary historians have concentrated too exclusively upon the "evolution of the end-product" and paid too little attention to the "evolution of the mechanism," while critics, in making detailed studies of structure and technique, too seldom consider the historical, developmental context of these mechanisms.

The chief importance of understanding evolutionary processes as "two-tiered," as Waddington has recognized, is that such understanding leads to the comprehension of "ethical belief"—or what the literary critic refers to as the "meaning" or "moral significance" of a work of art—as essential to the process of development itself.

I wish to urge in extension of the normal Humanist argument . . . that man's ethical feelings are essentially involved with, and in fact are actually a part of, the mental mechanism by which he is developed into a being capable of receiving and accepting socially-transmitted information. Unless some sort of authority-bearing system is developed in the mind of the growing individual, social transmission would break down because nobody would believe what they were told. . . .

The orthodox Humanist argument is that it would be a recognizably good thing if we took steps to see that our ethical beliefs effectively controlled the further course of evolution. What I am arguing is that our ethical belief *must* influence the course of human evolution, since that is based on a mechanism of which those beliefs are an essential part.[9]

Waddington's comments on the relation of "ethics" to biological evolution adapt to the evaluation of the moral sig-

[9] Waddington, pp. 77-78.

nificance of works of literature. In defining structural developments in works of fiction we inevitably become engaged with
the "meaning" which those structures convey. Yet, if we
accept the biological analogy, the meanings in each novel
ought *first* to be assessed not in isolation and not in direct
relation to "nonfictional" dogmas of politics, religion, and
so forth, but in relation to the meanings embodied in the
structures of associated works of fiction, because the "significance" of a work of fiction is integral to the nature of its
contribution to the developmental process (that is, the history
of fiction) of which it is a part, without which, indeed, it
would never have come into being. Only after this assessment
can we usefully consider a work of fiction's "moral importance" in relation to extrafictional attitudes and beliefs. A
critic, I am suggesting, will be most likely to arrive at genuinely humanistic judgments of fiction if he *begins* by studying
his texts in relation to one another. But to do this he needs
what I call "reasonably objective" methods of comparison and
contrast. The aim of the remaining chapters in this book is
to arouse interest in the possibility of devising such methods.

CHAPTER VIII

Resolution Scenes

IN PRECEDING chapters I have tried to illustrate how difficult it is to define fictional structures in a fashion which permits useful comparisons and contrasts. My purpose was to make it worthwhile to reconsider the usefulness of the kind of formalized, quantified analyses illustrated in Chapter Two. In that chapter I suggested that word choice in fiction will often depend upon an imaginative concept to be understood only in terms of the total design of a work of fiction. I want to pursue this thought by proposing that much larger elements than words need to be understood in terms of the same dependence. If this be true, there exists a possibility that one might be able to define the coherence which links different structures.

The possibility needs exploring, because unless we can devise means for comparing and contrasting relations between different kinds of fictional structure our comparisons and contrasts will not mean much. It is not especially helpful to observe that novelist A prefers an omniscient point of view whereas novelist B prefers a first-person point of view *and* that novelist A employs a rather abstract vocabulary whereas novelist B favors concrete words, unless we can establish a meaningful connection between A's omniscience and abstractness as well as between B's first-person form and concreteness. The connections, however, might usefully be compared. One factor in this situation is the difficulty of being sure what elements in a work of fiction are most nearly essential. We have no firm evidence, for example, as to whether point of view or word choice is more important in structuring fiction.

The first task, then, is to illustrate the "determinedness" of larger fictional units. One way of doing this is to distinguish the forms of those segments of different works of fiction which serve the same function. Merely for exemplification, I shall consider the manner in which the main line of action is resolved in *Mansfield Park*, in *Shirley*, and in *Felix Holt*.

I purposely abstain from dates on this occasion, that every one may be at liberty to fix their own, aware that the cure of unconquerable passions, and the transfer of unchanging attachments, must vary much as to time in different people.—I only entreat every body to believe that exactly at the time when it was quite natural that it should be so, and not a week earlier, Edmund did cease to care about Miss Crawford, and became as anxious to marry Fanny, as Fanny herself could desire.

With such a regard for her, indeed, as his had long been, a regard founded on the most endearing claims of innocence and helplessness, and completed by every recommendation of growing worth, what could be more natural than the change? Loving, guiding, protecting her, as he had been doing ever since her being ten years old, her mind in so great a degree formed by his care, and her comfort depending on his kindness, an object to him of such close and peculiar interest, dearer by all his own importance with her than any one else at Mansfield, what was there now to add, but that he should learn to prefer soft light eyes to sparkling dark ones.—And being always with her, and always talking confidentially, and his feelings exactly in that favourable state which a recent disappointment gives, those soft light eyes could not be very long in obtaining the pre-eminence.

(*Mansfield Park*, 48; or III, 17)

The terms of this resolution are generalized. What matters is less the specific character of the affection between Edmund and Fanny than the generic quality of their relation. However successfully individualized they may be in the novel, Fanny's and Edmund's marriage exemplifies a process by which "good" marriages take place. While it is true that marriage to Fanny runs counter to the prevailing notion of the best possible match for Edmund, his marriage is socially acceptable and is not unconventional. His is like the marriages of all Jane Austen's protagonists; it affirms not only individual preferences but also, perhaps more significantly, social patterns, yet social patterns which are not quite conventional. This is why it is possible for Jane Austen to resolve her novels appropriately and effectively in summary fashion using generalized terms and a distant perspective.

The resolution of Shirley Keeldar's story is of a different nature entirely. Her match shocks Sympson, a representative of good society—and Sympson is shown to be a vicious, impotent fool. In this he is like the representatives of "good" society in Brontë's other novels. Brontë's resolutions assert the superiority of two individuals over convention. In *Felix Holt*, Esther's marriage to Felix is of less importance as a marriage. It emblemizes Esther's choice of the difficulties of a "dim life" which promises to make some improvement in a society which is faulty, not because (like the society Shirley Keeldar and Louis Moore ignore) it sets up external barriers of "gold and station," but because it warps the best impulses of individuals; it creates inner obstacles. In the resolution of *Felix Holt* Esther denies her own former attitudes, her former personality as shaped by the inducements and threats of social conventions. In rejecting Harold Transome she rejects her earlier personality. Like Shirley, Esther asserts herself as an individual—but less against "exterior" society than against her former self as an individual, albeit one shaped by society.

The resolution of each novel provides a happy ending, but the happiness in each is of a special kind. The happy resolution of *Mansfield Park* is plainly the most conventional. For some of its effect it depends on the reader's recognizing its conventionality. The first paragraph of the passage quoted above, particularly its reference to the Northangerish "cure of unconquerable passions and the transfer of unchanging attachments," would lose some of its point for a reader unfamiliar with the *convention* of the happy ending of matrimony. Jane Austen's fiction never pretends to be anything but fiction. This openness permits the play on the word "natural" in this passage. However one interprets *Mansfield Park*, one recognizes that the "natural" is an issue at the center of the action. Leaving aside the problems posed by the acting of *Lovers' Vows* and the contrast between Mary Crawford's vivacity and Fanny's constitutional debility, one may recall the brilliantly written scenes of Fanny's visit to Portsmouth as representing how little hold "natural" ties have on the heroine. The natural bond of family is feeble in contrast to what might be termed the "nurtural" bond that links Fanny to Mansfield. What is most natural to a human being in Jane Austen's view is not fully comprehended in the instinctive, the physical, or the biological. Intuition and sensation are dangerous guides. It is "natural" for a human being to be civilized—to think, feel, and behave in accord with artifices of thought, emotion, and behavior which have been trained into him, encouraging some propensities and repressing others. For a civilized person, it is "natural" to be conventional.

The cool distancing of the entire passage of resolution in *Mansfield Park* expresses the power of the cultural world and structurally reinforces the author's assertion of the rewards of decorum. Yet, as I have remarked, the union of Fanny and Edmund is not utterly conventional. In a thoroughly civilized fashion Jane Austen pokes fun at Edmund— not only in the first paragraph quoted but also in a subsequent one. There we find that only at "a later period" does he learn "the whole delightful and astonishing truth" that Fanny has always loved him. The gentle suggestion of Edmund's lack of perception is particularly interesting because in *Mansfield Park*—perhaps more than in her other novels—Jane Austen presents the relations between the sexes as hierarchical. The hero is superior to the heroine in those attributes which their society ranks as most important. Yet each of her heroes needs the heroine and benefits from his marriage. This is not crude criticism of society but something more subtle, a dramatization of the complexities of interpersonal relations which must be observed if social decorum is to fulfill its aim. Jane Austen's society encourages differentiations in rank, function, and personality. Only if the worth of each of these is recognized can the hierarchical formality escape becoming pompous tyranny. It is notable that Edmund's "regard" for Fanny is founded on the "endearing" claim of "helplessness." At the end of the resolution passage being discussed we find a special distinction between Edmund and Fanny. If he is her superior, she is the happier. The difference is presented in terms generalized almost to the point of abstraction, so the language forces us to see the union not merely as a particular event but also as a representative one.

' His happiness in knowing himself to have been so long the beloved of such a heart, *must have been* great enough to warrant *any* strength of language in which he *could* clothe it to her or to himself; it *must have been* a delightful happiness! But there was happiness *elsewhere* which *no* description can reach. Let *no one presume* to give the feelings of *a* young woman on receiving assurance of that affection of which she has scarcely allowed herself to entertain a hope.

> (*Mansfield Park*, 48; or III, 17—my italics)

One must observe that these generalized terms refer to a discrimination, and a discrimination not usually attempted— between different kinds of happiness. And immediately following the passage I have quoted is an explanation of Sir Thomas's reasons for approving the match.

Sick of ambitious and mercenary connexions, prizing more and more the sterling good of principle and temper, and chiefly anxious to bind by the strongest securities all that remained to him of domestic felicity . . . the high sense of having realised a great acquisition in the promise of Fanny for a daughter, formed . . . a contrast with his early opinion on the subject when the poor little girl's coming had been first agitated. . . . Fanny was indeed the daughter that he wanted.

> (*Mansfield Park*, 48; or III, 17)

One notes that Fanny is Sir Thomas's daughter by nurture, not nature. This contrast focuses the contrast between the views of Sir Thomas, the supreme arbiter of Mansfield society, at the beginning and at the end of the novel. The change occurs because Fanny realizes the ideals of Mansfield better than Sir Thomas himself. The values of Mansfield are affirmed by being made subtle and more complex. In a word, Fanny alone can make the proprieties of Mansfield "tender." The resolution of the book can be presented in a cool, generalized, summary fashion because it does not simplify. The difficulties

which make up the action of *Mansfield Park* are really less
subtle and complex than the union which resolves them, which
is one reason why we go on arguing about what *Mansfield
Park* "means."[1]

There is little argument about what *Shirley* "means."
Charlotte Brontë uses the same general form as Jane Austen,
the romantic story with a happy ending, but Brontë shifts the
focus from marriage to love. The respectable and socially
sanctioned marriages which conclude *Shirley* confirm the
rightness of the protagonists' personal choices rather than
affirm the value of social decorum. There is little point in
arguing about personal preferences.

In *Mansfield Park*, as in Austen's other novels, the right
marriage is the only possible embodiment of the heroine's full
experience of love. The same is not true for Brontë's heroines:
Lucy Snowe does not marry Paul Emanuel; Jane Eyre's most
intense expression of her love for Rochester is her flight from
him. The resolution of a Brontë novel establishes a psychological contract between equals instead of a hierarchical social
contract between two people who *need* each other in complementary fashion. Hence the appropriate form of Charlotte
Brontë's resolutions is a theatrical scene, not a generalizing
summary.

To illustrate Brontë's form I shall refer to the resolution of
the Shirley–Louis Moore part of *Shirley*. Both Austen's summary and Brontë's scene treat of changes: Edmund turns
from Mary to Fanny, and Louis finally forgets Shirley's "gold
and station." At first he says,

---

[1] One phrase at least I cannot resist citing as evidence: that in
which Fanny is described as dearer to Edmund "by all his own importance with her *than anyone else at Mansfield.*" Without the words
I have italicized there would be only fine psychological insight; with
them the insight is made to contribute to the reorientation of Mansfield values which Fanny's presence brings about. For interpretations
of *Mansfield Park* different from mine, see the works of Edwards and
Fleishman cited previously, as well as Joseph M. Duffy, Jr., "Moral
Integrity and Moral Anarchy in *Mansfield Park*," *ELH*, XXIII (1956),
71-91; and Lionel Trilling, "Jane Austen and *Mansfield Park*," *The
Pelican Guide to English Literature*, vol. V, *From Blake to Byron*, ed.
Boris Ford (Harmondsworth, 1957), pp. 112-29.

Gold and her Station are two griffins, that guard her on each side. Love looks and longs, and dares not: Passion hovers round, and is kept at bay: Truth and Devotion are scared.

At the climax of the scene, however, he reports that

. . . out of her emotion passed into me a new spirit. I neither was crushed nor elated by her lands and gold; I thought not of them, cared not for them: they were nothing: dross that could not dismay me. I saw only herself; her young beautiful form; the grace, the majesty, the modesty of her girlhood.
"My pupil," I said.
"My master," was the low reply.   (*Shirley*, 36)

Brontë's scene is a theatrical one—even the personifications in the first passage above are posed dramatically. Sensory particularities are emphasized: the lovers touch, they address one another with sensuous imagery, and more than once Louis attempts to picture Shirley's appearence. Brontë's resolution is a specific sensory-psychological event. It has to be a concretely realized confrontation because what it resolves is an intensely personal conflict.

Although it sounds odd to say so, the love between Jane Austen's protagonists is not simply a matter of personal relation. Their relation is inseparable from their relations with others. The climax of Brontë's love stories, however, is a scene in which at last the lovers confront one another with all other relations excluded—usually literally. Yet a similarity between Austen and Brontë remains. For both, the representation of love as a social union of disparate personalities is the climax of all significant themes in their narratives. Whatever other issues and meanings appear in their novels, all are shaped so as to contribute to a celebration of a love which *deserves* the sanction of marriage. Yet differences remain. "I am poor; I must be proud," says Louis Moore. Such a speech is impossible for the heroine of *Mansfield Park*, which like all of Austen's novels, shows us an essentially undifferentiated social group. All the major characters are of one class, broadly speaking, the upper-middle class. Where another class is introduced—Fanny's family is the most celebrated example—

it is represented in the same terms which prevail elsewhere. Fanny's life at Portsmouth is very different from her life at Mansfield, but the two modes of living contrast because the processes of social existence in both places are represented in exactly the same fashion. What we learn about Portsmouth is what we learn about Mansfield, how people behave there, what their manners are. Portsmouth is not really a city in Jane Austen's novel, it is a way of behaving.

Louis Moore and Fanny Price are both dependents and both are conscious of their positions. Yet one cannot imagine Fanny saying to Edmund, "I know my place" and accepting his judgment that her apparent humility is the counterfeit for "monstrous pride." Yet why not? Some modern readers so interpret Fanny's character. When Fanny believes Edmund will marry Mary Crawford she believes that

To call or to fancy it a loss, a disappointment, would be a presumption, for which she had not words strong enough to satisfy her own humility. To think of him as Miss Crawford might be justified in thinking, would in her be insanity.

(*Mansfield Park*, 27; or II, 9)

Fanny's humility is genuine. She does not say "I know my place" because her existence is her way of behaving. Moore's statement, "I know my place," implies the potential inadequacy of his "place" to define his personality and aspirations. He feels that his place does not circumscribe his range of possible feeling and action. In Brontë's fiction, role and personality separate. Fanny Price's place must very nearly circumscribe her personality; in Jane Austen's fiction, role and personality must cohere because personality is realized through role. What tortures Louis Moore is the knowledge that it is not insane for him to think of Shirley as his wife. He sees the articulation of society which separates him from Shirley as a reality alien to the reality of his inner personality. There is no such conflict of realities in Austen's heroines.

Fanny Price is not like Louis Moore (or Edward Crimsworth or Jane Eyre or Lucy Snowe), a proud person who is forced to behave with humility because of social circumstances. Her humility is authentic. Were it not, the very foundation of Austen's concept of "society" would be shaken, since it depends on the presupposition that an individual best realizes his individuality through the exercise of his social role, and roles are hierarchic, superiors condescending, and inferiors humble. But it is not, finally, "insanity" for Fanny to think of Edmund as a husband, as something "dearer than a friend." How are we to explain this?

Psychologically, the hero and heroine in each of Jane Austen's novels fit perfectly in their differences: he is strong where she is weak and vice-versa. The action of the novels consists in the social matching of psychological opposites. In Charlotte Brontë's novels the action consists in the overcoming of social obstacles by the power of attraction between two psychological equals, and, therefore, two personalities which define themselves by "clashing." Brontë's protagonists strive to *prove* their independence. The economic independence sought by Edward Crimsworth, the Moores, Jane Eyre, and Lucy Snowe is obvious. But their "pairs" also have to achieve independence. Rochester must get free of Bertha (and all that she represents in himself); Paul must free himself from his Catholic family; Shirley must surrender her essentially irresponsible liberty. In Austen's novels, on the contrary, the protagonists search for someone on whom they can depend. This is what Edmund finds in Fanny. For better or worse, depending on one's opinion of Mansfield ideals, Edmund does not so much want Fanny as need her. Fanny marries Edmund not merely because she needs Mansfield but also because she is needed there.

I have remarked that the resolution of *Shirley* takes the form of a theatrical scene. Technically this is untrue, for it is presented as a passage written by Louis Moore in his diary. This device enables Brontë to render the scene from the first-person point of view, her preferred angle of representation. One reason she liked it, apparently, was that it enabled her to simplify; it helped her to be "theatrical."[2] In a colloquy,

[2] First-person point of view, of course, can be employed for aims other than theatricality—one thinks of Defoe's novels at once. Again

first-person narration permits representation of the intensity of the narrator's feelings, both expressed and unexpressed. Simultaneously, however, this point of view prevents too much probing into the other character's unexpressed motives and feelings.[8] The *relation* is presented in relatively simplified form. And the relations of Brontë's characters are, when compared to those of Austen's characters, simple.

A presupposition of most modern fictional criticism is that "dramatization" is superior to "telling," and that the history of the novel shows an advance from novelists who "tell" to those who "show." There is evidence of an increasing preference among novelists for showing, but, as the scene from *Shirley* may suggest, the movement is too complicated to be described as a simple "advance." Any fictional dramatization is a form of telling. Fiction is not drama but a story recounted on the pages of a book. The various devices of "dramatization" employed by novelists are not approximations of stage methods but autonomous fictional techniques whose interest lies less in their relation to the practices of the stage than in their function as means of realizing novelistic ends. Critical terminology derived from the language of stage drama applied to novels is metaphoric.

The resolution scene in *Shirley*, for example, is theatrical not in the literal sense of being stagy but in the metaphorical sense of clearly defining opposing forces and excluding everything which does not enhance the directness of the confrontation. The personalities of Louis Moore and Shirley are presented not as complex and many-sided but as concentrated, summarized in their commitment to the critical issue brought into focus by their confrontation. The language of the passage

---

we return to the observation made earlier that the specific function of point of view is more important than its category, "first-person," "omniscient," etc. On the other hand, Brontë's tendency toward "theatricality" helps to define the theatricality of Dickens (who did not prefer the first-person point of view) as essentially fictional and not, as some critics assume, a mere transposition into fiction of melodramatic stage techniques.

[8] This surely helps to explain why Henry James was attracted to the "central intelligence" rather than to the first-person point of view.

is appropriate, not only because it focuses the role-personality split but also because it is founded on simple, consistent pictorialization, with emphasis on personification and metaphor. First Shirley compares Louis and his brother to "homeless hunters" of "the loneliest western wilds." Moore seizes Shirley's imagery and develops it into the personification of Liberty accompanying him to America. He then transforms Liberty into the image of the "orphan girl" he seeks. Shirley recommends celibacy and, when he rejects the advice, suggests "any stout widow." He turns the tables by suggesting that she is the celibate, since she has rejected Sir Philip, whom she might have led and improved. Shirley retorts:

"Leading and improving! teaching and tutoring! bearing and forbearing! Pah! My husband is not to be my baby. I am not to set him his daily lesson and see that he learns it, and give him a sugar-plum if he is good, and a patient, pensive, pathetic lecture if he is bad. But it is like a tutor to talk of the 'satisfaction of teaching.' I suppose *you* think it the finest employment in the world. I don't—I reject it. Improving a husband! No. I shall insist upon my husband improving me, or else we part."

(*Shirley*, 36)

I do not wish to bog down the general contrast between the resolution of *Shirley* and that of *Mansfield Park* by calling attention to too many details, but the minutiae of this paragraph should be noted as extraordinarily revealing of Brontë's style in contrast to Austen's. This passage is highly exclamatory in a fashion that Austen's prose never is, because the exclamations are directed primarily to the ideas the speaker herself is *expressing* and not toward the person she is *addressing*. The alliteration of "patient, pensive, pathetic" is a formal device rarely, if ever, used by Austen. These details, as well as others which might be pointed out, are in large measure to be explained by the fact that the passage as a whole is a metaphoric image expressive of the speaker's "creativeness." This structuring is not found in Austen's fiction, where there are no "creative" people.

Moore accuses Shirley of taunting him with being a poor

teacher who has "nothing but a very plain person to offer the woman who may master my heart." She replies that he exaggerates his plainness to provoke compliments; though

> "Your face is nothing to boast of, certainly: not a pretty line, nor a pretty tint, to be found therein."
> "Compare it with your own."
> "It looks like a god of Egypt: a great sand-buried stone head; or rather I will compare it to nothing so lofty: it looks like Tartar: you are my mastiff's cousin: I think you as much like him as a man can be like a dog."

But Moore seizes the dog comparison (Austen's characters in their speech never seize on one another's language in this way):

> "In the winter evenings, Tartar lies at your feet: you suffer him to rest his head on your perfumed lap; you let him couch on the borders of your satin raiment; his rough hide is familiar with the contact of your hand; I once saw you kiss him on that snow-white beauty-spot which stars his broad forehead. It is dangerous to say I am like Tartar; it suggests to me a claim to be treated like Tartar."

When Shirley retorts that he may "extort as much" from his "orphan girl," he pursues the revived image by demanding that Shirley tell him "where she is." After wringing from her an admission of her love, he exclaims:

> "You must not smile at present. The world swims and changes round me. The sun is a dizzying scarlet blaze, the sky a violet vortex whirling over me."

To which extravagance Shirley responds that he has earlier called her a leopardess:

> ". . . remember, the leopardess is tameless," said she.
> "Tame or fierce, wild or subdued, you are *mine*."
> "I am glad I know my keeper, and am used to him. Only his voice will I follow; only his hand shall manage me; only at his feet will I repose." (*Shirley*, 36)

I have quoted extensively to make it clear that the "theatricality" of this resolution scene lies in the language used by the characters, not merely in their situation. In many earlier melodramatic works of fiction, such as Gothic novels, the melodrama is less truly fictional because it is solely a quality of the situation represented and does not penetrate into the language of representation. The entrance of melodrama into the language of fiction marks a decisive phase in the history of the British novel.[4] How decisive can be suggested by a consideration of George Eliot's work, which is realistic rather than romantic, illustrating nonetheless the enriching effect of the romance on the novel, and showing melodramatic elements "acclimated" to the needs of the novel's realism.

In the resolution of *Felix Holt*, Eliot combines detached authorial commentary with melodramatic confrontation. The resolution begins at the end of chapter 49, when Esther retires to her bedroom to consider her "final choice" between Harold and Felix, and concludes in chapter 50 with the description of Mrs. Transome's thoughts, her meeting with Esther, and Esther's final confrontation with Harold. All of this is foreshadowed at the end of chapter 49, the final paragraph of

[4] The novelist most responsible for this enrichment of fictional language was without doubt Charles Dickens. Merely to call Dickens' novels "melodramatic," and even to call attention to their indubitable relation to Victorian melodramas, is not, finally, very helpful. The poorest of Dickens' novels is superior to the best Victorian melodrama, in part because Dickens succeeds as had no one before in "melodramatizing" the language of fiction. The nature of this melodramatizing can be illustrated by the famous first sentence of *Little Dorrit*: "Thirty years ago, Marseilles lay burning in the sun, one day." The disturbing imbalance of time specifications at the two ends of the sentence, emphasized by careful mispunctuation, pivots on the word "burning," the "literal" sense of which is in fact metaphoric: "a burning day" is very hot. But Dickens' reference is also to the true literal meaning of the word. Anyone who will read the opening passage without preconceptions will see that Dickens' is not attempting a literal description. Any doubts on the matter can be dispelled by comparing this beginning of part I entitled "Poverty" with the passage about the St. Bernard Pass at the beginning of part II, entitled "Riches." Formal and structural contrast, not visual accuracy, is Dickens' chief concern. *Little Dorrit* treats, among other matters, of Hell on earth, as its first sentence tells us—through its melodramatic form.

which, out of context, some might identify as a piece of Dickensian theatricality.

> It was already near midnight, but with these thoughts succeeding and returning in her mind like scenes through which she was living, Esther had a more intense wakefulness than any she had known by day. All had been stillness hitherto, except the fitful wind outside. But her ears now caught a sound within—slight, but sudden. She moved near her door, and heard the sweep of something on the matting outside. It came closer, and paused. Then it began again, and seemed to sweep away from her. Then it approached, and paused as it had done before. Esther listened, wondering. The same thing happened again and again, till she could bear it no longer. She opened her door, and in the dim light of the corridor, where the glass above seemed to make a glimmering sky, she saw Mrs. Transome's tall figure pacing slowly, with her cheek upon her hand. (*Felix Holt*, 49)

This melodramatic situation is immediately preceded by a presentation which in its cool logicality seems closer to Austen than to Dickens or Brontë. The subject of the passage is Esther's self-examination, but it is, of course, a long way from "stream of consciousness." Like Austen, Eliot is unashamed of "telling," yet her aim in representing through analysis and commentary is quite different. Eliot wants us to understand the evolution of the inner impulses which make Esther's story significant, a story which is testimony to the worthwhileness of rejecting the rewards of conventionality. In this regard, Eliot seems close to Brontë. But Eliot does not celebrate the individual's mere assertion of self against social pressure. Esther rejects her former self more than she rejects others, and she joins with Felix in order to improve society.

The Victorianism of this motif ought not to absorb our attention so far that we fail to recognize the artistic problem involved. Eliot asserts the unusual person's duty not to accept one's society but to *change* it so that it will encourage the development of richer individual personalities. Eliot almost has to combine the summarizing and self-dramatizing techniques that are separate in Austen and Brontë.

It is fair to say that Eliot does not represent the processes of Esther's thoughts, as she does, for example, with Hetty Sorrel in *Adam Bede*. Instead of describing the processes by which Esther's thoughts and feelings fluctuate toward a decision, Eliot depicts the underlying configurations of these inner movements. She summarizes, making precise the significance of Esther's inner struggle rather than attempting to show the struggle itself. This is why the narrator's presence is appropriate: as author she provides an objective perspective that Esther cannot. For the same reason, Eliot needs the melodramatic paragraph which closes the chapter and embodies the larger significance of Esther's decision. In the mysterious sweep of Mrs. Transome's dress and the troubling enigma of her "tall figure," the intricate, unpredictable meshing of the effects of Esther's decisions on others is physically realized.

Unlike Brontë, Eliot does not merely focus on a clash between role and personality, and, unlike Austen, Eliot does not present role as a means of realizing personality. Instead she concentrates on how role and personality interact, sometimes reinforcing each other, sometimes conflicting, but always dynamically affecting each other. Esther's apparently private decision is not, after all, private. And not only does it affect (as well as being affected by) others at this moment, but it is also—inevitably—engaged with both the future and the past. Mrs. Transome's Gothic pose and situation are remarkably appropriate. What has led Esther to her present position is a strange chain of circumstances which climax in compelling her to examine her own past, to evaluate its doubts and turnings not merely in themselves but also as they serve as a guide to the future. Dramatically, even melodramatically, Eliot represents the connection of human circumstances in time as well as in space. In a subtle, sophisticated, meaningful fashion Esther's situation parallels that of the heroine of the Gothic romance: she is alone at midnight in a house with a strange history (Mr. Transome, one recalls, is feeble-minded) while her lover is far away in prison. The point is not, of course, that Eliot is in any sense imitating Gothic romances, but she does develop some of the more important implications of that crude form. One reason for her doing so is to emphasize how human actions interlink. Even at her most isolated, Esther is not alone. Any moment is an intersection of past and future. Human life *is* a connection of all dimensions, and the resolution of *Felix Holt* must simultaneously represent this connection while depicting life's diversity. "Realism" and "romance" are both relevant to *Felix Holt*.

Hence Eliot's "resolution" lacks the different consistencies of Austen's and Brontë's. It is composed of diverse parts, melodramatic scene and exposition. "Exposition" seems the best word, because Eliot's presence in the earlier paragraph is not a matter of occasional intrusion: it is essential to the form of the passage as a whole. The imagery is unlike the flamboyant intensifications of Brontë's characters. Eliot's imagery is her own, not Esther's, and it gives sensory embodiment to the *pattern* of Esther's thoughts, to the design underlying them, of which Esther herself is not fully aware. When Eliot writes "to know that high initiation she must often tread where it is hard to tread, and feel the chill air, and watch through darkness," she is neither rendering directly what Esther thinks nor merely generalizing. Her imagery embodies the direction and meaning of Esther's self-analysis. The same is true of the images of "the dim life of the back street," "the stony road," where Esther may be "alone and faint and be weary," the "silken bondage" of Transome Court, and the memory of Felix's kiss lying "on her lips like a seal of possession." The fact is that "love," in the sense in which "love" occurs in Austen's and Brontë's fiction, is not Eliot's primary subject. The conventional love story provides a general form for her novel, but she uses the form to explore a different topic. One might say that she explores complications which are obscured by the conventional form, above all, the complicated fashion in which social life is dense with personality-role interactions.

The resolution of *Felix Holt* involves Esther's choice between two reasonable if unequal possibilities. Fanny's choice between Edmund and Henry Crawford is part of the complication of the novel, not its resolution. In *Mansfield Park* choice is a feature of plot development; in *Felix Holt* plot development results in choice. The conventional form of the love story, culminating in "good" marriage (in which the "right" choice is of necessity virtually predetermined), is only superficially relevant for Eliot. After all, Esther's marriage, more than Shirley's, is a positive denial of the values of a "good" marriage; it is not a mere overcoming of obstacles but a reorientation of society. The social barriers dividing Shirley and Louis Moore are simplified and conventionalized and external. Those dividing Esther and Felix are not, which is why both analytical commentary and "theatricality" are necessary to Eliot, whose task is to represent the intertwining complexities which make personal choice socially significant. It is Esther's psychological attitude, the effect of her education and experience, which separates her from Felix throughout most of the novel. The obstacles to be overcome in *Felix Holt* are psychological, but they are created by social circumstances. Individual personality and social forms connect and interpenetrate. Esther's "inward resolution" has more than personal significance; it has social implications, specifically the affirmation that the "dim life of the back street" animated by Felix's idealism is superior to the "well-cushioned despair" of Transome Court. The contrary is also true. It is the sociopolitical convulsions narrated earlier in *Felix Holt*, convulsions which physically separate Esther and Felix by sending him to prison, which have initiated the transformation of Esther's personality. Because society is a changing medium, individual personalities change, and their changes affect the medium through which they interrelate. It is these mutually influential complexities which the resolution of *Felix Holt* strives to represent, without reducing them to an unreal stasis which could be portrayed by the kind of simple theatricality we see in the resolution of *Shirley*.[5]

[5] It is notable that Eliot has more difficulty attaining satisfying conclusions than has Austen. The difficulty is a sign of the underlying "unconventionality" of Eliot's fictional forms. Her most successful endings seem to me those (as in *Daniel Deronda*) which are new beginnings.

I HAVE TRIED in the last few pages to demonstrate how careful inspection of a segment of a novel larger than a sentence or a paragraph reveals the segment to be determined by the largest and most fundamental designs of the novel as an aesthetic whole. A segment such as a "resolution" is fully explicable, I submit, only in terms of this determinedness— just as, as I tried to illustrate in Chapter Two, even individual words in a novel have to be interpreted as part of a vocabulary of forms which depends on the total design of the novel. A drawback to analyses such as those just presented lies in the subjective definition of the formal "unit" being analyzed. One could argue cogently against my definitions of what constitutes the critical portion of each "resolution." Such a debate might be fruitful and might be a good means for developing our understanding of fictional art. Yet I wonder if we are not engaged in a hopeless task in trying to discuss comparisons and contrasts of elements such as "resolutions," let alone word choices, *in themselves*. It seems to me we need to find methods of comparing the *relations* between different elements, particularly those of different structural levels. Toward this end I propose that we experiment with the possibilities of establishing other units as the basis of comparisons and contrasts.

The method I have used as a first and tentative thrust into this unknown critical territory is based on the same line of thought underlying this chapter: the nature of smaller elements in fiction cannot be defined structurally except in relation to larger elements, this hierarchy leading ultimately to the total design of the novel. I therefore attempt first to give some "objective" description of fictional works as wholes, then try to derive from that description objective descriptions of progressively smaller units, with the hope of arriving finally at a somewhat systematized series of descriptions permitting definition of the coherence which gives distinctive unity to the fictional art of each novelist.

CHAPTER IX

The Total Design of Novels

MY TECHNIQUE for analyzing the underlying structures of novels was to discriminate four basic elements sure to be present in any work of fiction and to indicate something of each element's function on each page of every novel studied. The elements studied were: time or temporal ordering; location or setting; action, that is, narrative, dialogue, etc.; and characters. The fashion in which these elements were described, with some commentary on the limitations of the technique, will be found in the Tabulations Appendix.

The unit of the page is unsatisfactory, but practical considerations drove me to use it. Although the size of a novel (or of any subdivision of it) is measured most precisely and usefully by the number of words it contains, this method of measurement was too expensive and time-consuming for the limited resources at my disposal. One must bear in mind when examining my comparisons that pages in different novels not only contain varying numbers of words but also represent varying proportions of the whole novel: a 300-word page from a 200-page novel is a larger segment of that novel than is a 500-word page from a 600-page novel.

My hope was that by identifying, even if only by pages, different novelists' treatment of time, setting, action, and characters, I could define more-or-less objectively some generic characteristics of one author's larger structural patterns relative to another's. The hope was not fully realized, among other reasons because it proved difficult to devise effective measures of relation. Also objective measures tend to miss or to obscure nuances of representation which over the course of a long novel are probably decisive for establishing its predominant aesthetic. For example, it is easy enough to define the amount of time covered by the action of a novel, yet such a definition really tells us little about the temporal sequences within the work. Only rarely is the total time span of fictional action of much aesthetic significance. I found in the process of analysis, furthermore, that with the novelists with whom I was concerned there was no consistent patterning of total time spans of novels by each author, although some graphings indicate that there is probably a broad temporal range to which Austen, Brontë, and Eliot adhere—that is, there are no examples in their fiction of highly reduced time spans such as one finds in *Ulysses*.

I did discover, however, that Austen concentrates the time covered by her action more than do Eliot and Brontë and that Eliot prefers a larger time span than does Brontë [TIME 1]. (Titles in brackets refer to tables to be found in the Tabulations Appendix.) Interestingly, however, when we add up the number of pages in the novels on which "continuous time" alone occurs we find that Austen shows the lowest figure [TIME 3]. The reason appears to be not that Austen has less continuous time [TIME 4], but that she breaks up the temporal flow of continuous action with "indeterminate" time elements. About forty percent of Eliot's "indeterminate" time marks occur on pages with no other time indicated, whereas only about fifteen percent of Austen's indeterminate time marks occur in isolation (Brontë's figure is about twenty-five percent). Eliot tends to work with blocks of continuous time separated by "timeless" passages (often involving authorial commentary), whereas Austen interweaves indeterminate and continuous temporal orderings.

On the whole Brontë uses less indeterminate time than do the other two [TIME 6]. Her interruptions of temporal continuity spring from intrusions of "blank" weeks or months— the passage of some such span being merely referred to in a phrase or sentence. Eliot's "blank" time is more frequently of a longer span—months to years. Austen uses little blank time. Another fashion of pointing up these distinctions is to observe the kind of temporal ordering which characteristically occurs at the beginnings of chapters [TIME 5]. Eliot has a preference for beginning chapters with a passage which is temporally indeterminate; Brontë, with a passage which rapidly covers a considerable length of definite time; and Austen prefers relatively tighter continuity. The differences in themselves are of limited importance, because in all the novels considered between three-fourths and nine-tenths of the pages show temporal continuity [TIME 4]: a more precise analysis of the nature of each author's continuity is needed. Yet the differences do point to structural variations: Austen's and Brontë's novels both adhere to an underlying pattern of temporal continuity, Austen adhering more consistently than Brontë. Eliot relies less on this continuity of "real" time or ordinary chronology.

The analysis of settings reinforces the findings for temporal movement. Relative to Austen and Eliot, there is very little "indeterminate" setting in Brontë's novels [SETTING 1]. Indeterminacy of time and location is doubtless somewhat incompatible with first-person narration. It is notable, too, that Brontë is the least likely of our authors to shift settings at the beginning of chapters, whereas Eliot is the most likely to begin a new narrative unit with a change of scene [SETTING 2]. Eliot's preference for "block" structure is here reemphasized —and the structure becomes even clearer when we examine the continuity of characters between changes of setting. Whereas Austen changes settings relatively often but keeps two or more characters continuously "on stage," and whereas Brontë keeps one character continuously on stage (obviously a function of first-person narration), Elliot often changes settings and simultaneously changes her cast of on-stage characters completely [SETTING 3].

Something about the nature of the settings used by the novelists is indicated by the association of descriptive passages with the introduction of new locations [SETTING 4]. Here Brontë runs higher than Eliot, though both are markedly above Austen. Brontë is relatively fond of discriptive writing, but she also prefers initial "scene-setting." Initial scene-setting is a characteristic of the Gothic novel, where description also bulks large. Description, I believe, will frequently be found in fiction with a strong symbolical orientation. Eliot, however, tends to combine description with commentary. Her initial scene-setting often involves "attitude-setting." For Eliot a new scene is likely to serve as a means of establishing a new viewpoint for the reader. Of course, the decision as to what constitutes "description" is a thoroughly subjective one, as is the decision as to what constitutes a definable "setting." My markers agreed, however, that Austen uses distinctively fewer settings than Brontë or Eliot, and that Brontë uses more than Eliot, even though Brontë's novels are, on the whole, shorter [SETTING 5]. In isolation these findings are of limited value. *Silas Marner* has as few major settings as several of Austen's novels, but the nature and function of the settings in *Silas Marner* are clearly distinguishable from those in any Austen novel. Still, Austen's relative consistency is helpful; *Persuasion* has about the same number of major settings as the earlier novels. The emphasis on place and scene noticed by many critics seems to be a development within the pattern of Austen's established fictional imagining rather than a radical departure.

When one turns to the different kinds of narrative action one finds that Brontë stresses description; Eliot, exposition; and Austen, what we call "interiorized" narration [ACTION 1]. These kinds of action are congruent with the kinds of setting and temporal ordering favored by each author. It is notable, however, that the percentage of pages on which dialogue occurs runs pretty steadily from sixty to seventy, with Austen fairly consistently at the upper end of the scale. The pattern is sustained by the count of pages which are more than half dialogue [ACTION 2 and ACTION 3]. Whereas nearly forty percent of the pages beginning chapters in Austen's novels contain dialogue, the same figure for both Brontë's and Eliot's novels is thirty percent. The between-chapter continuity in time and the continuity in characters on stage favored by Austen tend to reinforce one another.

The interrelation between dialogue and the other kinds of narrative action is illustrated by cumulative figures [ACTION

4] which show that, once again, Brontë favors description and Eliot exposition. These numbers illustrate with special clarity that the tabulations referred to throughout this chapter do little more than delimit subjects worthy of detailed, *subjective* study. We have an indication that Austen associates interiorized action and dialogue more frequently than does Eliot. But, as I try to demonstrate in subsequent chapters, the texts of the novels show: first, that the kind of interiorized action associated with dialogue is definably different in the two novelists; and, second, that Austen's and Eliot's methods of making this association are impressively distinct. To me it is the dubious, sometimes even misleading, character of these measurements which makes them valuable. They act as irritants. They stimulate one to examine and justify one's intuitions.[1]

It is intriguing to me that of all the discriminations so far discussed, the clearest is probably the most nearly objective, the distinction between "dialogue" and "narration" (including description, exposition, and interiorized action). Of the four elements studied the most objective is indubitably that of "character," and here, too, we find clear-cut distinctions between the novelists. In the first place, simple listings of major characters (those who "appear" on at least five percent of the pages of their novel) show a surprising consistency throughout the work of each author [CHARACTER 1]. Not only are the cast sizes remarkably similar but the number of pages devoted to each role—protagonist, other woman, etc.—shows unexpected consistency, particularly in Jane Austen's works [CHARACTER 2]. These lists alone support the traditional attitude of regarding characters as the essential element in novels, but the figures suggest that "characters" are as vital a feature of form as of subject matter.

---

[1] It is worth pointing out that the very unreliability of the tabulations gives a value to the marking technique as an educational device. Two people independently preparing tabulations for the same novel end up with somewhat different markings. The discrepancies make excellent focal points for fruitful discussion not only of the text but also of the critical presuppositions and even the value-systems of the markers.

It is apparent that Austen's casts of major characters are larger than Brontë's or Eliot's, even though Austen's novels are, in general, shorter. This fact is probably related to Austen's relative preference for dialogue. But major characters are only part of the story. If one counts the number of characters appearing on two percent of the pages of each novel, the relative cast sizes shift [CHARACTER 3]. The trend of this shift is intensified when one adds to the foregoing figures, estimates (an exact count is virtually impossible in a large novel) for the total number of characters in each work [CHARACTER 4]. The context of "other" characters in which any one character appears is distinctively different in the fiction of our three novelists, but the difference is not just that of size. Austen's major characters move on and off "stage" much more frequently than do Eliot's or Brontë's. A gross measure of character movement is provided by a determination of the major characters' approach toward "total" movement, that is, a condition in which every major character would appear on every alternate page. (What a novel that would make!) By dividing the sum of the major characters' separate appearances by half the number of pages in the novel one arrives at a figure which indicates relative frequency of movement—the higher the figure the closer to total movement. Austen runs about .09, Brontë .05, Eliot .07.

Another dimension of character arrangement consists in the number of characters appearing simultaneously. This dimension can be given broad definition by a simple summing up for all "two-percent" characters of the pages on which each one appears. By dividing this sum by the number of pages in the novel, one arrives at comparable average character-per-page figures [CHARACTER 5]. Crude as these averages are, they distinguish our three authors clearly, and the importance of the distinctions is emphasized when one adds to them the percentage of pages on which one character only, two characters, and four or more characters appear [CHARACTER 6]. These figures indicate that Austen favors crowded scenes, that Brontë favors scenes with one or two characters only, and that of our three authors Eliot is the most balanced, although in terms of number of characters usually on stage at any given moment she is nearer to Brontë than to Austen.

Austen favors relatively large casts of major characters with few subordinate ones; she manipulates this cast so that the major characters move in and out of center focus frequently and so that large groups are often assembled together and only rarely do we see one character alone. Brontë uses a smaller cast of major figures with more subordinate figures and presents us with few crowded scenes but with many in which one character is alone or only two characters appear. Eliot uses a cast of major characters not much larger than Brontë's (even though her novels tend to be longer) but a much larger cast of subordinate figures. Eliot moves her characters on and off stage more frequently than does Brontë but not as frequently as does Austen. Eliot attains something close to an over-all balance between crowded scenes and those containing only one or two characters.

Austen's rapid movement of a large cast of major characters takes place in a few, stylized settings, transitions between which are often carried out by two or more characters. Austen's chief mode of action is dialogue, associated with the rendering of unverbalized (interiorized) attitudes and opinions, which follows a predominatingly continuous temporal progression. Brontë prefers the descriptive mode of action, just as she prefers the first-person narrative form. She employs a considerable variety of settings and does not use a great deal of dialogue. She maintains a degree of temporal— as well as spatial—continuity, a continuity which centers on her leading character, who is sometimes isolated, so that her "descriptions" are in fact often impressions. Her secondary characters tend to be quite minor; a sequential series of confrontations constitutes one of Brontë's major formal patterns —a pattern which contrasts with Austen's preference for fluid groupings. Eliot favors an interweaving of fairly independent subcomplexes of action. Compared to Austen and Brontë, she distorts temporal continuity rather freely, relying on an expository mode for linking episodes clearly separated through changes in setting and characters. Though never

147

focusing on any one character as Brontë does, Eliot usually gives major attention to at least two characters, who operate among a dense population of secondary and tertiary figures. This enables her to establish patterns through parallelism as well as through alternation, particularly between crowded scenes and those in which a major figure is isolated.[2]

None of the foregoing should be startling to a reader familiar with the fiction of Austen, Brontë, and Eliot—except the degree of abstraction in the presentation. The worth of such analyses lies in their depiction of familiar arrangements freed from the details of the stories of the novels. Formal analyses should articulate formal patterns. To my mind the foregoing analyses indicate that plots do possess structures which can, at least to a limited degree, be isolated and described.[3]

[2] Some supplementary figures on other novels with a brief commentary will be found in the Appendix of Tabulations, pp. 239-45.

[3] In the Bibliographical Appendix will be found a partial listing of linguistic and stylistic studies which I consulted in the course of my work. Doubtless I learned much from these materials, but I can cite only a few works—such as David Lodge's *The Language of Fiction* (New York, 1966)—which have been specifically helpful. Lodge emphasizes what most stylisticians, particularly those who are linguistically oriented, minimize in their attempts to set up systems of "discourse analysis": analysis of any partial segment of a work of fiction (whether a "vertical" unit, a chapter or a sentence, or a "horizontal" unit, a pattern of imagery) must be founded on an understanding of the segment's function in the work as a totality (Lodge, p. 79). From this emphasis derives the well-balanced quality of Lodge's criticisms and his recognition, for example, that "the significance of repetition" (his critiques of individual novels are based on evaluations of specific reiterated elements) "is not to be determined statistically" (p. 85). But Lodge is not interested, as I am, in trying to stimulate the development of techniques for giving reasonably objective structural definition to novels as total unities. Without such definition, comparative studies, the basis of the history of fiction, are difficult if not impossible. But this is not Lodge's concern: ". . . no treatment of the historical development of the language of fiction has been attempted [here]. . . . These chapters are essentially self-contained studies of particular texts . . ." (p. 91).

For investigations into the historical processes of style one must usually turn to art historians (some of whom I cite in the Bibliographical Appendix) and, upon occasion, scholars who are interested in folklore. Among the latter I may mention here (in addition to those such as Roman Jakobson referred to in the Appendix) Vladimir

But the value of such isolation and description depends on other matters. It ought to provide means for enhancing our appreciation of the detailed actualities of different novelists' styles by providing a context within which we can more rewardingly study and contrast specific passages. To test the context established so far, I propose to consider some aspects of three limited passages from the fiction of my three novelists. The passages were selected not at random but arbitrarily. I mean that novels representative of each author's mature art were chosen first. Then enough pages on either side of the mathematical center of each novel were marked off so that a continuous passage of twenty to twenty-five pages, about 1,000 lines of text, including at least two complete chapters, was established. Neither "typicality" nor function (climax, resolution, etc.) nor the nature of the subject matter played any part in the selection of the passages. I stress this arbitrari-

---

Propp, whose *Morphology of the Folktale*, translated by Laurence Scott, Publication x of the *International Journal of American Linguistics* (Bloomington, Indiana, 1958), attempts to define structural patterns in folktales so as to make systematically comparative studies among them possible. I'm afraid Propp is little more successful with his tales than I am with my novels. (An Italian translation of Propp's work, *Morfolgia della fiaba*, Torino, 1966, includes a penetrating critique by Claude Levi-Strauss, whose structuralist approach to language and myth contains much that ought to be of value to literary historians.) But I think literary critics concerned with style might do well to pay more attention to the folklorists, anthropologists, and art historians who have in recent years tried, as we have not, to define developmental processes in persisting art forms.

One literary critic who, if not as interested in developmental processes as I, has nevertheless carried out one of the most important studies of fictional form is J. Hillis Miller, whose brief book *The Form of Victorian Fiction* (Notre Dame, Indiana, 1968) may well become a landmark of criticism. While I often disagree with Miller (obviously I cannot accept as true for Eliot his statement that "the reader of a Victorian novel . . . is invited by the words of the narrator to enter into complicity with a collective mind which pre-exists the first words of the novel and will continue when they end, . . ." (p. 67), I have found in his work one of the few efforts to define the fictional form of an epoch in critically sophisticated and philosophic terms. His chapter on "The Ontological Basis of Form" is especially stimulating.

149

ness, because the discussion in the next chapter is not intended to define touchstones for the art of Austen, Brontë, and Eliot. It is intended only as an exploration into the question: To what degree can formalized analyses of the kind attempted in this chapter provide a useful basis for increasing our understanding, and appreciation, of diverse kinds of fictional art?

CHAPTER X

A Contrast of Passages from Emma, Villette, and Middlemarch

THE PASSAGES on which the discussion in this chapter and the next is based are: *Emma*, chapters 27-30 (or II, 9-12); *Villette*, chapters 22-23; and *Middlemarch*, chapters 40-42 (or IV, 7-9).

To a degree, the preferred forms of narrative action previously discussed reappear in the three passages identified above. The principal narrative action in the passage from *Emma* is conversation. Conversations are not so important in the passage from *Villette*, where Lucy's impressions are the central focus. In the passage from *Middlemarch*, impressions as well as conversations are overshadowed by authorial commentary, particularly on feeling, thoughts, impulses, and motives.

Austen tells us what is going on in Emma's mind, but what she tells us is largely that of which Emma herself is (or can readily become) conscious. In *Villette* we see from Lucy's point of view: what she tells reveals her conscious mind, and her way of telling reveals her subconscious mind.[1] A good example is provided by the first appearance of the "nun." Since the story is told in retrospect, a sentence such as the

---

[1] Neither "subconscious" nor "unconscious" is a satisfactory term. I should prefer to substitute "preconscious" for the former and use "subconscious" when discussing Eliot. But "preconscious" is a vexed term among psychologists and would only compound the confusion. I therefore use "subconscious" and "unconscious" inexactly, rather in the fashion in which most of us would employ the terms in ordinary conversation when we wanted to distinguish two degrees of psychic activity below the level of full consciousness.

following appears to be deceitful: "Say what you will, reader —tell me I was nervous or mad; affirm that I was unsettled by the excitement of that letter; declare that I dreamed; this I vow—I saw there—in that room—on that night—an image like—A NUN." At the time of writing the narrator knows the natural explanation of the phenomenon. Yet Brontë's trickery has justification. Dr. John's diagnosis of the nun is shrewd but incorrect: " 'You think then,' I said, with secret horror, 'she came out of my brain, and is now gone in there, and may glide out again at an hour and a day when I look not for her?' "

The nun is *not* a creation of Lucy's disordered psyche, but a real, objective phenomenon which permits Lucy to focus and to bring to the level of expression impulses which have previously been just below the reach of conscious articulation.[2] Brontë's justification for not "explaining" the nun immediately is twofold: not only did Lucy not understand it at the time but also she understood it "better" at the time than did Dr. John. Notice that later Paul Emanuel shares her experience with a similar vision, the sharing dramatizing that he is closer to Lucy than is Dr. John. The doctor does not convince Lucy that the nun is a "spectral illusion," and his failure to convince is connected with the fact that Lucy's insight into him is keener than his into her. In the passage with which we are concerned she comes to terms with and succeeds in verbalizing her feelings toward him. It is notable that in speaking of Dr. John, Lucy *exploits* her retrospective vantage point: "Dr. John, you pained me afterwards: forgiven be every ill— freely forgiven—for the sake of that one dear remembered good!" And later: "I have been told since that Dr. Bretton was not nearly so perfect as I thought him: . . . I remember him heroic. Heroic at this moment will I hold him to be."

In fact, the nun serves to reveal to Lucy the nature and significance of her ambivalence toward Dr. John. He is "heroic," as indeed he demonstrates at the fire in the theatre

[2] The nun, as I have already observed, functions symbolically in *Villette*. Were the nun not an objective phenomenon it could not function as it does.

(where he is, however, indifferent to Vashti's power which so stirs Lucy), yet his limitations provoke Lucy to a kind of ironic contempt for him. Notice the two final adjectives in the following quotation, which succeeds the nun's second appearance: "Of course with him it was held to be another effect of the same cause: it was all optical illusion—nervous malady, and so on. Not one bit did I believe him; but I dared not contradict: doctors are so self-opinionated, so immovable in their dry, materialistic views." The nun is not, however, a means for revealing what we would call Lucy's subconscious. Brontë does not go that deep. Her material is indeed suitable for debates between Reason and Feeling, for it is the matter of personal experience which can, with sensitivity and introspection, gradually be given shape, or, if one prefers, whose shape can gradually be comprehended through a process of verbalization. That process is the essential "story-line" of *Villette*.

Eliot *is* concerned with what we would call the unconscious. Her omniscience serves, among other purposes, to permit revelation of that which is concealed within her characters, concealed even from themselves. The vitality of Mr. Casaubon as a character depends upon this. He is unjust to others to the degree that he does not and cannot comprehend himself. After a very long description of Mr. Casaubon's motives, acts, and aspirations, Eliot remarks without irony: "This is a very bare and therefore a very incomplete way of putting the case. The human soul moves in many channels, and Mr. Casaubon, we know, had a sense of rectitude and an honourable pride in satisfying the requirements of honour, which compelled him to find other reasons for his conduct than those of jealousy and vindictiveness."[3] Most important in these sentences is

[3] I cannot resist calling attention to Eliot's reference to Casaubon as "the case." Unlike Brontë, Eliot sees her character as something close to what we would today call a "case." This view accompanies the profound insight expressed in the phrase "an honourable pride in satisfying the requirements of honour." The very form of the phrase dramatizes Eliot's interest in explicating the interaction of the social and the psychological, just as Brontë's inversions of conventional subject-predicate order express her focus on the personal in "mere" opposition to the social.

153

not Eliot's psychological shrewdness but the revelation of how she conceives of "character."

To her, character is a particular pattern of adjustment between the pressure of a social role (or, more accurately, roles) and a system of unconscious impulses exerting a different kind of pressure. It is fair, I think, to speak of unconscious impulses because they are not susceptible (as are Lucy Snowe's) to release through rationalization. When Eliot says of Casaubon "that he was not unmixedly adorable" and continues to comment, "He suspected this, however, as he suspected other things, without confessing it, and like the rest of us, felt how soothing it would have been to have a companion who would never find it out," she is not presenting a situation which could be improved easily. It would not help, for instance, for someone to say to Casaubon, "Look here, old chap, you ought to recognize that you're not unmixedly adorable." The sources of Casaubon's unattractiveness lie too deep for easy palliation. Hence Casaubon, like most of Eliot's major characters who are not protagonists, is defined as a personality by his idiosyncratic adjustment to the incongruous demands of two powers, society and unconscious impulse (or role and inner self), neither of which is fully within his control.

Again one sees why Eliot's fiction leads some readers to think of her as a "determinist." She is aware of how little the individual does control his life. Yet it is worth remembering that she also conceives of society as intrinsically changeable, and always presents us with changing societies. In every novel she shows us at least one or two unusual people struggling, without the aid of psychoanalysts or effective religious mentors, to reach a realistic comprehension of the powers of unconscious life which surge within them.

Austen is not as concerned with vitalizing her characters by exposing hidden psychic drives. She presents us with those inner activities which cause or come from social interactions. She portrays Emma's private thoughts and feelings only insofar as these are manifest, or will become manifest, in her social interrelations. When Frank Churchill is called away,

Emma "could not doubt his having a decidedly warm admiration, a conscious preference of herself; and this persuasion, joined to all the rest, made her think that she *must*[4] be a little in love with him, in spite of every previous determination against it. 'I certainly must,' said she. 'This sensation of listlessness, weariness, stupidity, this disinclination to sit down and employ myself, this feeling of every thing's being dull and insipid about the house!—I must be in love; I should be the oddest creature in the world if I were not—for a few weeks at least.' " As psychological analysis this is poor stuff, because Austen is not interested here in characterizing by revealing subconscious or unconscious impulses. Instead she characterizes with a lucid rendering of purely conscious mind, that part of the mind most active in the ordinary patterning of social interrelations. Since we today are so interested in "deeper" psychic activities, it is worth observing that accurate and effective fictional rendering of conscious processes is perhaps aesthetically the most difficult task of all. Any hack can represent an archetype.

Social interrelations are secondary to Brontë, whose focus is the private collection of memories and expectations which Lucy amasses during the course of her experience. It is the evolving pattern of these expectations and memories which constitutes the form of her story, which is "literally" a reconstruction of impressions, a memoir. And to Eliot social interrelations are but one of two competing forces out of whose competition "character" arises.

These differences accompany many others, of which one example may suffice here. The differing kinds of action require different language forms. Conversation is inherently "clear." That is, even if the speakers are muddle-headed (like Harriet

---

[4] The emphasis here, which is Austen's, calls attention to a little word which illustrates beautifully the difficulties inherent in statistical studies of fictional vocabulary. "Must" is one of Austen's favorite words, and by my estimate seventy percent of its occurrences in her work carry some degree of ironic implication. When one of Austen's characters (or the narrator) says or thinks something *must* be, the chances are it is not. Someone interested in the implications of common words could probably learn more from a careful study of Jane Austen than from Wittgenstein.

Smith) or deceitful (like Frank Churchill), a report of what they say is "just" a report. Fictional conversation is thus intrinsically transpicuous, although it may, of course, have complex implications. The language of impressions, however, calls attention to itself. Lucy's impressions could not exist except through her verbalizations. Her impression of Vashti can't be known except insofar as Lucy can verbalize it. The verbalization demands something like poetic expression, because the impression consists to a considerable degree in nonverbal experience. Metaphor becomes a necessity. More important, the language forces us to attend to what it connotes, the relevance of what it evokes to what it denotes.

Hence we find in *Villette* a tension between the narrator and her language. In a variety of ways Lucy Snowe keeps us alert to the inadequacies of ordinary discourse. For instance, of Vashti she remarks: "Suffering had struck that stage empress; and she stood before her audience neither yielding to, nor enduring, nor, in finite measure, resenting it: . . . I have said that she does not *resent* her grief. No; the weakness of that word would make it a lie. To her, what hurts becomes immediately embodied: . . ." Observe that it is the "weakness" of "resent" which disqualifies the verb—not so much what it "means" as its power or value.

Eliot, on the other hand, needs a language which will represent those movements of mind and heart of which the character himself can be only partially aware, which he misinterprets by attending only to their more superficial manifestations, or which he is compelled, as is Casaubon, to distort. What Eliot needs is not so much a poetic language as one of compassionate objectivity, a language conveying with both scientific precision and emotional vigor a sensitivity to hidden psychic causes and to nuances of feeling which would escape any but a deeply sympathetic yet penetrating observer. If there is something formalistic (I would prefer the term scientific) about much of Eliot's vocabulary and sentence structure, the cause lies—at least in part—in her desire to elucidate the underlying systems of psychic activity of which her actors cannot be conscious, except for transitory moments. When, for example, Casaubon questions Lydgate about his (Casaubon's) health, Eliot comments: "To a mind largely instructed in the human destiny hardly anything could be more interesting than the inward conflict implied in his formal measured address, delivered with the usual sing-song and motion of the head. . . . But Lydgate, who had some contempt at hand for futile scholarship, felt a little amusement mingling with his pity. He was at present too ill acquainted with disaster to enter into the pathos of a lot where everything is below the level of tragedy except the passionate egoism of the sufferer." The central point in these sentences is that Lydgate is unable to perceive "the inward conflict implied" by Casaubon's outward manner because there is a logic, a system, which Lydgate does not understand, and will not understand, until he himself experiences disaster. It is also worth pointing out that at the end of the passage Dorothea conquers her resentment and feels "thankfulness" that she has done so when she hears the "kind quiet melancholy" of her husband's voice, but there is no suggestion that she has plumbed the depths of his soul-torment. She is "able enough to estimate him," but that is not enough, as she discovers when she learns of the injunctions of his will.

When we turn from action to agents, we notice that although the passage from *Emma* begins with the heroine alone, a relatively small proportion of the passage as a whole depicts isolated individuals. In nearly four-fifths of the passage three or more characters are simultaneously on stage. The passage from *Middlemarch* shows approximately equal proportions for the presence of one, two, and three or more characters. *Villette* shows a slight bias toward two-character situations. The patterns fit with those we found to be characteristic of the novelists' works. But when we look at the passages and are forced to come to terms with details, we realize how tricky is the determination of the "presence" or "absence" of a character.[5] When Miss Bates and Mr. Knightley converse,

[5] Obvious as this problem may appear to be, it merits attention because it gives focus to an essential difference between fiction and drama. In drama characters must be either present or absent; in

she at a window and he on horseback in the street, are all or any of her guests who overhear (Harriet Smith is an especially problematic case) on stage? When Eliot presents Casaubon's thoughts of Dorothea and Will Ladislaw, are they not in some meaningful sense "present"? Is Lucy alone when she describes her impressions of Vashti? And who is "present" when she describes her impression of Dr. John's impression of Vashti? Another set of problems arises if one tries to decide who should be counted as a character. Are unnamed servants characters? Is Vashti a character? Is Mrs. Churchill, who never appears yet who so definitely influences the action of *Emma*, a character?

I do not think it necessary to answer all these questions here, although for specialists in fictional criticism they are important: Mrs. Gamp's imaginary friend Mrs. Harris, for example, raises problems of genuine critical significance. One can, however, concentrate instead on the more definable phenomenon of major-character movement, that is, how frequently characters who are indisputably important to a novel are at the focus of the immediate action and how frequently they recede from it.

In each of our passages, for example, there are nine important figures (if one counts the "nun" and Vashti in *Villette*). Austen's nine make thirty-seven clearly definable separate appearances; Brontë's, twenty; and Eliot's, only fifteen. Austen's characters move to the foreground and recede from it frequently. The *Villette* passage is of course dominated by Lucy, but Dr. John plays a not unworthy secondary role, making five separate appearances and being the focus of the action something over seventy percent of the time. All other characters in the passage appear only briefly. In the *Middlemarch* passage no one character dominates as does Lucy and even Emma, and none of the characters move into and out of the central focus of the action more than twice. In this respect

---

fiction ambiguity is possible. This is one reason why even the silent reading of a play by oneself is a quite different experience from that of reading a novel.

the general findings are not merely borne out: their significance is enriched by consideration of limited passages.

Character-movement in the passages in question draws one's attention to the fact that Eliot's chapters are more overtly functional units than are either Brontë's or Austen's. There is no connection through action between the three successive chapters in the *Middlemarch* passage. The separation suggests that Eliot's art is structurally unified on a different level, and a study of settings supports the suggestion. The settings in the *Emma* passage are unparticularized—to put it mildly. Lack of specificity permits remarkable fluidity of movement (economy of movement might be the more accurate term). Thoughts and even conversations can be continued without a break even though the scene changes and hours elapse. In Austen's fiction, places are virtually only names. Hartfield, Randalls, Donwell Abbey, Miss Bates' house, The Crown—the names signify social distinctions and relations but are void of concrete, physical specifications.

In *Villette* there is some particularization of settings, but less than one might at first imagine. Persons and meteorological phenomena tend to be more specifically and graphically described. The grenier, for instance, is a particular and important place, but its importance derives from Lucy's impressions there, impressions which are at least half psychological and which are, in any event, primarily the result of the actions of other characters, most notably DeHamal and Ginevra. Thus all we are told about the grenier in itself establishes its appropriateness for its role as hiding place for both the "poor English teacher" and the mysterious nun: "I mounted three staircases, reached a dark, narrow, silent landing, opened a worm-eaten door, and dived into the deep, black, cold garret. Here none would follow me—none interrupt—not Madame herself. I shut the garret-door; I placed my light on a doddered and mouldy chest of drawers; I put on a shawl, for the air was ice-cold. . . ." Settings in *Villette* tend to be symbolic, which means they are literally "settings," like the sets on a stage, that are structured by their appropriateness (occasionally by contrast) to the psychic action they encompass.

In the *Middlemarch* passage, however, settings are substantively and concretely particularized. We know where we are and how this place differs from that. Both the interiors and the grounds of Garth's home, Featherstone's house, and Casaubon's mansion are distinguished for us as places. There are more significant settings and more different kinds of significant settings in this passage than in the other two. As is conventionally remarked, Eliot is a "realist." It is just to call her a realist, but to do so may obscure major implications of her art. Many of the realistic details of her settings possess symbolic importance.[6] The realism of Eliot's settings, moreover, creates a dimension in her art that is absent from Austen's and Brontë's: an actuality to some degree independent of the forces of both social and individual human action. Because land, houses, objects, and so forth, exist in their own right, not merely as labels or as symbols, one can conceive of them as existing apart from the particular characters they presently surround (the significance of the Featherstone House, Stone Court, is that several people own it at different times, and others, such as Fred Vincy, might own it). In this sense, Eliot's fiction is dehumanized to a degree that Brontë's and Austen's fiction is not: this is the gain and loss of a "scientific" art.

It might also be observed that this "permanence" of setting makes it possible for Eliot to create a complex temporal "reality" unavailable to Austen and Brontë. When we turn our attention from space to time, we find the temporal ordering of the *Emma* passage to be surprisingly regular. The end of each episode in the passage is clearly identified as later than its beginning, and just as clearly identified as earlier than the commencement of the next, although we seldom know exactly how many hours or minutes elapse. Such rigorous adherence to the "normal" flow of time is more unusual in a novel than casual readers might think. In *Emma* it is sustained by a

[6] The few concrete details of place in *Emma* are not to any significant degree symbolic.

multitude of unobtrusive time indicators: "she was then interrupted . . . Emma watched them in, and then . . . beginning again when . . . soon afterwards he began again . . . but soon it came to be . . . two days of joyful security were immediately followed by . . ." and so forth. As our general findings indicated, the fictional time scheme of *Emma* follows the sequences of "normal" time, the pattern of ordinary social life as we conventionally think of it.

Villette, too, is keyed to normal time, but it includes irregularities. Moments of great intensity in which time is transcended or becomes irrelevant interrupt the chronological regularity of the memoir, as do stretches of "emptiness." Time in *Villette* is personal rather than social because it is controlled by Lucy's experiences. No one character in any of Austen's novels, not even Anne Elliot, can so shape the temporal pattern, which is that of social existence rather than the individual impression.

It is worth noting that in the *Villette* passage we have the "re-introduction" of Polly and her father, although at this point the reader cannot know that they are in fact characters he has previously encountered. This odd device, though only fully developed in *Villette*, has prototypes in Brontë's earlier fiction, being found even in her juvenilia, much of which, in fact, turns on the re-introduction of figures.[7] Re-introduction is Brontë's substitute, as it were, for the flashback, which she does not use, I believe, because she retains the chronological sequence of normal, social time as an underlying structure of her action. Lucy Snowe is defined in part by her idiosyncratic distortions of normal sequence. "Character" for Brontë (as is not true for Austen) *is* a special pattern of temporal disturbance of social norms. In the passage about Vashti quoted above, for example, one can observe a curious minor distortion of chronological regularity by which Brontë conveys Lucy's absorption (as contrasted with Dr. John's detach-

---

[7] The device recurs in miniaturized form many times in *Villette*. In our passage, for example, Lucy first sees Dr. John only as "a man" with his back turned, and she is surprised (as is the reader) when he speaks to her in the garret.

ment): "Suffering *had struck* that stage empress; and she *stood* . . . I *have said* that she *does* not *resent* . . . that word *would* make it. . . ." In a somewhat analogous fashion, the many extended similes in *Villette* disrupt "regular" progression.

Eliot uses flashbacks, but she is less fond of formal flashbacks than of those which give the illusion that the action is continuing forward. In each of the three chapters of the *Middlemarch* passage a normal chronological progression prevails; but authorial commentary, essentially timeless, often interrupts it; and the exact temporal relation of events is sometimes left deliberately vague. For example, the evening colloquy between Caleb and Susan Garth presumably occurs about concurrently with Mary's and Mr. Farebrother's conversation in the orchard and with his walk home. Even more interesting are the openings of chapters 41 and 42, which use the past perfect tense to carry us back into what are half flashbacks and half timeless analyses of characters and events. In contrast to that of *Villette* or *Emma* the time scheme of *Middlemarch* is complex. Without much distortion of our sense of conventional chronological ordering, Eliot manipulates temporal progressions into patterns of some intricacy. She can do so because her authorial presence allows her to move in and out of not merely one narrative but several interwoven narratives. The multiple-narrative form so popular between 1846 and 1876 (*Vanity Fair* to *Daniel Deronda*) accompanies the development of new intricacies in the temporal structuring of fiction.[8]

Eliot creates a "fictive" time not found in Brontë's or Austen's novels. Temporal order in their fiction has as its main referent "real" time, the chronology of ordinary, normal life, seen either from the aspect of society or from that of the individual. Eliot's principal time referent is the fictional time scheme of the novel as a whole, a unity subsuming diverse

---

[8] From this point of view *Wuthering Heights* is not a sport (as F. R. Leavis says it is); it is an early, original manifestation of a large mid-Victorian trend in fictional art toward the development of complicated narrative-temporal structuring.

and separate though interwoven "plots," an *artificial chronology*. This supernarrative chronology includes authorial commentaries. A high proportion of these portray either the ultimate genesis or the immediate causes of events that have just occurred or are about to occur. Often the commentaries suggest the general applicability or the broader significance of particularized acts or feelings. In all these circumstances the reader is made aware of a network of connections linking what has already happened in the novel, what is now happening, what will happen, and what could happen outside the particular plot lines of the book. This complicated and to a degree *reversible* system of patterns forms the primary time scheme of *Middlemarch*.

CURSORY AS THE FOREGOING discussion has been, it suggests that examination of limited passages in terms of larger, underlying structures of fiction is rewarding. This critical method enables us to study coherently units of fiction which are not defined solely by subjective impressions of their significance. Or, to put it another way, with this method, "significance" is not restricted merely to a unit's relevance to the substance, the subject matter, of the plot. Because novel plots are "original," that is, not primarily mythic or legendary, descriptions of novel segments defined in terms of plot or subject are intrinsically difficult to compare. I have tried to show how examination of limited, arbitrarily selected passages can enrich our understanding of the underlying conceptual structures of fiction. The method allows the critic to work from the small to the large as well as from the large to the small. Because of this flexibility, the method is adaptable to the study of plot material.

If, for instance, we look at the subject matter of the three passages, we notice that two of the four chapters in *Emma* are almost exclusively concerned with reminiscences of the party and with gifts to the Bates family. The other two chapters are concerned almost exclusively with preparations for the forthcoming dance. In the *Villette* passage Lucy's mind has many topics with which to occupy itself: Dr. John's letters, the nun, Ginevra, Vashti, the fire at the theater, and the injured Polly. All of these, to be sure, are unified by an underlying theme of the two chapters, Dr. John's "removal" from his position of potential lover to that of a dear friend.

An analogous but more subtle technique for attaining unity through the use of an underlying motif is used by Eliot in each of her three chapters. The overt subject matter of each is distinct from the other two: there is no obvious connection between the Garths, Rigg and Raffles, and the Casaubons. Each chapter, moreover, contains a considerable range of subtopics. Yet at the root of each chapter lies the question Eliot poses at the beginning of the second paragraph of chapter 41: "Who shall tell what may be the effect of writing?" Caleb Garth's letters and the letter signed by Bulstrode which Raffles picks up by chance are obvious illustrations of the *complicated* relevance of writing.[9] More important, though, are the wills, Featherstone's helping to establish the situations whose development is partly traced in chapters 40 and 41 and Casaubon's which is in part at least shaped by the events of chapter 42.

But writing is relevant in more indirect ways, particularly as it focuses the general problem of articulation. It is in relation to this problem, for instance, that Caleb Garth and Mr. Casaubon, narratively unconnected, are dramatically contrasted. Caleb is bothered by "a sense that words were scantier than thoughts" (for Casaubon the opposite is true). He articulates his personality through constructive deeds: "getting a good bit of contriving and solid building done—that those who are living and those who come after will be the better for. I'd sooner have it than a fortune. . . . It's a great gift of God. . . ." Casaubon, student of all gods, immersed in the past, a man of words and an investigator into language, is oppressed by his inability to get "a good bit of contriving and solid building done" in his scholarly profession.

[9] Just how complicated this relevance can be is illustrated by the fact that Caleb's letters are not essential to the plots of the novel, because he could be addressed orally, but Bulstrode's letter is essential —it has to be written.

Eliot is not merely praising the practical business man at the expense of the impotent pedant; she is also using the contrast to illuminate the diverse means by which humans can and cannot "express" and give order to their deepest impulses, those which by definition are most difficult to verbalize. Her argument is that "successful" individuals, psychically healthy and constructive (though not necessarily important) people are successful because they can in some fashion articulate these impulses. For such articulation, sophisticated language may be, as it is for Casaubon, an obstacle. Caleb "expresses himself" through actions rather than words. Somewhat analogously, Will Ladislaw will finally "succeed," that is, attain a happy marriage with Dorothea, by *not* becoming a publicly successful artist. In chapter 42 Dorothea's "meditative struggle" is only partially within the realm of verbalization, involving as it does "a litany of pictured sorrows and of silent cries." Her victory here is that she does not give in to easy articulation, she does not yield to the attraction of facile and conventionalized attitudes, she does not begin to hate. Emotionally and intellectually she works out the deepest significance of her unique situation, just as, finally, she comes closest to the attainment of St. Theresa by living a life superficially contrary to that of the saint.

INSOFAR AS the discussion in this chapter illuminates the style of the three passages it poses the question: Might it not be possible to establish some meaningful relations between the largest structures of a novel and the smallest? Can one discover "microscopic" structures *within* the passages which can be connected *through* their structuring *to* the "macroscopic" structures of the novels' total designs? In the next chapter I tentatively explore this possibility, which holds out hope for a systematized base upon which to build the stylistic comparisons and contrasts necessary to a genuinely aesthetic history of fiction.

CHAPTER XI

Narrative and Dialogue: Large and Small Structures

IN TRYING to suggest how we might connect the largest structures of a novel to the smallest, I shall concentrate on sentence forms. I largely disregard vocabulary because I wish to examine the structuring of narrative (here meaning sentences without explicit dialogue) and dialogue sentences. Although the points would seem to be obvious, no critic to my knowledge has considered, first, that interaction between narrative and dialogue in large measure defines "fiction" in its broadest sense as a literary type (distinguishing the novel, romance, and epic from drama on the one side and from the lyric on the other) and, second, that interaction between narrative and dialogue occurs at every level of fiction. Table XI-1 provides a basic narrative-dialogue sentence analysis of the passages discussed in the preceding chapter.

Let me immediately draw attention to circumstances which cast doubt on any quantitative analysis of fictional sentences. Leaving aside the vexing question of *whose* punctuation we are studying—part of the textual problem[1]—we must still face the difficulty of deciding what constitutes a sentence. Anyone who spends a little time examining nineteenth-century fiction will recognize, to single out the most obvious but by no means the only problem, that most novelists of the last century frequently employ semi-colons (or their equivalents,

[1] The extent and intricacy of the problems involved in establishing texts suitable for detailed statistical analyses of style are tremendous. In this study, in which I do nothing more than compare a few crude compilations of figures, textual difficulties can be ignored. But even slightly more sophisticated discriminations will require serious attention to textual difficulties I disregard.

such as a colon plus a dash) where we would use periods. In the table just cited, in which sentences are defined as groups of words terminated by some kind of full stop, Austen's sentences generally average out shorter than Brontë's. If, however, we define the sentence as a group of words terminated by semi-colons or their equivalents, as well as full stops, the figures change: the passage from *Emma* then contains 1031 sentences averaging 10.3 words in length; that from *Villette*, 934 sentences averaging 9.1 words; and that from *Middlemarch*, 682 sentences averaging 17.4 words. With this definition Brontë's over-all average sentence length is shorter than Austen's, and the proportional relation of Brontë's and Austen's average sentence length to Eliot's is significantly reduced.

The preceding will have to stand as a cautionary example of the many qualifications which ideally ought to be applied to any hypotheses developed from my figures. But some reasonably secure observations seem possible. For instance, it is clear that the three passages contain quite different proportions of dialogue: in terms of words, the *Emma* passage is sixty-one percent dialogue; the *Villette*, twenty-two percent; and the *Middlemarch*, thirty-two percent. The proportions correlate with the relative preferences previously found for the total work of the three novelists. It is plain, furthermore, that Eliot's dialogue and narrative sentences are both substantially longer on the average than Austen's and Brontë's (but see Table XI-2, which indicates that the proportional relation is somewhat different). That Eliot fairly *consistently* uses longer narrative sentences is indicated by the following figures, which describe the difference in length between successive narrative sentences (for comparative purposes converted to percentages by dividing the number in each category by the total number of successive narrative sentences). In the *Emma* passage forty-six percent of the successive narrative sentences have less than ten words, twenty-four percent have more than thirty words, and eleven percent have more than fifty words. The same figures for the *Villette* passage are forty-four percent, sixteen percent, and five percent; for the *Middlemarch* they are thirty-five percent, nineteen percent, and six percent, respectively.

The figures indicate that Austen varies the length of her narrative sentences more than do either Brontë or Eliot. One might speculate that because of her consistency of subject matter and language Austen introduces variety in this rather subtle fashion. Since there is a correlation between sentence length and sentence structure, long sentences being relatively complex (however complexity is defined) and short sentences being relatively simple, this form of variation is of some importance. It reminds one of Austen's device of concealing psychological complexity within lucidity of presentation (discussed in Chapter Two). The variation helps, moreover, in distinguishing between Austen's narrative sentence use and Brontë's, though their average narrative sentence lengths are nearly equal. Evidence that Austen employs more variety in narrative sentence form is congruent with the finding that she clusters passages of dialogue and narrative, whereas Brontë tends to mingle them. Eliot, however, clusters her narrative sentences even more than Austen, as Table XI-3 shows.

The distinctions in sentence groupings indicated by these figures probably correlate with some of our previous, more general findings, such as Eliot's preference for "block" organization. But before I turn to the "mixed" sentences, in which both narrative and dialogue occur, where one can perhaps see the significance of such correlations more clearly, I want to point to a small indicator of the relation between sentence form and transpicuousness or conspicuousness of language. A question mark or exclamation point tends to direct our attention toward the nature of the sentence it concludes. Of the narrative sentences in the passage from *Emma* only about one percent terminate with a question mark or exclamation point. Nearly five percent of the narrative sentences in the *Middlemarch* passage so terminate, as do some seven percent in the *Villette* passage. Austen's relative "declarativeness" even carries over into her dialogue, where the parallel figures are eight percent for *Emma*, eleven percent for *Villette*, and ten percent for *Middlemarch*.

Dialogue sentences, incidentally, pose several special problems for the analyst. For one thing, dialogue sentences are usually shorter and more fragmentary than narrative ones. A specific difficulty in our three passages is that the amount of dialogue differs so markedly from one to another that in compiling the figures in Table XI-4 and XI-5 for variation in dialogue sentence lengths I decided to consider only the initial portions of the *Emma* and *Middlemarch* passages so as to keep them numerically at least analogous to the *Villette* passage. Two features appear to emerge even from the truncated figures of XI-4 and XI-5. Austen's dialogue, unlike her narrative, seems to be less varied than Brontë's or Eliot's. All of Austen's characters do—from this point of view at least—talk alike. Eliot's dialogue is the most varied, reflecting, I think, the fact that although there are no more major characters in the *Middlemarch* passage (there *are* more minor ones), the groups of characters are more differentiated. It is plain, also, that the form by which each author presents a change from one speaker to another is distinguishable. Only a quarter of these changes in the *Villette* passage accompany a mixed sentence, whereas three-quarters of the *Middlemarch*'s changes of speaker involve a mixture of narrative and dialogue. The *Emma* passage is closest to a balance in this regard. The differences emphasize Brontë's tendency toward confrontation. Her dialogue is brief and formed into something resembling stichomythia. It is notable that she changes speakers more frequently than do Austen and Eliot. Of the 506 sentences containing dialogue in the *Emma* passage, 129 involve changes of speaker, as do 81 of the 173 sentences containing dialogue in the *Villette* passage. For the *Middlemarch*, the same figures are 96 changes in 269 sentences.

There are sixteen speakers in the passage from *Middlemarch* (including a one-sentence speech by Tantripp, two sentences by Letty, three by Jim, four by Ben, and five by Alfred). There are nine speakers in the passage from *Villette* (including one-sentence speeches by Goton, Rosine, an unidentified servant of the Bassompierres', and two-sentence "cries" by unidentified characters at Mme. Beck's and at the theater). In the passage from *Emma* there are ten speakers (including Mrs. Ford, who has two one-sentence speeches). These figures for speakers reflect to a remarkable degree our findings for the total cast sizes and the numerical distinctions between major, minor, and tertiary characters. To return to the original point, however, if Brontë favors rapid interchange, Eliot's heavy use of mixed sentences at the introduction of each "new" speaker emphasizes her attention to the "contexts" of dialogue. She is concerned with that which is not, perhaps cannot be, put into words but which is nevertheless essential to what is said. Austen's balance no doubt reflects her emphasis on dialogue in its "pure" form, but it also illustrates her concentration (vis-à-vis Eliot) on what is said rather than on the manner of saying it.

The functions and characteristics of mixed sentences may in the long run turn out to be most worthy of careful and extended investigation, if for no other reason than that they are more characteristic of fictional prose than of most other types of prose. The number of mixed sentences in our passages is unfortunately small, but the figures in Table XI-6 seem to indicate some clear differentiae. There is a higher proportion of mixed sentences in the *Middlemarch* passage than in the *Villette* passage, which in turn shows a higher proportion than the *Emma* passage. But the functions of the mixed sentences differ. In *Middlemarch* they are oriented more toward narrative than toward dialogue, in *Villette* the orientation is slightly in the opposite direction, and in *Emma* emphasis on dialogue is marked. In *Middlemarch* most of the mixed sentences consist of one narrative and one dialogue phrase, whereas in *Emma* a substantial majority contain three elements and in *Villette* two- and three-element sentences are employed about equally. A majority of the two-element sentences in *Emma*, moreover, begin with narrative, whereas only a small proportion of two-element sentences in the other two passages commence that way.

Much more data is needed to substantiate the potential validity of these differences, but even my limited figures suggest that mixed sentences may rather clearly reveal on the microscopic level, as it were, some basic designs of fictional art. If nothing else, attention to mixed sentences raises the possibility that critics of fiction might turn away from the definitions of sentence structure provided by grammarians and linguists to definitions of sentence structure in terms of *fictional form*. I do not mean merely that proportions of narrative and dialogue are intrinsically of much importance. Rather I suggest that careful analysis of the sorts of relations—on all levels—among the elements of narrative and dialogue could lead to a separating out of the patterns of form and structure which give a piece of fiction its distinctive aesthetic design. Much of the attraction of this possibility is that it depends on the comparison of relations between essential elements rather than of elements in themselves. For an understanding, and perhaps an ultimate definition of fictional form, it is, I believe, relations—not that which is related—which we must study. To reduce fictional art to the elements of which it is composed is finally self-defeating. Knowledge of the crystalline structure of the marble out of which a statue is carved is of limited value in defining the sculptor's art. All art is involved with patterning. It is the patterning of relations which constitutes form in art. We cannot significantly penetrate the secret of novelistic form through the mere analysis of words, syntax, imagery, character, setting, and so on, in themselves. We must devise methods for understanding the relations between these materials by which the novelist shapes his art. The shapes of fiction, its essential structures, may be rewardingly studied, I suggest, through systematized descriptions of the patterning of its most elementary materials, for example narrative and dialogue.

In the passages analyzed we have seen that, on the sentence level, Eliot mixes narrative and dialogue more than do Brontë and Austen. In this regard, her art may meaningfully be described as the most formally complex of the three. Further analysis shows, moreover, that it is Austen who most frequently uses abbreviated, stylized narrative elements; twenty-nine of her sixty-eight mixed sentences contain in their narrative portions only "he said" or its equivalent. In *Villette* only twenty-two of the sixty-one mixed sentences contain this minimal narrative and in *Middlemarch* only thirteen out of eighty-nine. Moreover, within the *Middlemarch* passage the mixed sentences tend to cluster distinctively, whereas in the *Emma* passage they tend to be more evenly distributed, with the *Villette* showing more clustering than *Emma* but less than *Middlemarch*. On the sentence level, then, we find a repetition of the general patterns of form we noted in the analysis of the novels as a whole. That is, to take the most obvious example, the organization of sentences in *Middlemarch* is analogous to the patterning of chapters or narrative in distinctive blocks or units separated from one another, with each block being composed of a relatively dense mixture of elements. Similarly, we find Austen's patterns of sentence form paralleling the consistency, evenness, and transpicuousness we have noticed at other levels in her writing. To illustrate the differences in mixed-sentence clusterings, I divide the total number of sentences in each passage into groups of twenty and then indicate the number of mixed sentences in each unit of twenty:

Emma: 0-1-1-4-2-3-0-2-0-2-4-3-2-0-3-2-2-4-2-5-1-2-1-1-3-4-0-1-2-3-2-2-3-1 (thirty-nine of the sixty-eight sentences occur in clusters of three or more)

Villette: 1-2-2-2-1-3-2-1-4-2-5-2-4-3-1-0-6-7-6-4-3-0 (forty-five of the sixty-one sentences occur in clusters of three or more)

Middlemarch: 6-8-11-6-6-5-8-3-4-3-7-4-2-2-2-4-0-1-3-3-0-0-0-1 (eighty-one of the eighty-nine sentences occur in clusters of three or more)

In short, distribution of basic elements differs in much the same way on each level in the fiction of Austen, Brontë, and Eliot.

This can be illustrated, I believe, even on the level of the word. Contrast, for example, the following lists compiled from the three passages of all the narrative portions of mixed sentences which contain brief comment on the voice, manner of speech, or tone of the speaker. Eleven of the sixty-eight mixed sentences in the *Emma* passage contain these comments:

rather hesitatingly; said he in a rather low voice; said Emma in a whisper; said she in a voice of forced calmness; Emma took the opportunity of whispering; said he in a deliberating manner; (raising his voice still more); he gravely replied; said Mr. Woodhouse rather warmly; said Mrs. Weston rather hesitatingly; said Emma laughingly.

Five of the sixty-one mixed sentences in the *Villette* passage contain these comments:

I panted and plained, almost beside myself; cried he irreverently; said a girlish voice; responded the patient demurely and with dignity; said the girlish voice faintly.

Twenty-one of the eighty-nine mixed sentences in the *Middlemarch* passage contain these comments:

said Mary good-humoredly, while she . . . ; said Mary with a grave air of explanation, so that . . . ; said Mrs. Garth, with a touch of her rebuke in her tone; said Mary, rather curtly; said Caleb, gently, looking . . . ; said Mrs. Garth magisterially, conscious of . . . ; said Caleb in a deep voice of assent, as if . . . ; said his wife with answering fervour; said Mrs. Garth rather coldly; he said with some enjoyment; said Mary quickly, fearing that . . . ; said Mrs. Garth, with decision; said Mrs. Garth decidedly; said Caleb, with the deep tone and grave shake . . . ; he was saying, in a full rumbling tone; returned Rigg, in his cool high voice; said Mr. Rigg, quietly without looking . . . ; he said in a cajoling tone; said Mr. Casaubon with his invariable polite air; he said, with a gentle surprise in his tone.

The lists show that Eliot is concerned with representing manner of speech in a fashion in which Austen and Brontë are not; even on the level of the word this is an expression of her concern with the medium of communication discussed earlier. Moreover, this concern allows for a kind of dramatic contrast not available to Brontë and Austen: characters are differentiated, paralleled, and contrasted by manner of articulation. (In the list above, Eliot's technique is most apparent in relation to Mr. and Mrs. Garth and to Rigg and Raffles.)[2] And, in the same terms used earlier, we see here that at word level Austen's essential focus is on *what* is said, not on the manner of speech.

What Brontë's mixed sentences show is something "negative," that is, that the relation of dialogue to narrative is not as significant as it is in the work of Austen and Eliot. Because *Villette* is a personal memoir, the distinction between dialogue and narrative, and thus the complexity of their relations, is of secondary concern. As was pointed out earlier, what is central in *Villette* is the verbalization of impressions. The principal clustering of mixed sentences in the *Villette* passage occurs with the re-introduction of M. Bassompierre and his daughter, where something closer to conventional plot briefly replaces the main lines of Lucy's story. In the *Villette* passage, out of twenty-two mixed sentences with brief narrative portions, only two such portions contain proper names, whereas in the *Emma* passage ten out of twenty-two such narrative portions contain proper names and in the *Middlemarch* passage there are seventeen in twenty-two. The absence of proper names in *Villette* is an indication of the tendency of its conversations to be limited to confrontations. The medium of communication is not at issue; interest arises from the representation of intense inner responses to what is said. The dialogue, as sentence-length averages show, is brief and pointed. It is also surrounded by narration. Dialogue is not per se the main focus and is not intricately interwoven with narrative.

Austen's distinctions of tone seem to apply predominantly to volume or to generic manner. Specific sensory qualities of speech are not important to aesthetic contrasts between characters. The impression one gets is that everyone speaks in more or less the same fashion—hence *what* each says is

[2] If the contrasts seem rather superficial, the reason is, as I suggested in the preceding chapter, that Eliot's fundamental interest is in likenesses and connections.

very important. What we are looking at here is the formal or structural aspect of the central substantive characteristic of Austen's novels: they are fascinating stories about trivialities. It is, however, the subjects of conversation which are trivial; the aesthetic form—that is, the distinctions between characters—depends not on *how* the characters discuss the trivia but *what* they say about it. This in turn is why there is such diversity within the tight unity of Austen's fiction and why her transpicuous language contains such complexity of implication. Both narrative and dialogue are regular, orderly, formalized, consistent, and they cohere smoothly. There is relatively little contrast and dramatic interaction between narrative and dialogue (just as there is little emphasis on the kind of "responsiveness" so important to Brontë). The narrator, like each of the characters, is distinguished less by her way of discussing than by what she says. I yield to no one in my admiration for Jane Austen's skill as a writer, but I feel that an impressive feature of her skill is her ability never to become a mere stylist—meaning rather than manner is invariably her primary focus.

I should pause here to say that I do not deny that Austen frequently distinguishes characters through their mannerisms of speech. My point is that such characterizations, and many of them are brilliant, occur as parts of a fictional art which is structured by other fundamental principles. The greatness of Miss Bates and Mrs. Elton, for example, is that *what* they say is aesthetically significant. One reason Jane Austen was able to adapt herself so easily to the conventions of the fiction of her day (and to adapt the conventions to her own interests so quietly) is that, to her, form on all levels is a means of establishing significance of content—not the reverse.

A microscopic indicator of this bias is Austen's skill at blending, which means "sustaining a formal coherence between," narrative and dialogue even though she as narrator is always distinguishable from any of her characters, just as they are usually distinct from one another even though they all adhere to the same rigid code of address. Brontë's narrators are usually characters within the action of her fiction, but this point of view is only an obtrusive symptom of her difference from Austen.[3] The microscopic evidence that Brontë does not blend narrative and dialogue and is relatively indifferent to subtleties of their formal interaction is perhaps more interesting. As I suggested earlier, as a writer of modern romances Brontë rejects the adequacy of received novelistic forms. In contrast to Austen's easy adaptation to novelistic conventions, Brontë had to struggle to establish her own appropriate form. Her fiction is anticonventional in the broadest sense. On the basis of our analysis of her treatment of narrative and dialogue it become possible to propose that her concern with impressions is symptomatic of her resistance to conventionalized, formal distinctions between (and relations among) the *forms* of narrative and dialogue.

When we turn to Eliot we find microscopic evidence of what I have described as her "subversiveness." Eliot's narrative and dialogue, unlike Brontë's, are closely interrelated formally, but, unlike Austen's, they do not cohere smoothly. To a degree they contrast, and to that degree they interact significantly. The narrative portion of Eliot's mixed sentences usually qualifies, extends, or even controverts the dialogue portion—and vice-versa. This is one reason why her novels require slow reading. There are important patterns of interplay between narrative and dialogue, and the more alert to the patterns we are, the more we find that we cannot take what is said at face value—not because it isn't true, but because its full meaning appears only in relation to something else.

One sees here a connection with Eliot's tendency to break down temporal regularity. To put it simply, a comment on the manner in which a speech was delivered carries us back to the time of the speech. We see on this level, too, why Eliot's block structuring is effective: each block is a dense intertangle of complexities. Indeed, because of the intertangling, some

[3] I am inclined not to attribute overwhelming significance to Brontë's first-person point of view for several reasons, probably the most important of which is that several of the impressive characteristics of her writing appear in intensified and really more interesting fashion in the fiction of Charles Dickens, who relatively rarely employed first-person narration.

arbitrary clarity of structure on a higher level is probably essential. And, in contrast to Austen, Eliot's concern with something more than what is said, stands out clearly. Not only is manner of speech stressed but also gestures and positions that express what is not easily verbalized are made important. These features are probably related to Eliot's heavy use of proper names in her mixed sentences, even though, altogether, Austen uses a higher proportion. In *Emma*, though most of the dialogue occurs in large groups, particular dialogue is specifically focused on two clearly defined speakers.[4] Or, to put it another way, in *Emma*, dialogue is dialogue. In *Middlemarch*, self-expression is more important than it is in *Emma*, as is the effect on others of a speech addressed to one person. At one point, Mary speaks "quickly" because she fears her father's remark that she "gets her tongue" from her mother will offend Susan Garth. Even in the doubly deceptive three-cornered conversation at the Bates' between Frank Churchill, Jane Fairfax, and Emma, such focus on interpreting the effect of words on others in relation to oneself and third-parties is absent. Jane Austen's characters only talk to one another; they are not involved in the complexities of communication and articulation which serve to characterize Eliot's people. These differences are as much structural as substantive. What is at issue is not relative sophistication in understanding sociopsychological relations (though there are expressed in the differences some important underlying philosophical divergencies) but systems of artistic organization, that is, structures. And, as I have tried to show, when the differences are considered this way it becomes possible, at least potentially possible, to understand the coherence between different levels of structure in a fine work of fiction. It is to that coherence which we primarily refer when we praise any novelist's art.

The foregoing discussion raises the question: how typical are the passages discussed? To answer this question I have tested some of my figures against random samplings from

---

[4] This situation, however, is quite different from Brontë's isolated confrontations.

other novels. Although the results depend on insufficient data for any absolute conclusions, in general the samplings support the validity of the findings for the three passages. I confess surprise at the degree to which the two sets of figures correlate, because the passages were selected arbitrarily, not for their typicality. Yet even where there is variation between figures for the passages and figures for the samplings, the differences are likely to clarify the meaning of tendencies detected in the passages. Because of the relatively impressive correlations (which, however, need more testing), I present the findings for the samplings (Tables XI-7 through XI-15 in the Tabulations Appendix) in as condensed fashion as possible with minimal comment here.

For successive narrative sentences the samplings (200 sentences per author) were used to test distribution by length (see Table XI-7). The samplings accentuate our findings for the passages: Austen varies the length of these sentences more than both Brontë and Eliot, though Eliot varies hers more than Brontë. Admittedly inadequate figures indicate that the reverse pattern may hold for dialogue, although to my mind the figures in Table XI-8 (in this case in numbers, not percentages) cast doubt on the significance of variations in the length of dialogue sentences. On the other hand, there appears to be little doubt that the patterns of sentence form which were observed in the passages to be characteristic of each author when introducing a new speaker are indeed typical (see Table XI-9).

Furthermore, comparison of the figures for the number of sentences containing dialogue in relation to the number of speakers shows good correlation between samples and passages. In Table XI-10 these figures are converted to sentences-per-speaker-change for comparative purposes. And the number of changes per major speaker is remarkably similar in the samplings and in the passages (Table XI-11).

For dialogue, then, a key to differentiation appears to be when and how and how often speakers change. The importance of the changes, for which there are no equivalents in pure narrative, perhaps explains why variation in sentence length seems to be of so little significance in dialogue. It is also obvious that manner of speech is a prime mode of characterization. Reasonably large figures more-or-less bear out the relative distinctions among the average sentence lengths manifest in the passages (Table XI-12). An interesting sidelight: of the total number of narrative sentences included in the count for Table XI-12, those which the markers distinguished as "descriptive," "expository," or "interiorized" were singled out and the results shown in Table XI-13. The results are interesting because they indicate that such a relatively low proportion of Eliot's nondialogue sentences are pure narrative—reflecting the formal complexity I pointed out earlier and on which I comment again in Chapter Twelve.[5] Relatively, Austen distinguishes her pure and impure narrative sentences in terms of length, which supports our earlier findings. By comparison, Brontë does not rely on this kind of formal differentiation.

As for basic sentence-length averages (Table XI-12), the samplings and the passages do not exactly agree. *Emma* apparently runs to shorter sentences in all categories than Austen's novels as a whole. *Proportions* of number and length for the different categories, however, hold surprisingly well, particularly as regards mixed sentences (Table XI-14). The only divergence from a fairly close correlation here is in the proportion of Brontë's mixed to her dialogue sentences. While the larger figure for the samplings is undoubtedly more "accurate," the important point, I believe, is that we have more evidence that Brontë is less consistent than the other two in her handling of pure dialogue in relation to mixed sentences. In other words, mixed sentences are not as im-

---

[5] It is this complexity of detail that gives us a basis for judging the relevance of findings such as those reported in Chapter Nine about Eliot's preference for "exposition." This complexity, as well as the figures in Chapter Nine, incidentally, make me doubtful about the validity of W. J. Harvey's ratios of "omniscient intrusions" to pages (*The Art of George Eliot* [London, 1961], p. 247): *Adam Bede* 1:10; *The Mill on the Floss* 1:14; *Middlemarch* 1:33. I think that Eliot's "omniscience" does not decrease but that her "intrusions" become more and more engaged in the texture of her prose.

portant to the formal designs of her action as they are—in opposite fashions—to Austen's and Eliot's designs. This belief is strengthened by figures for proportional lengths of the different kinds of sentences (Table XI-15). Again the one serious failure in correlation occurs in Brontë's dialogue. The failure is especially impressive because the correlation between forms of mixed sentences in the samplings and the passages holds about as well for Brontë as for Austen and Eliot.

Altogether, then, our samplings indicate that descriptions of characteristics in the passages from *Emma*, *Villette*, and *Middlemarch* are reasonably reliable. The reliability suggests that analysis of the relations among formal characteristics of fiction through examination of arbitrarily selected passages is feasible and can provide a useful (if hitherto unexplored) complement to the study of subjectively defined and selected passages. The findings, furthermore, sustain confidence in the hypothesis that formal interactions between dialogue and narrative constitute excellent focal points for examinations into the relation of large and small, underlying and detailed, structures of fiction.[6]

[6] I have accentuated positive results in this chapter because I believe development of some method for defining the structural patterns of "speech" and "narration" would be helpful to the study of fictional history. I must, however, add a cautionary note. There exist no norms, either statistical or critical, against which to test such results. To establish norms we need, I suspect, less data collecting (particularly of my simple-minded kind) and more informed theorizing about the nature of fictional structures. My limited reading in the literature of recent stylistics and linguistics (for which, see the Bibliographical Appendix) has taught me that the shrewdest and most experienced practitioners in these disciplines are exceedingly cautious in making claims that their work will soon be of much help to sophisticated literary criticism.

CHAPTER XII

Evaluations

IT HAS NOT been my purpose in this study to provide definitive answers. It has not been my intention to arrive at conclusive definitions of the styles of Jane Austen, Charlotte Brontë, and George Eliot. I have attempted, instead, to initiate development of systematic methods of fictional criticism which will enable us to study individual novels more fruitfully and to build up more exact and helpful comparisons and contrasts between novels and between novelists. I hope that others will take up my tentative suggestions and improve on them so that before long my work will seem little more than the historical curiosity that beginnings of large enterprises inevitably become. I hope, in particular, that others will prove far more significant than I have been able to demonstrate the premise that valuable comparative-contrastive studies of fictional art must concentrate on the patterns of relations which make fictional structures cohere. This premise has supported my impoliteness in devoting so many pages to the illustration of inadequacies in existing critical assumptions, methods, and aims.

I was motivated to begin this undertaking, and sustained as it dragged its slow length along, by the conviction that, at this time, what the humanities desperately require is the development of subdisciplines which will render humanistic studies cumulatively effective. One of the great achievements of the natural sciences in the past century has been the establishment of premises and methodologies which make it possible for many scientists to feel justifiable satisfaction in contributing, however minutely, to a growing body of information, knowledge, and even wisdom which is vaster, more enduring, and more significant than the greatest individual scientist. The principal objections to modern literary criticism, my special sphere within the humanities, are that it is separatist, egocentric, and committed to perfection. The work of even the best critics is of very little *use* to subsequent critics. Too often our criticism is either a gathering of personal insights unorganized by a methodology which would enable someone else interested in the same topic to build upon those insights, or a thinly veiled philosophical, religious, or political polemic. Very little of our criticism is honestly exploratory. How often do we read an article about a humanistic investigation that admittedly turned out to be less than successful? Scientists admit that at least nineteen out of twenty of their efforts go for naught. Apparently nothing in literary criticism ever fails. Our best critics do literary criticism a disservice by so seldom telling us of their mistakes, their intuitions which went sour, their theories which broke down. They could afford such admissions. An elegant humility of manner affected by many academic critics today is a poor substitute for a genuine desire to work with others in a task the scope and significance of which is as grand as that of the sciences.

It is not, then, modesty which makes me unwilling to claim much importance for my results. I am perhaps arrogant in asserting the necessity for tentativeness and incertitude, for insisting, above all, that my findings are dubious, their implications not fully clear, and that most of what I have been able to discover about structural relations in Austen's, Brontë's, and Eliot's fiction ought soon to be superseded. But any reader who has followed me this far deserves the ambiguous reward of knowing what I think the work of the previous chapters adds up to. What follows is, without any pretense at being a "final" evaluation, a summarized presentation of how, at this point, I understand the fictional styles of Jane Austen, Charlotte Brontë, and George Eliot.

Early in the book I suggested that a discrepancy between "superficial" and "concealed" form is a special characteristic of all fictional styles. For Jane Austen, superficial form may be termed the conventional. Her manner of presenting the conventional subtly reveals what it masks, not, one must add, to expose it as evil but to reveal the virtues of properly functioning conventions. For Charlotte Brontë, superficial form is the anticonventional, the "truth," but her manner of telling it reveals that the truth is more complex than is suggested by the mere claim of breaking through established falsifications. Perhaps the best way to illustrate her revelation of what I have called the subconscious is to point out that the total impression created by a Brontë novel is considerably more powerful than the sensationalism of the parts of its plot. In *Jane Eyre*, for example, the mad-wife-in-the-attic part of the novel is effective in large measure because, structurally, it is of secondary importance. It is not the climax of the novel; it is "preparation" for an even worse horror—the perversity of St. John Rivers' religious zeal. Sensational as are the events which occur at Thornfield, Rochester's house is not a trap, but Moor Cottage, for all its pleasant respectability, *is* a trap. Odd though it may seem to some readers, I believe Brontë could have found no device for saving her heroine more appropriate to the "hidden" form of *Jane Eyre* than the one she actually uses: the mysterious cry in the night, which is the subconscious call of Rochester to Jane.

George Eliot, as I have remarked, works at a deeper level than Brontë and represents a more complex vision of society than does Austen. The superficial form of Eliot's fiction is realism, the presentation of things as they really are. Yet, unlike Brontë, Eliot attempts no illusion of literal truth in her manner of telling. She never, for example, employs first-person narrative. Eliot is a little like Austen in not straining to disguise the fact that she is writing fiction. In this mixture of realism and storytelling a subversive truth gradually takes shape—the truth that there is a superpersonal logic to the accidents of life and that there is a connectedness of a different kind from that by which we customarily order and evaluate the circumstances of ordinary living. To a degree at least, Eliot's writing challenges our usual conception of the principles by which the world works. Her prose is not the best of my three authors,[1] but to me it is the most interesting

---

[1] In my personal judgment, Jane Austen's fictional prose is the "best." It is the most economical, elegant, and precise. It is consistent but flexible, graceful, controlled, and harmonious, yet almost never

because it strives to make us aware of the very process by which we understand it. Eliot's aim is to articulate the systems of communication which underlie and in some measure control human relations but which cannot be expressed by ordinary, that is, nonfictional, means. She is in this respect a forerunner of several important late nineteenth- and early twentieth-century novelists.

These may seem generalized terms in which to speak of so concrete a matter as style, but as I tried to make clear in earlier chapters, one must begin with such macroscopic distinctions if one wishes to avoid the futility of adjectives such as "formal," "poetic," "ponderous," and the like. Such adjectives may be accurate, although, as Louis Milic has shown in his study of Swift's style, when adjectives are piled up by various critics over the years their meanings change and often become contradictory. The intuitive evaluations expressed by such descriptive terms, particularly when enunciated by an experienced scholar, are not "wrong." They are just not helpful. They are private. They sum up a complex of personal experiences. In the long run they tell us more about the critic than about the art he criticizes.

More useful stylistic judgments begin with assessments of the central purpose of the style in question, and such judgments can be related to small details in limited passages. To illustrate this I chose virtually at random (I looked for brief paragraphs of narrative only) one paragraph from each of the

---

rigid or dry. Austen fails to attain her aims less frequently than any other English novelist, and her aims, though limited, are not superficial. All in all, I judge Eliot to be a better writer of fictional prose than Charlotte Brontë, who is uneven and was only attaining mastery of her art at the time of her death. But as a writer of fictional prose Brontë has gifts denied to Eliot. In her novels there are passages of subtle evocativeness lacking in Eliot's art. Eliot's tendency not merely to be intellectual but also to seek out the deepest connections of life probably prevents her from achieving anything equivalent to Brontë's most intense paragraphs, which are usually centered on stark confrontations between antagonistic forces. The strengths and weaknesses of Eliot's prose style might be most succinctly defined as closely analogous to the strengths and weaknesses of Wordsworth's poetic style.

segments of *Emma, Villette,* and *Middlemarch* discussed in Chapters Ten and Eleven. Examination revealed that there are other similarities between the paragraphs chosen: all center on the novel's heroine and a major male figure who is not the protagonist, and all three deal with the aftermath of a significant event. The extra similarities are unimportant except insofar as they validate the comparability of the paragraphs in themselves with minimal reference to their contexts. I stress the casualness of my selection because I think that few critics would choose these short passages on which to focus the central significance of each novel or by which to reveal the main characteristics of the authors' styles.

My difficulty in discussing the paragraphs is in resisting the temptation to go on at too great length, because I find these few sentences richly illustrative. The wealth of significance in these unremarkable passages is evidence that my method eliminates the problem of deciding which part of a novel is the best part for analysis. Almost any part will serve. I need not juxtapose opening paragraphs or passages of plot resolution or scenes comparable in action, number of characters, and so forth. And I believe that the first test of the effectiveness of a method of stylistic criticism is whether or not it is applicable—within reasonable limits—to any segment of a text.

Frank Churchill had danced once at Highbury, and longed to dance again; and the last half hour of an evening which Mr. Woodhouse was persuaded to spend with his daughter at Randalls, was passed by the two young people in schemes on the subject. Frank's was the first idea; and his the greatest zeal in pursuing it; for the lady was the best judge of the difficulties, and the most solicitous for accommodation and appearance. But still she had inclination enough for shewing people again how delightfully Mr. Frank Churchill and Miss Woodhouse danced—for doing that in which she need not blush to compare herself with Jane Fairfax—and even for simple dancing itself, without any of the wicked aids of vanity—to assist him first in pacing out the room they were in to see what it could be made to hold—and then in taking the dimensions of the other parlour, in the hope of discovering, in spite of all that Mr. Weston could say of their exactly equal size, that it was a little the largest.

(*Emma*, 29, ¶2; or II, 11)

On first reading, Jane Austen's paragraph strikes one as being clear and simple, although somewhat stylized. Probably a first reading also conveys an impression of consistency: nothings stands out as markedly different from anything else. Yet closer inspection reveals some interesting intricacies within the lucid regularity. The latter portion of the first sentence, for example, shows ingenious ordering. It might have been written: "Emma and Frank planned for another dance during the last half hour of an evening visit to Randalls." One element lost by such an arrangement is regularity of progression, but a more important loss is that of the context in which the "schemes" take place. Although Mr. Woodhouse is mentioned apparently only in passing and the Westons are not mentioned by name at all, the presence of all three is relevant because their attitudes toward the schemes will be decisive. Though not so defined, these are older people. Much of *Emma* turns on the relations between young and old. The patterns of tyranny through dependence center on older people's dependence on younger people.[2] Thus the first sentence is constructed so as to convey economically the context which

[2] Even the casual detail of Knightley's age, "thirty-seven or eight," is germane. Young enough to dance well and to be embarrassed by innuendoes about his feelings toward Jane, he is mature and responsible. Knightley is simultaneously the most independent character in the novel and the one most willing to undertake the burdens of older "dependents." Today when we are so concerned with the "generation gap," *Emma* is especially fascinating. One subject of the novel is how such gaps are bridged, and it is treated with remarkable sophistication. For instance, the literal age of a character is sometimes of secondary importance. Mr. Woodhouse is not as old as he appears to be. Mr. and Mrs. Elton are younger than, respectively, Mr. and Mrs. Weston (just what Mrs. Weston's age may be poses an interesting problem), yet the Eltons strive to appear older than they are. The Eltons try to separate themselves from their "agemates," whereas the Westons retain their links with youth. Jane Austen perceives the social equating of "age" with power or position to be at least as determinative of how people behave as the number of years they have lived.

compels Frank and Emma to scheme rather than plan. Mr. Woodhouse has had to be "persuaded" to spend an evening with his best friends, and only during the final "half-hour" of the visit is even so determined a dancer as Frank able to broach his project. This construction focuses attention on Frank and Emma together, but they are together within a complex of interrelations, not in isolation.

Frank and Emma are discriminated as individuals by their relations with other major characters. The second and third sentences of the paragraph both unite Frank and Emma and distinguish one from the other in terms of such relations. Sentences, paragraphs, chapters, all units of an Austen novel are ordered so as to form a series of patterns which make possible discriminations—discriminations which could not exist without the patterns. Austen's word choices, which are simultaneously delicately precise yet abstract, contribute to this discrimination-through-patterning. Just one example: Emma is more "solicitous for accommodation" than Frank. The quoted phrase seems abstract, yet it would be difficult to find substitutes for the words which would convey as precisely (and as economically) both Emma's attitude toward her society (she does not, for instance, "worry about" accommodation) and the values of that society, which is not concerned with display or magnificence on the one hand, nor with issues and undertakings of a "serious" nature on the other. Emma's society's ideal is unostentatious elegance of accommodation (although "elegance" has a moral as well as a decorative connotation here), which requires solicitousness.

What has just been said is testimony to Austen's preference for rationalized, declarative prose.[3] Her emphasis falls on

[3] At least four excellent studies of Jane Austen's style which complement my description deserve notice: Frank W. Bradbrook, "Style and Judgment in Jane Austen's Novels," *Cambridge Journal*, IV (1951), 515-37; Tudja Crowder, "The Rational Treatment of Emotion: An Essay on Jane Austen's Style," *Spectrum*, II (1961), 91-96; Mary Lascelles, *Jane Austen and Her Art* (London, 1939). The last is a splendid work which has been quietly plundered by most subsequent critics and which contains a superb chapter on style. Also, Norman Page, "Standards of Excellence: Jane Austen's Language,"

denotation rather than connotation. Granted that she uses a specialized subject matter, Jane Austen tells it like it is, as the modern phrase has it. Her honesty may account for her concentration. The paragraph just quoted, like the chapters I discussed previously, has a single subject, a social activity, dancing. This singleness of subject permits the regularity and continuity of normal, "social," time flow to operate throughout the paragraph: Frank has danced, wants to dance again, and schemes to dance in the future. We see here another dimension of Austen's representation of diversity within unity. Singleness of subject also serves to reinforce the point that Austen stresses what is said rather than the manner of speech. It is noteworthy that our paragraph is the narration of a conversation—or, more accurately, of several conversations—in conjunction with Emma's thoughts. It is the subject of conversation that is dwelt upon. We are not told, for example, how Mr. Weston addressed the young people but only his factual contribution: that the parlors are of the same size.[4]

One final small but significant point is Emma's thinking of herself as "Miss Woodhouse." This kind of detail encourages critics to describe Jane Austen's writing as "formal." "Stylized" would, in my view, be a better term. The crux of the matter is that we are being told of Emma's thoughts, we are inside her mind, but what we learn is what she thinks about how she appears to others and about her relations with others, such as Jane Fairfax, in the context of Highbury society. Austen's prose aims at revealing the coherence of Emma's personality and her social role. The discriminations Austen

---

Review of English Literature, VII (1966), 91-98, is particularly good on Austen's precision in her use of abstractions.

[4] This point exemplifies how Jane Austen's economy enables her to make small touches effective. Because there is so little specific and detailed information about the houses in *Emma,* the fact that Mr. Weston knows precisely the size of his two parlors can function as indicator of his character. We read the remark not as an indication of what Randalls looks like but as an indication that Mr. Weston is a responsible, even meticulous, home-owner. This quality, which rather contrasts with his tendency toward boyish enthusiasm, helps us to respect, as well as like, him.

makes among characters are discriminations among such coherences. This is why her prose always works toward a transpicuousness which is neither dull nor flat and which enjoys the advantages of abstractness without being indefinite.

> A warm hand, taking my cold fingers, led me down to a room where there was a fire. Dr. John and I sat before the stove. He talked to me and soothed me with unutterable goodness, promising me twenty letters for the one lost. If there are words and wrongs like knives, whose deep-inflicted lacerations never heal— cutting injuries and insults of serrated and poison-dripping edge— so, too, there are consolations of tone too fine for the ear not fondly and for ever to retain their echo: caressing kindnesses— loved, lingered over through a whole life, recalled with unfaded tenderness, and answering the call with undimmed shine out of that raven cloud foreshadowing Death himself. I have been told since that Dr. Bretton was not nearly so perfect as I thought him: that his actual character lacked the depth, height, compass, and endurance it possessed in my creed. I don't know: he was good to me as the well is to the parched wayfarer—as the sun to the shivering jailbird. I remember him heroic. Heroic at this moment will I hold him to be. (*Villette* 22, ¶25)

I suppose the most obvious contrast between Austen's paragraph and Brontë's lies in the latter's several vigorous metaphors. Yet, as I tried to make clear in Chapter Six, we must get beyond the mere observation that there are metaphors and metaphoric patterns if we wish to discuss fictional style usefully. We must define the specific nature and function of the metaphors. We must see how their patterns relate to patterns of other elements.[5] For example, the metaphors in

---

[5] One advantage of concentrating on a limited passage is that it precludes undue concern with "image patterns." Perhaps the chief procedural weakness of modern fictional criticism is its tendency to assume that the mere description of a pattern (or patterns) of imagery is sufficient basis for broad judgments of the "meaning" of a novel. Image patterns are important, but their importance can be asesssed properly only in relation to the other kinds of patterns that, altogether, constitute the artistry of a novel. In their anxiety to assert the evaluative function of their discipline, many critics forget the dangers of inadequately based judgments. Poorly founded evaluations give rise to an industry of counter-critiques focused not on works of litera-

Brontë's paragraph contribute to its temporal distortion. The diversion from straight narrative chronology is in the direction of Lucy's psychological history. Her judgment of Dr. Bretton "then," which is the immediate present of *Villette*'s action, is reaffirmed by her evaluation "now," the moment of composition, in the light of what she learned subsequent to the scene in the warm room, the time between "then" and "now." Metaphor enables Brontë to free her narrator from the tight chronological progression we have noticed in Jane Austen's writing. The metaphors, moreover, enable Brontë to characterize her narrator by the fashion in which she distorts regular chronology. Not only do the metaphors take us far from the room where Lucy and Dr. John converse, but they also emphasize Lucy's contrasting yet related conceptions of life, what some modern psychologists would describe as the "set" of her expectations which determine the character of her perceptions. Lucy conceives of life as extended pilgrimage or a prison. What relates the "shivering jailbird" to the "parched wayfarer" are the empty stretches of existence each must endure before the sun shines or the well appears.[6]

Even more characteristic of these metaphors is the absoluteness of their oppositions. The "serrated and poison-dripping edge" contrasts with the "tone" of "caressing kindnesses"; the "shine," with the "raven cloud" from which it comes; and, of course, the "parched wayfarer" is the opposite of the "shivering jailbird." Charlotte Brontë's style consists in confrontation on every level. Dr. John's "warm hand" takes

---

ture but on the shortcomings of equally partial analyses. The perpetuation of this industry at least in part validates the complaint of many students today that literary scholars are not really interested in literature.

⁶ Anyone familiar with *Jane Eyre* will immediately recognize the applicability of the symbolic dialectic of prisoner-wayfarer to the protagonist of that novel. The pattern, in fact, recurs throughout Brontë's fiction, appearing frequently even in her juvenilia. The most detailed study of Charlotte Brontë's language I know, and one which deals perceptively with patterns of recurrence, is Mrs. Margo McCullough Peters' doctoral dissertation, "Four Essays on the Style of Charlotte Brontë," University of Wisconsin, Madison, 1969.

Lucy's "cold fingers"; the room with the fire contrasts with the icy garret of the preceding paragraph; Lucy and Dr. John are opposites in sex, personality, position, and experiences; the time of writing is juxtaposed with the time of the event; Dr. John's character is presented as amenable to opposed evaluations; even the sentence forms in the paragraph are vigorously diversified. In these antagonisms the vitality of Brontë's art resides. Out of them arises the symbolic force of her prose. For instance, the room in which Lucy and Dr. John converse is not described: it has a fire and in it Lucy and Dr. John can be alone together. The significance of these two features of the paragraph's setting is their relation to the warmth-refuge and isolation-union patterns of symbolism which link all portions of the novel.

The symbolism, however, cannot be separated from the narrative point of view. The paragraph represents Lucy's impressions. Impressionism contributes to the breakdown of conventionalized, formal order. Logically and chronologically the paragraph does not progress. Our knowledge of Lucy increases. Or, to put it another way, the conflict between incongruous characteristics of her personality is meaningfully intensified. For this reason one is tempted to call Brontë's writing expressive.

Brontë's expressiveness takes the form of a tension between the narrator and her language. The tension is revealed in the clustering of metaphors; the extremeness of much of the vocabulary, ranging from *"unutterable* goodness," *"deep-inflicted* laceration," and *"Death* himself," to the "heroic" qualities of Dr. John; the use of negatives which affirm; and the arrangement of words so that parallelism of sound, structure, and function are nearly as significant as meanings— "loved, lingered," "unfaded tenderness . . . undimmed shine." The tension also involves other levels, for it links up with the patterns of antagonism mentioned before. Dr. John is "heroic" because he speaks kindly to a flustered young woman, and his kindness provokes Lucy's exclamations about "poisoned" knives, "Death," the "shivering jailbird," and the like. What is

191

represented is, in the terms I have used before, a split between the character's role and his personality.[7] It is the split that counts. There is almost no ambiguity, only contrast, which is why many readers find little subtlety in Brontë's writing. The strength of her prose lies in the intensity of the conflict it presents, a conflict which at its deepest level expresses the vital rivalry between what an individual intrinsically is and what his social role presses him to become.[8]

Dorothea had been aware when Lydgate had ridden away, and she had stepped into the garden, with the impulse to go at once to her husband. But she hesitated, fearing to offend him by obtruding herself; for her ardour, continually repulsed, served, with her intense memory, to heighten her dread, as thwarted energy subsides into a shudder; and she wandered slowly round the nearer clumps of trees until she saw him advancing. Then she went towards him, and might have represented a heaven-sent angel coming with a promise that the short hours remaining should yet be filled with that faithful love which clings the closer to a comprehended grief. His glance in reply to hers was so chill that she felt her timidity increased; yet she turned and passed her hand through his arm.   (*Middlemarch*, 42, ¶28)

Both the paragraph from *Emma* and that from *Villette* are

[7] The chief means of representation is the impressionistic mode, which enables Brontë to make us aware of the contrasts in her narrator-protagonist and those in the character (Dr. John) with whom the narrator-protagonist deals simultaneously. Because Brontë is primarily concerned with vivid contrasts she favors two-person confrontations. In this regard she is clearly distinguishable from more truly "impressionistic" writers (such as Conrad) later in the century. On the other hand, the function of Brontë's first-person narrator is structurally distinguishable from that of most of her predecessors who organized their fiction around a first-person point of view. One could speak of Charlotte Brontë as an expressionistic-impressionist.

[8] At the risk of undue reiteration, I want to make it clear that I am trying to describe at least sketchily the special character of Charlotte Brontë's symbolic fiction. It is true, broadly speaking, that both Charlotte Brontë's and Charles Dickens' fiction is symbolic when contrasted to the fiction of Jane Austen and George Eliot. But to decipher the significance of that similarity one must recognize that there are impressive differences in the symbolic styles of the two. Dickens, for example, does not as a rule exploit a tension between a narrator and his narrative language (the obvious signal of this is Dickens' rare use of the first-person form), nor does he concentrate on absolute antagonisms as Brontë does.

narratives of conversations (although Austen's is far more "conversational" than Brontë's). The paragraph from *Middlemarch* differs absolutely from both, for Eliot narrates a dialogue that does not occur. Eliot is concerned with defining the communications between people, their interrelatings, which cannot be reduced to verbalization. Her language is directed toward representation not merely of manner of speech but also of manner of not speaking. It is not surprising that her emphasis falls on the ambiguities of the situation: Dorothea resists her "impulse"; her "ardour" is the source of her "dread"; she "might" have "represented a heaven-sent angel" to Casaubon, but at his "chill" response she feels her "timidity increased," yet she passes "her hand through his arm." The entire scene dramatizes an intricate *interplay* between two characters. The role and personality of each neither cohere nor conflict simply but, instead, interact complexly. The characters are a husband and his wife who can only partially be husband and wife despite their adherence to certain codes of "husbandly" and "wifely" behavior.

Just as the subject of the narration alternates between physical and psychic movements, so the language of the paragraph includes both concrete and abstract elements, both "the nearer clump of trees" and "a comprehended grief." The concrete details are "realistic" rather than symbolic, that is, they provide substantial actuality, and much of the detail depicts bodily movements. The concrete language, in fact, consistently tends toward tactileness, as when Dorothea "passes her hand through his arm." Touching, like gesturing, is probably the most basic nonverbal language.

The abstract language does not lean toward personification (contrast Eliot's "a comprehended grief" with Brontë's "Death himself"), nor does it possess the *type* of exactitude found in Austen's abstractions. Eliot's abstractions elucidate the interplay of psychological processes rather than define social conditions. The second sentence illustrates her representation of behavior through a rendering of psychic causes and physical consequences: Dorothea "wanders slowly" because she fears "to offend" by "obtruding," her dread being intensified by previous rejections of her "ardour." This language is adjusted to reveal primarily sensitive psychological, not social, awareness. The intricacies of the cause-consequence system are complicated even by the form of the sentence, which refers first to present time (the whole passage is in the past tense),[9] "she hesitated"; then to the future, "fearing to offend"; then, in the next twelve words, to the past; then the "timelessness" of a simile is introduced; and finally the sentence spirals back to a kind of progressive present, "wandered . . . until. . . ."[10] Detailed temporal relations are clearly if intricately developed because the underlying system being defined is that of a process, not a static condition.

The quality of psychological awareness established by the prose can perhaps be characterized by the word "obtruding." This sort of polysyllabic, latinate word offends many readers today. On the other hand, "obtrude" is not a word favored by Jane Austen. It is difficult to find a synonym appropriate to Eliot's context. Dorothea does not merely fear that her physical presence will "offend" her husband; she is also afraid that her presence will remind him of their unsatisfactory psychological relationship. "Obtruding" conveys the sense that Dorothea recognizes that she will be an object of perception

[9] The difficulty in describing appropriately the temporal elements in the sentence is evidence of the importance in Eliot's novels of what I have called a "fictive" time scheme.

[10] The last sentence of the paragraph exhibits much the same form in a simplified fashion. The syntactic complexity, psychological interconnectedness, and emphasis on unverbalized communication which I am discussing are closely related to Eliot's developed skill at using what the Germans call *erlebte Rede*. This characteristic of Eliot's style was first pointed out, I believe, by Lisa Glauser in *Schweizer anglistische Arbeiten* (Berne, 1948). Derek Oldfield in his essay "The Language of the Novel: The Character of Dorothea," *Middlemarch*, ed. Barbara Hardy (London, 1967), pp. 63-86, provides a perceptive discussion of the function of indirect discourse in the novel. This fictional mode deserves intensified examination. I think it can be shown for example, that Eliot's career displays her increasing use of, and skill at using, *erlebte Rede—Daniel Deronda* being climactic for this technique. Eliot's predecessors, with the possible exception of Thackeray, use less indirect discourse and employ it differently. Dickens, for instance, tends to favor dramatic, attention-seizing indirect discourse concentrated in distinctive passages instead of attempting Eliot's unobtrusively interwoven complexity.

for Casaubon, and that his perception will arouse unpleasant feelings in him. One notices that the entire paragraph centers on the unverbalized perceptions and responses-to-perceptions of Dorothea and her husband, and the patterning of perception-responses *is* the process of their interrelation.

One has to stress "process," because it is a developing relation. Even in this minor paragraph there is change: Dorothea's timidity is increased. Arm-in-arm at the end of the paragraph, Dorothea and Casaubon are psychically farther apart than at the beginning when Dorothea goes into the garden "with the impulse to go at once to her husband." The discrepancy between outward appearance and inner reality has widened.

All I have said about this paragraph from *Middlemarch* might be summed up by the observation that everything in it functions to reveal the particular manner in which Dorothea and her husband relate. We are made to see the true meaning beneath apparently random actions (Dorothea's "wandering" is a sign of her inner distress) and beneath what might be called conventional poses (the linking of arms conceals incompatibility). Here, almost literally, "the medium is the message"; the prose works to define the system which explains how the forms of relation operate—even if sometimes by concealment—to express the evolving processes of response and counter-response.

The prose connects. The paragraph contains not only the internal connections to which I have been alluding but also similes which compel us to see the specific situation in relation to other possibilities. We see this process as analogous to others. It is not *Dorothea's* "thwarted energy" which "subsides into a shudder"; it is "abstract" energy which changes that way when balked.[11] And there is still another kind of connectedness in the paragraph, which, one should note, includes several specific actions. Dorothea, aware that Lydgate has left, steps into the garden, hesitates, wanders between the

[11] The length and relative complexity of the sentence reveal, I believe, Eliot's desire to associate rather than to distinguish, even when her subject is the growing rift between a particular man and his wife.

trees, and finally goes toward her husband when she sees him advancing.[12] The coldness of his glance frightens her, but she turns to walk arm-in-arm with him. Granted that the subject matter is psychological, a good deal has "happened" in 134 words. The happenings are bound together by the language which represents them. In sentence two we find "fearing" and "dread" and "shudder." In the third sentence "grief" appears; and in the fourth, "chill" and "timidity." Dorothea's "intense memory" helps to "heighten" her dread; at her husband's coldness her "timidity *increased*." These various words contribute to the underlying *motif* of the paragraph's action: the intensification of Dorothea's anxieties. I suggested in Chapter Eleven that methods of subterraneous linking make it possible for Eliot to unify many apparently unrelated actions. The same tendency to make diversities cohere is visible in microscopic form in this paragraph and is, in my view, a central characteristic of Eliot's style.

I HOPE MY characterizations may help the reader to appreciate the art of Jane Austen, Charlotte Brontë, and George Eliot. More significant paragraphs, and paragraphs richer in examples of the authors' stylistic techniques, could be cited. But I have tried to demonstrate that by approaching fictional style through a tracing of the relations between macroscopic and microscopic structural systems it is possible to find rewarding critical foci even in ordinary passages. At the risk of exposing my naïveté, I confess that until I undertook this work I had not realized how consistently complex the organization of a good novel is. I had not fully realized, in other words, how marvelous is the creation of a fictional work of art. The severest test of any critical procedure is whether or not, finally, it enhances our wonder at and delight in the art it criticizes. For me, at any rate, there has been such enhancement in analyzing structure in fiction to discover its styles.

---

[12] The authorial suggestion at this point that Dorothea "might have represented a heaven-sent angel" does not, I feel, jar at all, because the preceding sentences are not presented from "inside" Dorothea's mind; they are authorial elucidations of the shifting patterns of her feelings, patterns of which she is herself only partially aware.

BIBLIOGRAPHICAL APPENDIX

APPENDIX OF TABULATIONS

INDEX

Bibliographical Appendix

I HAVE CITED relatively few general references in this book because most of my particular observations were derived from the novels themselves. Doubtless what I observed and how I evaluated what I noticed owes more to the influence of critics I have read than to my originality. I try to indicate here a few of the works which I know must have shaped my responses to the novelists I studied and contributed to the development of my analytical techniques. I apologize for omitting, in order to be brief, many relevant items, especially journal articles. I do not normally repeat here citations in footnotes, nor do I include references to the many fine introductions to inexpensive reprints of nineteenth-century novels. Editions of the novels I have used which are not cited here are listed in the Tabulations Appendix.

Novel

If a student were restricted to reading only one general book on the novel, I should recommend E. M. Forster's *Aspects of the Novel* (New York, 1927), which is filled with brilliant insights but is also uproariously funny. Forster's book is a kind of answer to Percy Lubbock's *The Craft of Fiction* (London, 1921), which, in turn, is a systematization and simplification of some of Henry James' ideas about fiction, which may be found in *The Art of the Novel* (New York, 1934), edited by R. P. Blackmur, who provides a brilliant introduction, and *The Future of the Novel: Essays on the Art of Fiction*, edited by Leon Edel (New York, 1956). Lubbock, a sensitive writer and perceptive reader, stimulated many less accomplished critics to attack problems of point of view from a more-or-less Jamesian slant, though the master would be horrified at some of the intellectual vulgarizations of his subtle speculations on fictional craftsmanship. Wayne Booth's *The Rhetoric of Fiction* (Chicago, 1961) laboriously endeavors to correct the worst excesses of this line of criticism,

199

and several thoughtful works published during the past fifteen years have carried fictional studies beyond the narrowness of point-of-view polemics.

F. R. Leavis' *The Great Tradition* (London, 1948), for example, demonstrated that close reading and detailed structural analysis can be applied rewardingly to many different kinds of novels and can accompany serious interest in moral problems other than those in which Henry James specialized. Intellectually more significant than Leavis' work, however, is Erich Auerbach's *Mimesis* (English translation by Willard Trask, Princeton, 1953). Auerbach proves that linguistically detailed analyses of quite brief passages of literature can be used as the groundwork for evaluations of the character of profound cultural and philosophical changes in "the representation of reality," and his ideas and techniques have influenced most subsequent theoretical studies of fiction; for example, Robert Scholes' and Robert Kellogg's *The Nature of Narrative* (New York, 1966). Scholes and Kellogg also reflect the influence of Northrop Frye, who has been successful in directing attention to archetypal features of even aggressively "realistic" works.

In an entirely different tradition, George Lukacs, the great Hungarian Marxist, in *The Historical Novel* (English translation by Stephen and Hannah Mitchell, London, 1962) as well as in (to my mind a less significant though better known work) *Studies in European Realism* (English translation, London, 1950) shows a remarkable breadth of responsiveness and provides a pleasant antidote to the pallid academicism of much contemporary American writing about fiction. One American who has read Lukacs with profit (and in some ways gone beyond him) is J. Hillis Miller, whose impressive *The Form of Victorian Fiction* (Notre Dame, Indiana, 1968) is discussed briefly in footnote 3 in Chapter Nine.

Ian Watt's *The Rise of the English Novel* (London, 1957), is disappointing, even irritating, in its treatment of Fielding—whose prefatory discussions in both *Joseph Andrews* and *Tom Jones* contain profound insights into the nature of the novel. Fielding has been much underrated as a critic, probably because he writes so beautifully and amusingly. His definition of the novel, a comic epic in prose, for example, when understood in the context of his "critical essays" remains the most penetrating definition of the relation of fictional to epical art. Despite the oddly superficial response to Fielding, Watt's book is the best yet written on both the philosophical and sociological origins of the modern novel, and his essay "The First Paragraph of *The Ambassadors*," *Essays in Criticism*, x (1960), 250-74, is not merely an elegant example of practical criticism at its best but is also one of the sanest and most significant discussions of the nature of fictional style. Though his approach differs from Watt's, Simon Lesser's *Fiction and the Unconscious* (Boston, 1957) probably ought to be read in conjunction with Watt's work, because Lesser explains, I believe brilliantly, how and why a reader responds to subtleties of fictional style.

Of special interest to anyone concerned with style in fiction and with the relevance of recent developments in linguistics and stylistics is David Lodge's indispensable *The Language of Fiction* (New York, 1966). Lodge's explanations of the newest techniques of stylistic description are models of lucidity and his critiques of several popular methods are sympathetic but penetrating. Robert J. Donovan's *The Shape of Fiction* (Ithaca, 1966) is not as detailed or profound but contains much stimulating material. Robert A. Colby's *Fiction With a Purpose: Major and Minor Nineteenth-Century Novels* (Bloomington, Indiana, 1967) is the first systematized study of the relations between major and minor fiction and is a thoroughly rewarding work of scholarly criticism. Among histories of the novel, E. A. Baker's monumental ten-volume *The History of the English Novel* (London, 1924-39) is the most complete; Walter Allen's succinct *The English Novel* (New York, 1955) is the liveliest and most original; and Lionel Stevenson's *The English Novel: A Panorama* (Boston, 1960) is probably the most judicious of the publications in this subgenre.

Finally, I should mention a few works which have been of special interest to me as a student of style in fiction. R. S.

Crane's "The Concept of Plot and the Plot of *Tom Jones*," republished in *Critics and Criticism, Ancient and Modern*, ed. R. S. Crane (Chicago, 1952) is a deservedly famous essay which first appeared in 1945; Dorrit Cohn's "Narrated Mono-logue: Definition of a Fictional Style," *Comparative Litera-ture*, XVIII (1966), 97-112, is one of the most intelligent studies of a topic which should increasingly attract the atten-tion of fictional critics; John Holloway, *The Victorian Sage* (London, 1953), has a fine chapter on George Eliot's rhe-toric; Philip Stevick, besides editing an excellent anthology of criticism with an unusually complete bibliography, *The Theory of the Novel* (New York, 1967), has in "The Theory of Fictional Chapters," *Western Humanities Review*, XX (1966), 231-41, raised some original questions about an im-portant segment of fictional form.

Quotations in the text are from the following inexpensive editions of the novels studied, although, as is explained in footnote 3 in Chapter Two, some analyses were performed on different texts. Virtually all of these editions contain valuable critical introductions.

Northanger Abbey, edited by Andrew Wright, Holt, Rine-hart and Winston (with *The Castle of Otranto* and selections from *The Mysteries of Udolpho*); *Sense and Sensibility*, in-troduction by David Daiches, Modern Library (with *Pride and Prejudice*); *Pride and Prejudice*, edited by Mark Schorer, Houghton-Mifflin, Riverside; *Mansfield Park*, edited by Reuben A. Brower, Houghton-Mifflin, Riverside; *Emma,* edited by Lionel Trilling, Houghton-Mifflin, Riverside; *Per-suasion*, edited by David Daiches, The Norton Library; *The Professor*, introduction by Margaret Lane, Everyman Library; *Jane Eyre*, edited by Mark Schorer, Houghton-Mifflin, River-side; *Shirley,* introduction by Margaret Lane, Everyman Library; *Villette*, Dell Laurel edition; *Adam Bede*, edited by Gordon S. Haight, Holt, Rinehart and Winston; *The Mill on the Floss*, edited by Gordon S. Haight, Houghton-Mifflin, Riverside; *Silas Marner*, introduction by Jerome Thale, Holt, Rinehart and Winston; *Romola*, Everyman Library; *Felix Holt,* introduction by F. R. Leavis, Everyman Library; *Mid-*

dlemarch, edited by Gordon S. Haight, Houghton-Mifflin, Riverside; *Daniel Deronda*, introduction by F. R. Leavis, Harper Torchbook.

Stylistics

Much has been written about style in literature, as the reader may discover by consulting Louis T. Milic's excellent bibliography *Style and Stylistics* (New York, 1967), or Josephine Miles' "Works on Style" in *Style and Proportion* (Boston, 1967), pages 164-212, or *English Stylistics: A Bibliography*, edited by Richard W. Bailey and Dolores Burton, S.N.D. (Cambridge, Mass., 1968). The journal *Style* now publishes annually a helpful bibliography of stylistic studies. My own thinking about style has been much influenced by art historians, most notably George Kubler, whose *The Shape of Time* (New Haven, 1962) is a genuinely exciting work of scholarship. Equally exciting are E. H. Gombrich's *Art and Illusion* (London, 1960) and *Meditations on a Hobby Horse* (London, 1963). Meyer Schapiro's essay "Style," one of the best known general discussions of the subject, has been reprinted more than once, recently in J. V. Cunningham's handy anthology *The Problem of Style* (New York, 1966), but originally appeared in *Anthropology Today* (Chicago, 1953), edited by A. L. Kroeber.

At least three other essays which frequently fail to appear in literary bibliographies seem to me of importance. Leonard Meyer's *Emotion and Meaning in Music* (Chicago, 1956) is a difficult work primarily concerned with form in music, but which, nonetheless, contains many insights of value to the literary scholar. James S. Ackerman's philosophical article "A Theory of Style," *Journal of Aesthetics and Art Criticism*, xx (1962) 227-37, proposes the stimulating concept of style as "a class of related solutions to a problem—or responses to a challenge." The most lucid brief introduction to the problems of style in literature is, to my mind, R. A. Sayce's "The Definition of the Term 'Style,'" *Proceedings of the Third Congress of the International Comparative Literature Association* (The Hague, 1962), pages 156-66. Another valuable essay by the same author is "Literature and Language," *Essays in Criticism*, VII (1957), 119-33.

Two other works which I found enlightening but which have attracted little notice are Giacomo DeVoto's *Linguistics and Literary Criticism* (English translation by M. F. Edgerton, New York, 1963), and Nils Erik Enkvist's "On Defining Style: An Essay in Applied Linguistics," in the useful little volume *Linguistics and Style*, edited by John Spencer (London, 1964), pages 3-56. Although I have not found some of the more frequently cited works, such as Herbert Read's *English Prose Style* (London, 1928), René Wellek and Austin Warren's "Style and Stylistics" in their *Theory of Literature* (New York, 1949), pages 177-89, Richard M. Ohmann's "Prolegomena to the Analysis of Prose Style" in *Style in Prose Fiction*, edited by Harold C. Martin (New York, 1959), pages 1-24, or W. K. Wimsatt's "Verbal Style: Logical and Counterlogical," *PMLA*, LXV (1950), 5-20 (reprinted in *The Verbal Icon*, Lexington, Ky., 1954, with other relevant material), as helpful as I had hoped, I was surprised by how much of interest there is for the literary scholar in Colin Cherry's *On Human Communication* (New York, 1957), and in G. Udny Yule's *The Statistical Study of Literary Vocabulary* (Cambridge, 1944). These latter works of course carry us into the realms of information theory and quantification and imply at least linguistic competence. Before turning to this complex of topics, I should mention the work of two scholars who have significantly influenced most modern stylistic studies: Leo Spitzer, whose *Linguistics and Literary History* (Princeton, 1948), is only the best-known of his many publications, for a review of which see René Wellek, "Leo Spitzer (1887-1960)," *Comparative Literature*, XII (1960), 310-44; and Helmut Hatzfeld, two of whose articles deserve special notice, "Stylistic Criticism as Art-minded Philology," *Yale French Studies*, II (1949), 62-70, and "Methods of Stylistic Investigation" in *Literature and Science* (Oxford, 1955), pages 44-51.

Probably the best introduction to the technical literature of linguistically oriented stylistics is provided by the works of

Stephen Ullman, notably *The Principles of Semantics* (Oxford, 1961), *Style in the French Novel* (Oxford, 1964), and *Language and Style* (Oxford, 1964). Ullman combines sensitivity with sensibleness, is an admirable expositor of leading theories, and supplies a wealth of bibliographical references for every topic. The proliferation in recent years of new theories and methodologies in linguistics makes this important discipline a difficult and daunting one for a mere humanist, particularly because many linguists have taken to expressing themselves in a scientific (or, alas, more often a pseudo-scientific) jargon. To my mind the most significant and impressive work in linguistics in this century is Ferdinand de Saussure's *Course in General Linguistics*, admirably translated by Wade Baskin (New York, 1959), first published in 1915. My reasons for specially recommending Saussure in preference to many more recent scholars are set forth in a note at the end of this commentary.

The chief difficulty in applying linguistic techniques and hypotheses to sophisticated literary texts for the purpose of developing significant critical insights is succinctly stated by Angus McIntosh in "Saying," *Review of English Literature*, VI (1965), 9-20. McIntosh correctly observes that linguists have not been successful in going beyond the sentence as a primary unit of analysis and that "quite often where the impact of an entire work may be enormous, yet word by word . . . sentence by sentence, there may seem to be nothing very unusual or arresting . . . any approach . . . which looks at anything less than the whole text as the ultimate unit has very little to contribute. Whatever it may be in linguistic analysis, the sentence is not the proper unit here" (p. 19). F. W. Bateson argues more generally and more passionately against linguistics in "Linguistics and Literary Criticism," *The Disciplines of Criticism*, edited by Peter Demetz, Thomas Greene, Lowry Nelson, Jr. (New Haven, 1968), pages 3-17. Some of the intellectually most significant efforts to move beyond the sentence in linguistics have been carried out in Eastern Europe. Victor Erlich provides a history and analysis of the Russian "school" in *Russian Formalism: History, Doc-*

trine (2nd edn., The Hague, 1965), and Lubomír Doležel provides an excellent brief survey in "Russian and Prague School Functional Stylistics," *Style*, II (1968), 143-58. These eastern "schools" derive from principles first enunciated by Saussure, and, unlike many of their western counterparts, have followed Saussure's lead in associating linguistics with anthropological theories and findings. During the past fifteen years there has been considerable feedback, appropriately enough through French linguists, critics, and anthropologists, most notably Barthes and Levi-Strauss. The chief source of this movement, apparently, is the work of the great Russian scholar Roman Jakobson. Among his enormous bibliography one might cite *Fundamentals of Language*, with M. Halle (The Hague, 1956).

An American linguist who has tried to go beyond the sentence is Kenneth L. Pike, whose fundamental assumptions are succinctly set forth in his two essays in *Tagmemics: A Study of Units Beyond the Sentence*, a pamphlet issued by the National Council of Teachers of English in 1964 containing, in addition to reprints of the two articles by Pike, some related ones which originally appeared in the May and October, 1964, issues of *College Composition and Communication*, and in "Language Where Science and Poetry Meet," *College English*, XXVI (1965), 283-92. Pike's work has attracted less attention than that of Noam Chomsky. Chomsky's achievement is difficult for the nonspecialist to assess; his documentation not infrequently refers to unpublished material, and his later works often drastically modify, even refute, theories and presuppositions presented in his earlier works. Two of his best-known and most influential books are *Syntactic Structures* (The Hague, 1957) and *Current Issues in Linguistic Theory* (The Hague, 1964).

For the literary scholar I should recommend as the most persuasive introduction to the joys of transformationalism Richard Ohmann's "Generative Grammars and the Concept of Literary Style," *Word*, XX (1964), 423-29, and the same author's essay "A Linguistic Appraisal of Victorian Style" along with the excellent companion piece by Norman N.

Holland, "Prose and Minds: A Psychoanalytic Approach to Non-Fiction," in *The Art of Victorian Prose*, edited by George Levine and William Madden (London, 1968).

Among relevant works which literary scholars might overlook, I should mention especially Seymour B. Chatman, "Linguistic Style, Literary Style and Performance: Some Distinctions," *Georgetown Monographs*, XIII (1962), 73-81, and "On the Theory of Literary Style," *Linguistics*, XXVII (1966), 13-25; Vernon Lee (Violet Paget), *The Handling of Words and Other Studies in Literary Psychology* (New York, 1923), a genuinely pioneering work; Thomas A. Sebeok, editor, *Style in Language* (Cambridge, Mass., 1960), a valuable volume with several useful articles, notably those of John B. Carroll, "Vectors of Prose Style," pages 283-92, and Rulon Wells, "Nominal and Verbal Style," pages 213-20; C. B. Williams, "A Note on the Statistical Analysis of Sentence-Length as a Criterion of Literary Style," *Biometrika*, XXXI (1940), 356-61, and "Statistics as an Aid to Literary Studies," *Science News*, XXIV (1952), 99-106. All of Williams' work is interesting, even for the statistically unsophisticated, but Rander Buch in "A Note on Sentence-Length as a Random Variable" (first published in 1952 and now reprinted, with the first Williams article cited, in the useful *Statistics and Style*, edited by Lubomír Doležel and Richard W. Bailey, New York, 1969, pages 76-80) has raised doubts not merely about the validity of Williams' early findings but also about many other statistical analyses of literary material. I would be the first to admit that until such doubts can be thoroughly dispelled the value (as the basis for literary judgments) of even such crude tabulations as I have compiled is questionable. On the other hand, by doing something rather stupid one can sometimes inspire more intelligent critics to worthwhile endeavors.

IT SEEMS TO ME that most of the fundamental ideas of modern linguistics are explicitly or implicitly brought forth in Ferdinand de Saussure's lectures (which were delivered before the first world war) and that Saussure's work therefore provides an excellent basis for judging the originality and significance of many later linguistically-oriented works, particularly ones that claim theoretical importance. The lectures are also an excellent stylistic touchstone. Saussure exhibits the French gift for expression at its best. Though he frequently deals with complex matters, often paradoxes, he is unfailingly precise, lucid, succinct.

Interestingly, the *Course in General Linguistics* was not written by Saussure. It was compiled by his disciples from the notebooks of students in the courses he presented. I do not wish to detract from the excellence of the work of the editors, but I think the remarkable *form* of Saussure's work deserves thought. His fundamental distinction was between *langue* and *parole*, "language" and "speaking." Upon that distinction rests a large portion of subsequent linguistic work. It is intriguing that the man responsible for this distinction left as his principal testament not a written work but the report of his speaking. I believe that Saussure's clarity and precision and perhaps even the profundity of his thought owes much to the fact that he *talked* about linguistics.

It is a grim thought for the last paragraph of a long book, but I have begun to wonder if the inadequacies of much stylistic criticism may spring from our contemporary tendency to evade the problems posed by the oral definition of stylistic procedures and aims. Critics and linguists alike may have underestimated the value of oral discourse as an intellectual mode especially appropriate to their disciplines. Perhaps only when we can speak gracefully and effectively about written language can we hope to capture in our descriptions the vitality intrinsic to all significant language forms.

APPENDIX OF TABULATIONS

TABLE II-1

Words referring to parts of the body
and bodily movement

Novelist	Novels sampled	Total nouns in sample	Nouns referring to parts of body	Ratio
Austen	*Northanger Abbey*	539	28	.05
	Sense & Sensibility	267	2	.01
	Mansfield Park	198	12	.06
	Emma	591	18	.03
	Persuasion	791	19	.02
	Total	2386	79	.03
Dickens	*Oliver Twist*	591	53	.09
	David Copperfield	425	69	.16
	Bleak House	171	19	.11
	Great Expectations	412	91	.22
	Our Mutual Friend	237	35	.15
	Total	1836	267	.15
Brontë	*The Professor*	169	25	.15
	Jane Eyre	124	32	.26
	Shirley	252	28	.11
	Villette	447	52	.12
	Total	992	137	.14
Eliot	*Adam Bede*	443	19	.04
	Mill on the Floss	363	39	.11
	Silas Marner	506	48	.09
	Romola	214	22	.10
	Middlemarch	397	10	.13
	Daniel Deronda	348	41	.12
	Total	2271	179	.08

TABLE II-1 (continued)

Novelist	Novels sampled	Total verbs in sample	Verbs of bodily movement	Ratio
Austen	5	2032	13	.006
Dickens	5	3106	78	.025
Brontë	4	1487	30	.020
Eliot	7	2537	38	.015

TABLE II-2

Words referring to parts of the body

Novelist	Novels sampled	Total nouns in sample	Nouns referring to parts of body	Ratio
Richardson	*Pamela*	285	11	.04
Fielding	*Tom Jones*	454	17	.04
Lawrence	*Sons and Lovers*	460	68	.15
Woolf	*Jacob's Room*	991	106	.11

TABLE II-3

"Abstract" nouns

Novelist	Novels sampled	Total nouns in samples	Selected nouns	Sample in which noun occurs	Occurrences
Austen	7*	2427	feelings	7	26
			love	7	24
			spirits	7	23
			happiness	7	17
			manners	7	17
			visit	6	13
			attention	6	12
			pleasure	6	10
			account	6	9
			connection	6	7
			sensibility	6	7
			beauty	5	7
			journey	5	7
					179

TABLE II-3 (continued)

Novelist	Novels sampled	Total nouns in samples	Selected nouns	Sample in which noun occurs	Occurrences
Dickens	5	1673	manner	4	9
			look	4	8
			influence	4	6
			course	3	7
			death	3	7
			nothing	3	5
			point	3	4
			matter	3	4
			silence	3	4
					54
Brontë	5*	1270	love	3	12
			nature	3	8
			degree	3	7
			taste	3	5
					32
Eliot	7	2327	sense	7	17
			feelings	6	14
			love	6	13
			pleasure	5	15
			opinion	5	14
			presense	5	11
			experience	5	10
			consciousness	5	9
					103

---

* In this count Brontë's "fifth" novel is her juvenile work *The Spell,* and Austen's "seventh" novel is *Lady Susan.*

TABLE II-4

Verbs representing "psychic" action

Novelists using word	Verb	Austen	Eliot	Dickens	Bronte
All four	believe	5/11*	3/8	4/7	3/7
Three	hope	5/13	4/5		3/4
	know	4/8		4/6	3/4
	like	3/7	4/12	4/9	
Two	mean	3/9	3/6		
One	mind		3/4		
	love			5/16	
	learn			3/4	
	wonder			3/4	
	forget			3/4	
	care				3/6
	dare				3/4
	desire				3/4
	doubt				3/4
	suffer				3/4

TABLE II-5

Descriptive adjectives

Novelist	Novels sampled	Total adjectives in sample	Selected adjectives	Samples in which adjective occurs	Occurrences
Austen	8	2084	dear	7	38
			sure	7	35
			happy	7	33
			handsome	6	16
			agreeable	6	11
			amiable	6	9
					142

*These figures are based on a common base of approximately 350 words from five samples for each novelist. The number before the slash indicates the number of samples in which the word occurs; and the number after the slash, the total number of occurrences.

TABLE II-5 (continued)

Novelist	Novels sampled	Total adjectives in sample	Selected adjectives	Samples in which adjective occurs	Occur-rences
Dickens	5	1035	strong	5	11
			dark	5	9
			sure	4	11
			hard	4	9
			open	4	7
			general	4	7
			blue	4	7
			usual	4	7
			cold	4	6
			quiet	4	6
			afraid	4	6
			dear	3	9
			beautiful	3	7
			different	3	6
			heavy	3	6
			mysterious	3	6
			natural	3	6
			pale	3	6
					132
Brontë	5	885	human	5	11
			strange	5	9
			true	5	7
			white	5	6
			calm	4	6
			strong	4	6
			quiet	4	5
			cold	3	7
			dim	3	7
			wild	3	6
					70
Eliot	7	1747	strong	5	11
			painful	5	10
			fine	4	12
			ready	4	10
			true	4	8
			human	4	7
					58

213

TABLE II-6

Simple adverbs ending in "-ly"
answering the question "how?"

Novelist	Novels sampled	Total nouns in samples	Selected nouns	Sample in which noun occurs	Occurrences
Austen	5	741	hardly	4	9
			entirely	4	6
			merely	4	4
			scarcely	3	8
			directly	3	7
			equally	3	7
			perfectly	3	7
			happily	3	5
			heartily	3	5
			particularly	3	4
			properly	3	4
			absolutely	3	3
			comfortably	3	3
			easily	3	3
			evidently	3	3
			exceedingly	3	3
			instantly	3	3
			nearly	3	3
			separately	3	3
			warmly	3	3
					93
Dickens *	5	716	suddenly	4	7
			slowly	4	6
					13
Brontë * *	5	417	wildly	3	6
					6
Eliot	6	587	simply	5	5
			hardly	3	7
			gradually	3	4
			quickly	3	4
			alternately	3	3
			chiefly	3	3
			evidently	3	3
			thoroughly	3	3
					32

* "Scarcely" appears five times in two samples and "faintly" four times in two samples; all other adverbs appear in one sample only.

** "Hardly" appears five times in two samples, "especially" and "nearly" three times in two samples; all other adverbs in one sample only. apper

Tabulations for Chapter Nine

The abbreviations used in the left-hand column in each table have the following significance:

P = *Persuasion*
E = *Emma*
MP = *Mansfield Park*
PP = *Pride and Prejudice*
SS = *Sense and Sensibility*
NA = *Northanger Abbey*
AC = cumulative figures for Austen's six major novels

V = *Villette*
S = *Shirley*
JE = *Jane Eyre*
P₁ = *The Professor*
BS = cumulative figures for Brontë's four major novels

DD = *Daniel Deronda*
MM = *Middlemarch*
FH = *Felix Holt*
R = *Romola*
SM = *Silas Marner*
MF = *The Mill on the Floss*
AB = *Adam Bede*
EC = cumulative figures for Eliot's seven major novels

As indicated at the beginning of Chapter Nine, four elements were discriminated: Time, Action, Setting, and Character. For each element sheets of graph paper containing thirty-five vertical columns and fifty horizontal rows were prepared by numbering the left-hand margin so that each horizontal row of the graph paper would correspond with a page in the novel to be analyzed and each column would represent an item of information about the element being studied.

The simplest way to describe our procedure is to reproduce the core of instructions which we devised for each element to be sure that each of us was operating in the same fashion. It is obvious, however, that the instructions leave a good deal of room for subjective judgment (as well as simple error). I wanted to find out something about how subjective judgments functioned in the analysis of fiction. Altogether a dozen people marked two or more novels, and some novels were marked twice, independently by different people. In the long run the most interesting feature of this work may well be what it reveals about individual variations in response to fiction. The core of the instructions for marking each element follows.

Setting or Location

Number the columns consecutively. In column 1 write vertically "indefinite" and in column 2, "negative." Together these columns constitute "indeterminate" setting; for the distinction between "indefinite" and "negative," see instruction on Time. Each column after 2 will be used to identify each separate location or setting that occurs in the novel in the order in which it occurs. Identify each location by writing a descriptive name in the appropriate column vertically.

Character

The procedure for marking Location is used for Character. The character name, written vertically in the appropriate column, should follow the ordinary mode of address; for example, Sir Walter Elliot. If the character is not identified by name, identify him by means of a descriptive phrase; for example, "man who pours beer on Parson Adams."

216

Mark a 1 instead of an X in the appropriate column if a character is "present" in a scene but not participating, that is, not speaking or not having his actions narrated.

Time

Fifteen columns are needed for marking this element. The columns should be labeled in the following manner:

col. 1: minutes—continuous action   col. 8: indeterminate
     2: hours   9: negative
     3: days   10, 11, 12: "meanwhile"
     4: weeks   13: flashback
     5: months   14: flashforward
     6: years   15: multiple falshbacks
     7: seconds

Columns refer to the amount of time "covered" by the action on the page to which each particular row refers. Several time periods may occur on a single page. For example, a conversation may be followed by a rapid narrative summary of several weeks and this in turn may be followed by narration of a few hours' activities: in this case an X would be placed in columns 1, 2, and 4. Conversation is ordinarily marked as minutes, column 1, unless there is special reason for marking it otherwise. Column 9, negative, is used only when there is no action of the novel-plot itself, as when an author philosophizes (again, in a first-person narrative, however, such philosophizing may not be negative).

Action

Action is marked in the same way as Time, but there are only seven regular categories of action:

col. 1: narration   col. 5: dialogue
     2: description   6: quoted letter, poem,
     3: exposition   etc.
     4: "interiorized"   7: narrative within
                                          narrative

Column 1, narration, is the most commonly marked category, and in many novels is marked for almost every page. If a page is nearly all dialogue, however—except for such bits of narration as "She thoughtfully said. . ."—do not mark narration. The same is true in reverse—if only half a sentence of dialogue appears on a page, do not mark column 5. But, as with Time, markings in more than one column for a page are not uncommon, and in some cases all the Action columns will be marked for a single page. Exposition, column 3, means the comments by an omniscient author (this column is not infrequently marked in George Eliot's novels). Description, column 2, is usually distinguishable from narration, but not infrequently narration and description are intermingled, in which case both columns 1 and 2 should be marked. Column 4, "interiorized," refers to the representation of psychic actions, the thoughts of a character, his soliloquies, and so forth. This column is marked when there is a stream-of-consciousness passage, for example, and also when there is a formal soliloquy presented in quotation marks. Column 6 refers to quotations and also to the reproduction of letters and the like, when the novel is not epistolary in form. Notice that in some cases you will mark both columns 6 and 7, when a long letter tells a story, for example. Column 7 is used for all narratives within narratives, or narratives within narratives within narratives, etc. Again, a mark in column 7 may be accompanied by marks in other columns.

TIME 1

Number of pages, omitting first and last ten, on which passage of time indicated is equal at least to weeks, months, or years

	Weeks	Months	Years
P	3	4	2
E	3	1	0
MP	4	7	0
PP	5	0	0
SS	5	0	0
NA	0	0	0
V	7	4	1
S	15	0	0
JE	23	5	3
Pr	10	1	0
DD	19	9	7
MM	10	2	4
FH	4	1	4
R	4	13	5
SM	1	2	3
MF	4	6	9
AB	10	2	1

TIME 2

Percent of total pages in which some "distortion" of regular temporal order occurs

P	10%
E	5
MP	3
PP	6
SS	12
NA	0
V	4
S	9
JE	5
Pr	17
DD	30
MM	23
FH	8
R	35
SM	32
MF	15
AB	29

TIME 3

Percent of total pages on which continuous action only is marked

AC	56%
BC	64
EC	68

TIME 4

Percent of total pages on which continuous action occurs (other time marks may occur on same page)

P	82%
E	84
MP	76
PP	89
SS	82
NA	83
V	90
S	82
JE	94
Pr	74
DD	82
MM	85
FH	76
R	83
SM	74
MF	81
AB	88

TIME 5

*Percent of pages containing chapter beginnings with longest
span of time as indicated ("indeterminate" = 'longest')*

Author	Chapter beginnings counted		Contin- uous	Hours	Days	Continuous through days	Weeks or more	Indeter- minate
Austen	263	P	14%	18%	18%	50%	5%	45%
		E	37	17	20	74	2	24
		MP	23	25	10	58	2	40
		PP	21	31	16	68	6	26
		SS	42	24	8	74	10	16
		NA	16	19	36	71	0	29
		AC	*28*	*24*	*17*	*69*	*3*	*28*
Brontë	142	V	19	14	31	64	14	22
		S	38	27	7	72	14	14
		JE	24	24	16	64	24	12
		Pr	20	24	16	60	32	8
		BC	*25*	*22*	*18*	*65*	*20*	*15*
Eliot	423	DD	17	10	30	57	4	39
		MM	10	18	9	37	2	61
		FH	17	23	2	42	4	54
		R	22	15	13	50	15	35
		SM	26	26	4	56	9	35
		MF	22	4	15	41	3	56
		AB	23	27	9	59	14	27
		EC	*18*	*16*	*13*	*47*	*8*	*45*

TIME 6

Percent of total pages containing indeterminate time

P	25%
E	16
MP	29
PP	28
SS	12
NA	18
V	16
S	8
JE	8
Pr	7
DD	24
MM	35
FH	26
R	23
SM	25
MF	25
AB	15

SETTING 1

Percent of total pages containing indeterminate settings

P	16%
E	22
MP	17
PP	15
SS	9
NA	9
V	2
S	1
JE	5
Pr	8
DD	25
MM	17
FH	7
R	8
SM	10
MF	7
AB	9

SETTING 2

Percent of shifts in setting coincidental with chapter beginning

P	24%
E	27
MP	40
PP	43
SS	33
NA	29
V	25
S	19
JE	31
Pr	27
DD	57
MM	57
FH	67
R	53
SM	37
MF	56
AB	57

SETTING 3

Percent of shifts in setting with varying degrees of character continuity

	No characters continuing	One character only continues	Two or more characters continue
P	less than 10%	31–40%	51–60%
E	less than 10	31–40	61–70
MP	less than 10	31–40	61–70
PP	less than 10	21–30	71–80
SS	less than 10	21–30	71–80
NA	less than 10	21–30	71–80
V	less than 10	61–70	31–40
S	11–20	71–80	less than 10
JE	less than 10	71–80	21–30
Pr	less than 10	61–70	31–40
DD	11–20	31–40	41–50
MM	21–30	41–50	21–30
FH	41–50	41–50	less than 10
R	21–30	31–40	41–50
SM	31–40	51–60	less than 10
MF	41–50	31–40	21–30
AB	41–50	11–20	31–40

SETTING 4

Percent of setting changes coincident with description

P	18%
E	7
MP	25
PP	17
SS	25
NA	14
V	54
S	56
JE	56
Pr	37
DD	28
MM	48
FH	33
R	53
SM	47
MF	44
AB	31

226

SETTING 5

Type and number of major settings

	Country or outside	Public bldg. urban	Room or special part, private house	Bldg. general	Conveyance	Total
P	3	4	0	8	1	16
E	3	1	0	8	2	14
MP	2	1	1	5	1	10
PP	2	1	0	9	1	13
SS	2	1	0	5	1	9
NA	2	6	4	8	2	22
V	5	9	8	11	4	37
S	7	2	5	8	0	22
JE	8	1	4	6	1	20
PR	6	5	7	10	0	28
DD	6	10	1	10	3	30
MM	4	13	5	13	0	35
FH	2	6	2	8	0	18
R	4	7	5	12	0	28
SM	4	4	0	4	0	12
MF	6	4	4	10	1	25
AB	12	7	5	14	0	38

ACTION 1

*Percent of total pages containing different
kinds of narrative action*

	Description	Exposition	Interiorized narration	Total—only narrative and/or dialogue on other pages
P	7%	9%	26%	42%
E	1	3	23	27
MP	12	4	21	37
PP	6	2	22	30
SS	10	2	24	36
NA	9	6	8	23
V	27	7	26	60
S	23	11	9	43
JE	19	1	31	51
Pr	24	3	14	41
DD	7	14	42	63
MM	12	25	30	67
FH	17	9	16	42
R	16	13	15	44
SM	20	12	12	44
MF	11	15	13	39
AB	14	24	13	51

ACTION 2

Percent of total pages containing dialogue

P	71%
E	79
MP	71
PP	77
SS	73
NA	64
V	62
S	69
JE	69
Pr	48
DD	69
MM	63
FH	63
R	62
SM	61
MF	66
AB	66

ACTION 3

*Percent of pages containing dialogue on which dialogue
constitutes fifty percent or more of the page*

P	44%
E	76
MP	79
PP	68
SS	66
NA	70
V	42
S	58
JE	47
Pr	55
DD	59
MM	62
FH	63
R	64
SM	55
MF	60
AB	66

ACTION 4

*Percent of total pages containing dialogue in conjunction
with other kinds of narrative action*

	Description	Exposition	Interiorized Narration
AC	3.0%	1.0%	10.0%
BC	9.0	2.5	5.0
EC	3.0	6.0	7.5

CHARACTER 1

Characters appearing on at least five percent of total pages of their novel followed by the percent of total pages of novel on which the character appears, and the number of the character's separate appearances.

Persuasion: 18 characters

Anne Elliot 91, 6; Mary Musgrove 39, 14; Captain Wentworth 33, 13; Henrietta Musgrove 25, 13; Charles Musgrove 24, 14; Sir Walter Elliot 19, 18; Louisa Musgrove 18, 11; Mrs. Clay 17, 11; Elizabeth Elliot 17, 14; Mrs. Musgrove 16, 10; William Elliot 14, 12; Lady Russell 12, 13; Mrs. Croft 9, 7; Captain Harville 8, 3; Mrs. Smith 8, 4; Admiral Croft 7, 5; Mr. Musgrove 5, 6; Mr. Shepherd 5, 3.

Emma: 14 characters

Emma Woodhouse 92, 11; Mr. Knightley 32, 31; Harriet Smith 30, 26; Mrs. Weston 28, 32; Mr. Woodhouse 28, 36; Frank Churchill 24, 15; Mrs. Elton 20, 15; Mr. Weston 18, 25; Jane Fairfax 18, 21; Miss Bates 13, 20; Mr. Elton 13, 20; Mr. John Knightley 9, 10; Isabella Knightley 6, 8; Mrs. Bates 6, 8.

Mansfield Park: 17 characters

Fanny Price 84, 26; Edmund Bertram 47, 39; Mary Crawford 34, 22; Henry Crawford 31, 21; Mrs. Norris 27, 29; Sir Thomas Bertram 25, 22; Lady Bertram 19, 29; Maria Bertram 18, 19; Julia Bertram 14, 17; Mr. Rushworth 11, 15; Mrs. Grant 10, 17; Tom Bertram 12, 13; Susan Price 9, 8; William Price 9, 8; Mr. John Yates, 8, 10; Mrs. Price 6, 10; Dr. Grant 6, 16.

Pride and Prejudice: 19 characters

Elizabeth Bennet 95, 12; Jane Bennet 37, 20; Mrs. Bennet 33, 27; Mr. Darcy 32, 13; Mr. Bennet 23, 20; Reverend Mr. Collins 20, 10; Mr. Bingley 19, 13; Mrs. Gardiner 17, 9; Kitty Bennet 15, 19; Lydia Bennet 14, 13; Charlotte Lucas 12, 12; Mr. Gardiner 11, 7; Miss Bingley 11, 8; Mrs. Hurst 11, 7; Lady Catherine de Bourgh 7,5; Mary Bennet, 7,11; Mr. Wickham 7, 6; Mr. Hurst 5, 4; Sir William Lucas 5, 6.

Sense and Sensibility: 15 characters

Elinor Dashwood 84, 16; Marianne Dashwood 50, 36; Mrs. Jennings 27, 33; Mrs. Dashwood 23, 24; Miss Lucy Steele 15, 14; Colonel Brandon 15, 21; Edward Ferrars 14, 11; Mr. Willoughby 13, 11; Mr. John Dashwood 12, 11; Sir John Middleton 9, 17; Miss Anne Steele 8, 9; Lady Middleton 8, 14; Mrs. John Dashwood (Fanny) 7, 9; Mrs. Palmer 6, 8; Margaret Dashwood 5, 9.

Northanger Abbey: 10 characters

Catherine Morland 94, 3; Mr. Henry Tilney 32, 14; Miss Elinor Tilney 28, 14; Isabella Thorpe 21, 15; Mrs. Allen 13, 13; General Tilney 13, 12; John Thorpe 13, 8; James Morland 9, 10; Mrs. Morland 5, 2; Mr. Allen 5, 8.

Villette: 8 characters

Lucy Snowe 100, 1; John Graham Bretton 27, 17; Paul Emanuel Beck 26, 20; Pauline Bassompierre 17, 10; Mrs. Bretton 16, 8; Ginevra Fanshawe 16, 11; Madame Beck 14, 18; Mr. (Home) Bassompierre 5, 7;

Shirley: 10 characters

Caroline Helstone 53, 31; Shirley Keeldar 40, 15; Mr. Robert Moore 25, 25; Mr. Louis Moore 16, 10; Mr. Helstone 15, 24; Mrs. Pryor 12, 15; Mr. Yorke 11, 16; Hortense Moore 7, 14; Mr. Malone 6, 11; Mr. Donne 5, 11.

Jane Eyre: 10 characters

Jane Eyre 100, 1; Edward Fairfax Rochester 38, 15; St. John Rivers 17, 8; Miss Fairfax 10, 10; Adele Varens 10, 13; Diana Rivers 8, 9; Mary Rivers 7, 9; Blanche Ingraham 5, 5; Helen Burns 5, 5; Mrs. Reed 5, 7.

The Professor: 6 characters

William Crimsworth 100, 1; Frances Henri 26, 13; Henry Hunsden 19, 7; Mlle. Reuter 13, 7; M. Pelet 8, 5; Edward Crimsworth 7, 4;

Daniel Deronda: 14 characters

Daniel Deronda 50, 25; Gwendolen Harleth 47, 24; Henleigh Grandcourt 20, 24; Mirah Lapidoth 17, 20; Mrs. Davilow 15, 32; Mordecai Lapidoth 14, 19; Sir Hugo Mallinger 10, 18; Mrs. Meyrick 8,

12; Herr Klesmer 8, 11; Reverend Gascoigne 7, 18; Hans Meyrick 6, 9; Mrs. Gascoigne 5, 13; Rex Gascoigne 5, 5; Thomas Lush 5, 10.

Middlemarch: 16 characters

Dorothea Brooke 33, 16; Tertius Lydgate 29, 31; Rosamond Vincy 19, 27; Will Ladislaw 16, 20; Fred Vincy 14, 18; Mr. Brooke 13, 25; Mr. Casaubon 13, 19; Mr. Bulstrode 12, 14; Celia Brooke 10, 16; Mary Garth 10, 13; Sir James Chettam 9, 21; Mr. Farebrother 8, 16; Caleb Garth 7, 10; Mr. Vincy 6, 16; Mrs. Vincy 5, 14; Mrs. Garth 5, 9.

Felix Holt: 9 characters

Esther Lyon 35, 16; Harold Transome 28, 14; Rev. Rufus Lyon 27, 18; Felix Holt 26, 15; Mrs. Transome 18, 17; Mr. Jerymn 16, 14; Maurice Christian (Henry Scadden) 15, 11; Mrs. Holt 7, 10; Mr. Johnson 6, 8.

Romola: 13 characters

Tito Melema 68, 40; Romola 52, 35; Savanarola 31, 45; Baldassare 19, 33; Bardo Bardi 18, 29; Tessa 16, 20; Nello 13, 14; Bernardo del Nero 11, 33; Cugina Brigida 9, 14; Fra Luca 8, 21; Piero di Cosimo 7, 21; Lillo 6, 11; Bratti 5, 10.

Silas Marner: 13 characters

Silas Marner 49, 14; Godfrey Cass 34, 13; Eppie 27, 7; Nancy Lammeter 25, 6; Dolly Winthrop 14, 8; Squire Cass 12, 8; Mr. Macey 11, 6; John Snell 8, 4; Dunstan Cass 8, 3; Aaron Winthrop 7, 4; Mr. Crackenthorp 6, 4; Priscilla Lammeter 5, 4; Dr. Kimble 5, 4.

The Mill on the Floss: 12 characters

Maggie Tulliver 41, 30; Tom Tulliver 26, 24; Mrs. Tulliver 16, 24; Mr. Tulliver 14, 19; Lucy Deane 11, 13; Philip Wakem 10, 11; Stephen Guest 10, 8; Mrs. Glegg 9, 6; Bob Jakin 7, 8; Mrs. Pullet 7, 9; Mr. Glegg 6, 6; Mr. Deane 5, 6.

Adam Bede: 10 characters

Adam Bede 49, 32; Hetty Sorrel 29, 31; Dinah Morris 22, 18; Arthur Donnithorne 20, 16; Mrs. Poyser 20, 30; Mr. Irwine 18, 18; Martin Poyser 17, 27; Seth Bede 12, 27; Lisbeth Bede 11, 16; Bartle Massey 8, 14.

CHARACTER 2

How characters in similar roles appear on equivalent percents
of total pages in Jane Austen's novels

Role	Character	Percent of total pages on which character appears
Heroine	Catherine Morland	94%
	Elinor Dashwood Marianne	91
	Elizabeth Bennet	95
	Fanny Price	84
	Emma Woodhouse	92
	Anne Elliot	91
Male	Henry Tilney	32
Protagonist	Edward Ferrars Col. Brandon	29
	Fitzwilliam Darcy	32
	Edmund Bertram	47
	Mr. Knightley	32
	Capt. Wentworth	33
Other man	John Thorpe	13
	Willoughby	13
	Mr. Collins Wickham	27
	Henry Crawford	31
	Frank Churchill	24
	William Elliot	14
Other women	Isabella Thorpe	21
	Lucy Steele	15
	Caroline Bingley	11
	Mary Crawford	34
	Jane Fairfax	18
	Louisa Musgrove	18

CHARACTER 3

*Number of characters appearing on at least
two percent of total pages of each novel*

P	24
E	18
MP	20
PP	28
SS	19
NA	17
V	17
S	26
JE	32
Pr	21
DD	33
MM	52
FH	36
R	29
SM	29
MF	27
AB	36

CHARACTER 4

Estimated total number of characters in each novel

P	39
E	33
MP	32
PP	44
SS	38
NA	27
V	70
S	66
JE	57
Pr	39
DD	71
MM	103
FH	76
R	103
SM	42
MF	69
AB	99

CHARACTER 5

Average number of characters per page of novel
(counting characters from Character 3)

P	3.9
E	3.5
MP	3.8
PP	4.0
SS	3.0
NA	3.1
V	2.5
S	2.3
JE	2.5
Pr	2.0
DD	2.6
MM	2.8
FH	2.6
R	3.0
SM	2.5
MF	2.7
AB	3.0

CHARACTER 6

*Percent of total pages on which varying numbers of
characters appear (counting characters from Character 3)*

	1 character only	2 characters	1 or 2 characters	4 or more characters
P	6%	30%	36%	57%
E	5	31	36	41
MP	5	26	31	45
PP	6	23	29	54
SS	3	41	44	38
NA	11	22	33	35
V	24	38	62	22
S	17	50	67	11
JE	12	47	59	22
Pr	28	54	82	3
DD	11	46	57	22
MM	14	40	54	24
FH	15	44	59	16
R	12	24	36	35
SM	19	37	56	22
MF	12	43	55	22
AB	19	36	55	29

The following figures, which supplement those discussed in Chapter Nine, are intended to show that even such scattered, crude results (which are doubtless "inaccurate" in more than one fashion) support generally accepted ideas of the development of the novel from the eighteenth to the twentieth centuries. That the figures provide no startling revelations is encouraging, because relatively "objective" measures ought to be means of refining our subjective impressions—not of overturning them. Indeed, measures which controvert established views of formal developments in fiction must be strongly suspect. Where the figures confirm our subjective impressions they may provide points of entry into meaningful criticism. For instance, if one considers Jane Austen a "novelist of manners," the figures we have compiled for characters might be useful in confirming that judgment and explaining its value. My figures show that she characteristically presents the reader with an unusually large "cast" of major characters who move in and out of the central focus of the action with remarkable freedom. She designs her novels, one might say, so that there are many opportunities for manners to be displayed. And, as I have suggested, it is the density of social interrelations in her novels which permits her to discriminate her characters in the fashion which distinguishes her art from that of other novelists of manners.

That the value of such compilations of figures depends upon our having available comparable analyses of several novels by each author is made plain by a comparison of the following tables with the material presented in Chapter Nine. It is certainly difficult to define the relation between changes in verbal devices and changes in total design unless one can trace developments in both cases. For this reason no sweeping conclusions can be derived from the following figures. It is obvious, too, that our methods of analysis must be sharpened. To devise appropriate and adequate refinements, to apply them broadly, and to describe the results would require a study as large and time consuming as the one elaborated in this book. We need, I feel, not so much to eliminate subjective factors in analysis (what constitutes "interiorized" action, description, etc.) as to develop means of more accurately classifying subjective choices. A practical, mathematical difficulty is that of establishing a unit other than the page as the basis of

239

comparison. And, as I have already pointed out, only when we analyze large portions of a given author's work do we escape "distortions" introduced by the fact that each work of fiction is a unique entity whose uniqueness is the chief characteristic of its artistry.

An interesting aspect of the following figures is that they appear to point toward stylistic distinctions between eighteenth-century, nineteenth-century, and modern fiction. Simultaneously, even these few figures illustrate that no novel can be adequately defined by such broad categories. If we contrast the group of eighteenth-century novels with the group from the twentieth century, recognizing that some of the works are deliberately inventive in form and that several pose controversial problems for the marker, we can discern some patterns of differentiation. As a rule there is, as we would expect, more indeterminate time in the eighteenth-century group. This raises a point about the reader's relation to fiction: in both the eighteenth and twentieth centuries a reader is forced to make temporal shifts mentally—but the shifts are of different kinds (see Table IX-A).

That there is not a relatively higher proportion of indeterminate locations in the eighteenth-century group (perhaps expectable in the light of some of these novelists' fondness for authorial exposition) emphasizes the significance of the large number of identifiable locations in these novels. More refined analyses contrasting ways of identifying locations would, I think, be quite rewarding. One observes that, although the modern group uses less exposition and rates significantly higher in the category of "interiorized" action, the moderns also use more description. Even allowing for subjective discrepancies introduced by the markers, the figures are striking enough to focus attention on something which is occasionally forgotten—that modern fiction simultaneously stresses interiority and immediate exteriority. And the proportion of dialogue in both eighteenth-century novels and modern novels is distinctively lower than that in the nineteenth-century novels. The broad development of British fiction seems to be from eighteenth-century expositional narration through nineteenth-century expositional dramatization to modern interiorized description.

The numbers of major characters in each novel run parallel in the eighteenth-century and modern groups (although this means that the eighteenth-century major casts are smaller in proportion to the size of the novels in which they appear) and below the nineteenth-century average. Of course the eighteenth-century novels tend to have larger "casts" of secondary and tertiary characters. The character-per-page averages are in general higher for the earlier group, though they do not reach the extremes of Austen and Dickens, doubtless because the eighteenth-century novelists utilize tertiary figures more fully. The percentages for pages on which one character only appears are higher for the modern group, but the eighteenth-century figures are perhaps surprisingly high. The moderns, however, are distinctly "ahead" in the two-character-a-page category and "behind" in the four-or-more category. It seems fair to speculate that an important aspect of the dramatic quality of modern fiction lies in its emphasis on two-person confrontations—in this respect Charlotte Brontë's fiction is a kind of prototype of modern developments, as is its stress on "impressions."

There is one generalization derived from these figures which I should like to propose. Granted that there is a tendency for novels of the same general "kind" to reveal similar patterns regardless of chronology—for example, *Roderick Random* and *The Power and The Glory* are in some respects closer to one another than to their "contemporaries"—it strikes me that there is an underlying movement toward increased repetition in fictional style from the eighteenth to the twentieth century. To cite one observation not indicated by the figures, all eighteenth-century novels contain a considerable number of characters who appear only once. Such single appearances are relatively rare in modern novels, with nineteenth-century novels about midway between the extremes. The tendency toward repetition is discernible in the handling of time and space, too. Repetition is clearly germane to the development of "the novel as poem," the tendency of novels to become shorter and to be organized increasingly by image patterns, recurrent metaphors, and verbal leitmotifs. I suspect one might even be able to detect increasing emphasis on repeated syntactic structures—or nonstructures. In other words, the modern novel tends to be horizontally structured—the "three-decker" and serial publication being obtrusive symptoms of nineteenth-century "verticality." It is notable, too, that the typical contemporary critic of fiction seeks out recurrent items whereas the typical nineteenth-century critic of fiction calls attention to scenes, characters, and actions in themselves. And it does not seem to me far-fetched to suggest that such differences in total form and in reader-response point to significant shifts in the social functions of fiction.

241

If my hypothesis is valid, it points up fiction's increasing stress on "pattern"—as distinct from "life" in Arnold Kettle's formulation of an old and continuing fictional problem—because repetition means patterning. The so-called "vitality" of the earlier novel (a function of its "verticality") simply cannot exist in the forms of modern fiction. I am not arguing for life against pattern or vice-versa. Instead, I'm interested in the possibility that if, as I have suggested earlier, fictional structures are partly determined by the "sociological position" of the author in relation to his readers, continued study of structure will lead to definitions of fictional style dependent in some measure on a placement of works in their sociopolitical context. It is plain that many of the refinements needed to make my figures meaningful would require delineation of "historical" elements to which the novels refer—for example, what social types predominate among characters. In other words, a continued pressing toward formal descriptions may carry us rapidly, rather than slowly, back to increased concern with the role of fictional prose in the larger life of society. But we shall be seeking the profounder rather than the more superficial aspects of that role. The specific issues which agitated Dickens, for example, a century ago simply cannot be revitalized for us. But his social involvement and the involvement of his art, through the forms which specific issues take in his fiction, may become increasingly important to us, even as students of style.

Because I have included figures for four of Dickens' novels, it is possible to make a few special comments on patterns discernible in his work. The figures show that Dickens did not utilize serial publication to spread out the time of his action; his temporal ordering stays within the general limits we find in Brontë's and Eliot's fiction. It is interesting, too, that Dickens employs considerable time distortion, but within these distortions he uses more continuous action than the three authors who are the main focus of this study. Like Charlotte Brontë, Dickens uses relatively little indeterminate time, and about twenty percent of his indeterminate time occurs without other time indicators. Dickens is also close to Brontë in his infrequent use of indeterminate settings.

There is no doubt that Dickens favors description, but the proportion of his pages containing dialogue is greater than that of any other author studied. The combination of a great deal of description with a great deal of dialogue appears to delineate the broad outline of his fictional style as a kind of descriptive dramatization. The convergence of Jane Austen and Dickens in their preference for dialogue is sustained by some characteristics of their preferences for characters on stage. Dickens' average number of characters-per-page runs close to the figures for Austen, and his liking for crowded scenes, with a complementary de-emphasis on single-figure scenes, parallels hers. Like Austen, too, he uses a large number of major characters. These similarities are specially interesting because Dickens' and Austen's fiction differ in so many obvious ways.

TABLE IX—A

Time

Percent of total pages marked with:

Novel	Time distortion	Indeter- minate time	Indeter- minate time only	Day	Week, month, year*	Continuous time
Moll Flanders	4	51	13	16	12	74
Pamela	0	34	10	10	1	89
Joseph Andrews	11	14	9	3	1	87
Tom Jones	24	25	13	1	0	84
Roderick Random	0	17	14	24	5	93
Tristram Shandy	18	70	40	4	4	51
Old Mortality	6	3	2	1	1	82
Rob Roy	2	7	6	3	2	79
Vanity Fair	32	53	23	10	8	60
Oliver Twist	22	14	2	4	2	93
David Copperfield	6	22	5	4	6	91
Great Expectations	8	15	4	3	2	91
Our Mutual Friend	27	17	3	2	1	95
Nostromo	43	30	4	2	4	71
The Ambassadors	2	22	11	5	1	83
Sons and Lovers	12	26	3	8	12	89
Women in Love	4	13	3	3	2	88
Mrs. Dalloway	26	8	4	0	2	90
Absalom, Absalom!	91	52	28	2	24	42
The Power and the Glory	13	3	0	1	0	93

*The first and last ten pages of each novel were excluded from this count.

TABLE IX–B

Location and Action

Percent of total pages marked with:

Novel	Total number of locations	Indefinite location	Description	Exposition	Interiorized action	Dialogu
Moll Flanders	64	10	3	21	1	40
Pamela	22	3	1	2	24	70
Joseph Andrews	28	8	7	37	6	62
Tom Jones	36	11	6	24	8	62
Roderick Random	98	4	6	5	1	58
Tristram Shandy	13	54	9	55	0	41
Old Mortality	28	2	12	5	4	62
Rob Roy	23	3	9	4	2	60
Vanity Fair	29	11	24	24	4	66
Oliver Twist	33	3	31	13	8	88
David Copperfield	42	8	18	10	9	85
Great Expectations	27	6	25	3	16	79
Our Mutual Friend	30	5	38	4	10	86
Nostromo	18	9	17	3	12	62
The Ambassadors	11	3	18	7	18	67
Sons and Lovers	25	5	25	5	10	81
Women in Love	17	8	16	8	17	75
Mrs. Dalloway	10	13	16	4	53	31
Absalom, Absalom!	13	17	12	1	18	86
The Power and the Glory	27	0	25	0	30	78

TABLE IX–C
Character

Novel	Number chars. appear 5% pp.	Number chars. appear 2% pp.	Total number chars.	Average chars. (2%) per p.	% pp. with 1 char. only	% pp. with 2 chars.	% pp. with 4 or more chars.
ll Flanders	4	32	130	2.3	23%	49%	18%
nela	12	35	64	2.8	14	38	24
eph Andrews	12	42	103	2.9	8	27	28
m Jones	11	62	156	2.5	4	31	22
derick Random	9	50	278	2.9	12	39	26
stram Shandy	6	30	63	2.6	35	14	33
l Mortality	14	45	64	2.8	9	37	28
b Roy	12	26	54	2.7	6	38	22
nity Fair	17	56	190	2.8	9	29	31
ver Twist	17	44	78	3.2	5	31	32
vid Copperfield	21	65	104	3.6	5	22	46
eat Expectations	13	48	71	3.2	5	37	31
r Mutual Friend	25	35	127	3.2	5	41	29
stromo	11	35	69	2.1	28	47	11
e Ambassadors	7	12	26	2.2	14	62	11
ns and Lovers	10	32	71	2.5	20	47	17
men in Love	10	26	74	2.6	10	50	22
s. Dalloway	10	23	58	1.9	40	38	8
salom, Absalom!	13	20	44	2.3	22	46	14
e Power and the Glory	11	25	97	2.2	17	54	6

Tabulations for Chapter Eleven

TABLE XI–1

	Emma	Villette	Middlemarch
Total number of sentences	672	439	488
Total number of words	10,576	8,847	11,876
Average sentence length	15.5	19.2	24.2
Narrative			
Number of sentences	166	266	219
Number of words	3,714	6,259	6,940
Average sentence length	22.4	23.6	31.7
Dialogue			
Number of sentences	438	112	180
Number of words	5,525	1,193	2,934
Average sentence length	12.6	10.7	16.3
Mixed (Both dialogue and narrative)			
Number of sentences	68	61	89
Number of words narrative	494	635	1,110
Number of words dialogue	843	760	892
Total number of words	1,337	1,395	2,002
Average sentence length	19.7	22.5	22.5

TABLE XI–2

	Emma	*Villette*	*Middlemarch*
Length of dialogue sentences relative to narrative	.56	.45	.52
Length of "mixed" sentences relative to narrative	.88	.96	.71
Length of dialogue sentences relative to mixed	.64	.48	.73

TABLE XI–3

	Emma	*Villette*	*Middlemarch*
Narrative Sentences			
Number of groups of 10 or more successive sentences	6	4	6
Percent of all narrative sentences in foregoing groups	50%	26%	72%
Dialogue Sentences			
Number of groups of 10 or more successive sentences	18	7	11
Percent of all dialogue sentences in foregoing groups	81%	48%	77%

TABLE XI–4

	Number of sentences		
	Emma	*Villette*	*Middlemarch*
Variation in number of words between successive dialogue sentences			
0–4	57	16	25
5–9	31	12	26
10–14	21	10	18
15–19	4	2	12
20–24	1	1	7
25–29	1	1	6
30 or more	1	2	7
Total successive dialogue sentences	116	44	101

TABLE XI–5

	Number of sentences		
	Emma	*Villette*	*Middlemarch*
Variation in number of words between successive dialogue sentences in which speaker changes			
0–4	15	16	3
5–9	7	12	6
10–14	7	10	4
15–19	1	2	1
20–24	1	1	0
25–29	0	1	1
30 or more	0	2	3
Total number of dialogue sentences in which speaker changes	31	44	18
Number of mixed sentences in which speaker changes	16	15	48
Total number of changes in speaker	47	59	66

TABLE XI–6

Mixed Sentences	Emma	Villette	Middlemarch
Total number of mixed sentences	68	61	89
Percent of total sentences	10%	14%	18%
Percent of words narrative	36%	45%	56%
Percent of words dialogue	64%	55%	44%
Percent of all sentences which contain dialogue	13%	35%	33%
Number in which narrative portion contains more than 9 words	14(21%)	11(18%)	45(51%)
Number in which words in dialogue exceed narrative	51(75%)	39(64%)	42(47%)
Number in which dialogue exceeds narrative at least four times	25(37%)	18(30%)	13(15%)
Number in which narrative exceeds dialogue at least four times	4(6%)	10(16%)	72(81%)
Number with 1 part narrative & 1 dialogue (2-element sentences)	29(43%)	32(52%)	62(81%)
Number of 2-element sentences beginning with narrative	17	7	12
Number with three or more elements (3-element sentences)	39(57%)	29(48%)	17(19%)

TABLE XI–7

Percent of successive narrative sentences

Variation in length of successive narrative sentences	Percent of successive narrative sentences					
	Samplings			Passages		
	Austen	Brontë	Eliot	Austen	Brontë	Eliot
Less than 10 words	30%	51%	27%	46%	44%	35%
More than 30	15	11	17	24	16	19
More than 50	15	4	6	11	5	6

TABLE XI–8

Number of successive dialogue sentences

Variation in length of successive dialogue sentences	Samplings			Passages		
	Austen	Brontë	Eliot	Austen	Brontë	Eliot
0–4 words	37	32	14	57	16	25
5–9	25	21	16	31	12	26
10–14	22	14	13	21	10	18
15–19	11	1	8	4	2	12
20–24	11	9	6	1	1	7
25–29	8	8	4	1	1	6
30 or more	5	11	11	1	2	7

TABLE XI–9

Number of sentences

Variation in length of dialogue sentences in which speaker changes	Samplings			Passages		
	Austen	Brontë	Eliot	Austen	Brontë	Eliot
0–4 words	8	34	2	15	16	3
5–9	14	22	0	7	12	6
10–14	12	10	2	7	10	4
15–19	4	6	0	1	2	1
20–24	4	10	2	1	1	0
25–29	0	0	0	0	1	1
30 or more	4	10	0	0	2	3
Total number of dialogue sentences in which speaker changes	46	92	6	31	44	18
Number of mixed sentences in which speaker changes	52	6	54	16	15	48
Total changes of speaker	98	98	60	47	59	66

TABLE XI–10

Average number of sentences containing
dialogue per speaker change

	Samplings	Passages
Austen	3.5	3.9
Brontë	2.3	2.1
Eliot	3.0	2.8

TABLE XI–11

Number of changes per major speaker

	Samplings	Passages
Austen	15	14
Brontë	23	20
Eliot	11	9

TABLE XI–12

Average number of words per sentence

	Samplings			Passages		
	Narrative	Dialogue	Mixed	Narrative	Dialogue	Mixed
Austen	31.5	15.3	25.7	22.4	12.6	19.7
Brontë	23.4	15.8	22.5	23.6	10.7	22.5
Eliot	32.6	17.5	23.6	31.7	16.3	22.5

TABLE XI–13

	Number of descriptive, expository, interiorized sentences	Ratio of descriptive, etc., sentences to pure narrative sentences	Average length of descriptive, etc., sentences (in words)	Ratio of average length of narrative sentences to average length of descriptive etc., sentences
Austen	78	.14	36.2	.87
Brontë	51	.15	24.6	.95
Eliot	123	.29	34.7	.94

TABLE XI–14

	Samplings		Passages	
	Proportion of mixed sentences to total number of sentences	Proportion mixed sentences to pure dialogue sentences	Proportion of mixed sentences to total number of sentences	Proportion mixed sentences to pure dialogue sentences
Austen	.09	.20	.11	.16
Brontë	.10	.24	.16	.54
Eliot	.16	.45	.22	.49

TABLE XI–15

	Samplings			Passages		
	Austen	Brontë	Eliot	Austen	Brontë	Eliot
Proportion of average sentence lengths						
Dialogue to narrative	.49	.68	.54	.56	.45	.52
Mixed to narrative	.82	.96	.72	.88	.96	.71
Dialogue to mixed	.60	.70	.74	.64	.48	.73
Percent of mixed sentences containing 3 elements	51%	42%	15%	57%	48%	19%
Percent of mixed sentences containing 2 elements	49%	58%	85%	43%	52%	81%

FIGURES COMPILED FOR PARTS OF SPEECH

I have tried to make clear in this book why it is that quantitative compilations of the parts of novels can be of only minor use to the historian of fictional style. But because there have been few quantitative studies of fiction, we possess very little information which would enable us to test new methods of analysis and description which might enrich existing critical techniques. I present the figures which follow primarily to help plug this informational gap. Yet at least two observations about the figures suggest the possibility that they may have further relevance. In the first place, my figures are mere compilations. Statistical analyses of this material might well open up some new critical pathways. This potential ought not to be ignored, because the compilations indubitably reveal marked variations between the different novelists. This leads to the observation that the difficulty in making quantitative studies of fiction is not in compiling enough information to discover differences but in compiling enough information to define the significance of differences. Most statisticians and students of stylistics who have dealt with prose have assumed that approximately 10,000 *words* is an adequate base, and 10,000 words may be an adequate base for attribution and authorship studies. For studies of fictional prose, an adequate base, I estimate, is a minimum of 10,000 *sentences* per novelist. If my estimate is sound, quantitative studies of fictional prose will require the assistance of electronic computers. Although my own experiments with using a computer were not efficient, my experience has convinced me that computers can be used economically and effectively to assist in this work.

The basis used for the marking of grammatical features was traditional, "analytical" grammar, most of the distinctions in our system being based on the well-known handbook of Porter Perrin, at the time of our marking a required text for freshman English at the University of Wisconsin. We used traditional grammar for several reasons, one of which is implied by the conclusion of the preceding sentence: traditional grammar was familiar to all of the markers. It was closest to the grammar known by the novelists studied. Some of the systems developed by modern linguists were attractive, but they were not as well known, and most of them are still the subject of controversy and are undergoing processess of modification and refinement. In any

255

event, the particular system of marking used seemed to me less important than the fact that it should be easily comprehensible. Anyone who has had a high-school course in either grammar or composition can understand the distinctions of our system.

The process of marking was as follows. The text to be marked was typed on prepared sheets in columnar form, one word or mark of punctuation per line. The marker then indicated, by a numerical code in the proper column, information (part of speech, sentence type, kind of clause, etc.) about the item on each line.

The figures reported below represent only a part of the total compiled. For the reported figures most of the distinctions are self-evident and, as indicated above, follow Perrin's classifications. Thus, for example, the distinctions between concrete, abstract, and proper nouns follow the definitions on pages 652-53 of Porter Perrin, *Writer's Guide and Index to English,* revised edition (Chicago, New York, etc.: Scott, Foresman and Company, 1950). A few special selections and classifications we used require mention.

We distinguished between verbs of "physical action," (including gestures, movements, etc.) and those of "psychic action" (for example, "thinking," "wishing"). A third category, "other," was marked, unless a "physical" or a "psychic" action classification was obvious and clear. It is noteworthy that this third, catch-all category of an admittedly subjective classification system produced some useful results: Jane Austen regularly scored high with "other" verbs.

Although we distinguished separate tenses in our study, the figures reported below are categorized by three general groupings we also employed. "Simple" verbs include those occurring in the indicative of the present, past, future, and present-, past-, and future-perfect tenses. "Progressive" verbs represent continuing indicative action in the six tenses just cited. We included the emphatic forms involving some form of "do" in the progressive group. What we called "modal" verbs included all subjunctive and conditional forms.

Finally, in the word counts reported below multiword verbs were never counted as more than two words, regardless of the number of auxiliaries involved. Thus both "am going" and "have been going" were counted as two words. Analogously, the "to" in an infinitive construction was disregarded in counting verbals.

Our adjective classifications follow Perrin (pages 417-18), although we introduced some further distinctions, such as dividing "descriptive" adjectives into those of measure (or degree) and those of quality: a *huge* tree as opposed to a *green* tree. We also distinguished among limiting adjectives the definite and indefinite articles, demonstrative, numerical, and pronominal adjectives.

Our term "descriptive adverb" applies to Perrin's first five groupings (pages 421-22): adverbs of manner, time and succession, place and direction, degree and measure, cause and purpose. We discriminated, however, among members of his sixth group, distinguishing negatives from affirmatives ("yes," "indeed," "certainly"), "intensifiers" ("very" and "too" when followed by an adjective or adverb), and, lastly, what is sometimes called the "explicative" or "filler-word" ("there" in the phrase *"there* is. . .").

Although our experience in marking supports C. C. Fries' contention that the conventional distinction between "subordinating" and "coordinating" conjunctions is a meaningless one (see Fries' *American English Grammar,* New York, 1940, pages 206-40, for his discussion of conjunctions), we did discriminate these as well as correlatives and conjunctive adverbs. In the following figures for conjunctions where subordinating and coordinating conjunctions are contrasted, conjunctive adverbs have been omitted.

In marking clauses in sentences containing both dialogue and narrative, we treated dialogue as grammatically independent of the narrative, even when the dialogue was fragmentary, so that the material within quotation marks (or their equivalent) would not be marked as a clause completing a narrative verb, as in "He said, 'Go ahead. . . .' " In discriminating among subordinate clauses we followed Perrin except that among adverb clauses we identified separately only those of time, place, and cause, lumping all other types under the handy rubric of "other."

In most cases figures in the following tables are derived from samples consisting of passages from near the center of each novel, usually containing at least one full chapter and both dialogue and narration and providing at least 1500 words of continuous text. Occasionally we used groups (fifteen to fifty) of five consecutive sentences selected at random from throughout a novel. Such cases are indicated by the word

257

"random" in the list below, which provides the number of the chapter or chapters involved in the sample passages from which tabulations were derived. An asterisk indicates that for one reason or another we were unable to use material from the entire sample for some or all of our counts.

Northanger Abbey, random, I, 15, and II, 1; *Sense and Sensibility,* 26, 27; *Pride and Prejudice,* II, 7-9; *Mansfield Park,* II, 3, 4; *Emma,* random, II, 11; *Persuasion,* random, I, 12, and II, 1,4; *Lady Susan,** Letters 18-21; *The Professor,* 16; *Jane Eyre,* random, 21, 27; *Shirley,** 18; *Villette,* random, 21, 22; *The Spell** (edited by G. E. MacLean, London: Oxford University Press, 1931), 5; *Scenes from Clerical Life** (Cabinet edition), "Amos Barton," 5, "Mr. Gilfil," 5; *Adam Bede,** 23 and 24; *The Mill on the Floss,* random, 28, 29; *Silas Marner,* 10, 11; *Romola,** 23; *Felix Holt,* 22; *Middlemarch,* random, 41-44; *Daniel Deronda,* random, 35; *Oliver Twist* (introduction by J. Hillis Miller, Holt, Rinehart, Winston), 28, 29; *David Copperfield* (edited by George H. Ford, Houghton-Mifflin, Riverside),* 29, 30; *Bleak House* (edited by Morton D. Zabel, Houghton-Mifflin, Riverside),* 31, 32; *Great Expectations* (Doubleday, Dolphin Books),* 29, 30; *Our Mutual Friend* (afterword by J. Hillis Miller, New American Library, Signet),* 32; *Moll Flanders* (edited by James R. Sutherland, Houghton-Mifflin, Riverside), pp. 148-60; *Pamela* (introduction by William M. Sale, Jr., Norton, Norton Library), pp. 258-70; *Joseph Andrews* (edited by Martin C. Battestin, Houghton-Mifflin, Riverside), II, 4-5, 14-15; *Tom Jones* (introduction by George Sherburn, Random House, Modern Library College Edition), IX, 7-X, 2; *Evelina* (introduction by Lewis Gibbs, Everyman Library), Letters 46-48; *Old Mortality* (preface by W. M. Parker, Everyman Library),* 21, 22; *Wuthering Heights* (edited by V. S. Pritchett, Houghton-Mifflin, Riverside), 15, 16; *Agnes Grey* (introduction by Margaret Lane, Everyman Library),* 6-8; *The Tenant of Wildfell Hall* (introduction by Margaret Lane, Everyman Library),* 30; *Vanity Fair* (edited by Geoffrey and Kathleen Tillotson, Houghton-Mifflin, Riverside),* 32-34; *The Way We Live Now* (Oxford University Press, World's Classics),* I, 49-50; *Far From the Madding Crowd* (edited by Richard L. Purdy, Houghton-Mifflin, Riverside), 29, 31; *Jude the Obscure* (introduction by William E. Buckler, Dell, Laurel), IV, 1; *A Portrait of the Artist as a Young Man* (Viking Press, Compass Books),* pp. 124-46 (omitting sermon); *Jacob's Room* (Harcourt, Brace and World, Harvest Books), random, 6-8; *Sons and*

Lovers (Viking, Compass Books),* 8; *The Power and The Glory* (Viking, Compass Books),* II, 2.

Tables 1 and 1A show that proportions of various parts of speech do not significantly vary from one novelist to another; mere quantity in these categories does not permit stylistic discriminations (compare Tables 17 and 17A). It is true that Jane Austen employs relatively few concrete nouns and a relatively high proportion of proper nouns, and that, unlike Charlotte Brontë and George Eliot, she uses more concrete nouns in dialogue than she does in narrative (Table 2). These characteristics are doubtless of stylistic interest. More specific definition of "concreteness" and "abstractness" might well lead to useful insights—as might different kinds of categorization. But nothing in these talbles (or the others) refutes my assumption that in fictional style larger units are more important than smaller ones. In reading Tables 3 and 3A one must remember, for example, that first-person narrative will tend to produce a heavy weighting of "thing" subjects, because proper names are so often replaced by the pronoun "I."

Table 4 (and to a lesser extent 4A) indicates that verbals are useful as discriminators—although the significance of the discriminations they establish remains uncertain. Table 5 points up Jane Austen's preference for passive and copulative verbs. Table 6 reveals her relative fondness for verbs difficult to classify as those of either "physical" or "psychic" action. Table 7 shows that in relation to Brontë, Eliot, and Dickens, Jane Austen uses a high proportion of "modals" and a low proportion of "progressive" verbs. In all these verb counts one notices a tendency toward convergence in the figures for Austen and Eliot as against those for Brontë and Dickens, a convergence stylistically interesting because some elements, the modals and progressives, for instance, probably reflect long-term drifts in general language use. Although verb figures for other authors are too small for significance, Table 6A suggests that more specific categorizations, like a more specific distinction between concrete and abstract nouns, might produce stylistic discriminators of value.

Figures for adjectives and adverbs, Tables 8 through 12 and 8A through 12A, are difficult to evaluate, but they suggest that more intensive study of the *placement* and types of adjectives and adverbs favored by different novelists might be helpful. Of the four novelists for whom we have the largest figures, Charlotte Brontë most favors descriptive adjectives of quality, clusters these most densely, and least frequently employs the comparative and superlative degrees.

In some respects George Eliot's work stands out in the figures of Table 14, which indicates her heavy use of subordinate clauses and her tendency to interrupt them frequently. Reflected by these figures is her use of syntactic structures which do not adhere to simple sequential ordering. Characteristics such as these need to be considered in any evaluation of the figures in Tables 15, 15A, 16, and 16A, which of course do not indicate the critical feature of the positioning of clauses.

In Tables 19 and 22 I have tried to put together reasonably comparable sets of figures which will place the works of Jane Austen, Charlotte Brontë, and George Eliot in a "frame" of an eighteenth-century predecessor and a twentieth-century successor. Three observations are pertinent. First, Table 21 confirms the view that gross figures for major parts of speech are not of much use for stylistic analysis. Second, more precise and restricted discriminations within parts of speech, although these would require the analysis of large bodies of material, might also lead to insights into patterns of style. The positioning of elements would have to be studied carefully, and the frequency of their occurrence in relation to other elements would have to be systematically described. The need for such refinements is suggested, for example, by columns one and three in Table 22, in which are observable Virginia Woolf's low proportion of pronouns to nouns in both narrative and dialogue. But the relation of the prounoun-noun proportions in narrative and dialogue is about the same for all the novelists, suggesting that this is one of those situations of "dissimilitude in similitude" which ought to be of special interest to the student of style.

Finally, Tables 19 and 20 illustrate that in general the most widely varying figures are those for *Joseph Andrews* and *Jacob's Room* but that there is almost never a simple, orderly chronological progression from Fielding to Virginia Woolf. As so often with these figures, it is the negative finding that is most interesting. In this case failures of simple chronological progression suggest that elements of fictional style work against, or to some degree mitigate, the effect of "general" writing style, the currents in social conventions of language use which doubtless influence fictional art. In sum, though they are as yet undefined, there do seem to be historical patterns within the language of fiction distinctive enough to make their presence felt even amidst gross quantitative compilations of simple syntactic elements and structures.

1. PARTS OF SPEECH–GENERAL

	Austen	Brontë	Eliot	Dickens
Nouns	3955	2812	5564	4149
Pronouns	2318	1882	3038	3156
Verbs	2543	1983	3531	3117
Prepositions	2377	1428	3144	2383
Adjectives	4185	2994	5889	4187
Adverbs	2062	1123	2270	2154
Conjunctions	1574	933	1960	1716
Verbals	1127	837	1527	1211
1-word verbs	1583	1403	2199	2290
Compound verbs	960	580	1332	827
Descriptive adjectives	1575	1135	2369	1467
Descriptive adverbs	1107	759	1261	1465

1A. PARTS OF SPEECH–GENERAL

	Defoe	Richardson	Fielding	Burney	Scott	E. Brontë	A. Brontë	Thackeray	Trollope	Hardy	Woolf	Lawrence	Greene	Joyce
Nouns	769	660	1618	790	718	835	1245	1361	805	941	2212	810	447	220
Pronuons	890	828	919	767	301	700	1016	492	546	582	756	607	218	104
Verbs	750	690	938	681	320	689	866	700	560	587	1130	745	289	122
Prepositions	534	427	917	443	470	472	769	715	417	526	907	312	219	124
Adjectives	920	797	1538	729	681	892	1365	1354	663	1027	1882	799	478	197
Adverbs	502	454	702	511	199	408	625	379	303	449	607	419	170	75
Conjunctions	529	495	548	321	225	358	690	451	292	357	681	202	114	67
Verbals	251	241	456	250	162	344	354	215	149	225	354	233	71	46
1-word verbs	503	428	607	439	198	482	537	455	319	404		592	201	79
Compound verbs	247	262	331	242	122	207	329	245	241	183		153	88	43
Descriptive adjectives	134	310	489	138	234	267	486	418	244	315	434	273	110	64
Descriptive adverbs	256	235	406	388	87	322	458	205	227	347	523	294	149	62

2. NOUNS—CONCRETE AND ABSTRACT, IN NARRATIVE AND DIALOGUE

	Narrative		*Dialogue*	
	Concrete	Abstract	Concrete	Abstract
Austen	838	1242	439	355
Brontë	370	422	247	321
Eliot	221	553	136	248

3. NOUNS—SUBJECTS OF SENTENCES AND CLAUSES WHICH ARE THINGS AND PERSONS

	Total number of nouns subjects	Number of subjects things	Number of subjects persons
Austen	898	379	519
Brontë	478	303	175
Eliot	1218	455	763
Dickens	688	327	361

3A. NOUNS–SUBJECTS OF SENTENCES AND CLAUSES WHICH ARE THINGS AND PERSONS

	Total number of nouns subjects	Number of subjects things	Number of subjects persons
Defoe	97	42	55
Richardson	59	32	27
Fielding	289	86	203
Burney	194	67	127
Scott	116	51	65
E. Brontë	146	86	60
A. Brontë	160	73	87
Thackeray	287	113	174
Trollope	174	47	127
Hardy	185	111	74
Lawrence	254	71	183
Greene	96	45	51
Joyce	53	35	18

4. VERBALS

	Total verbals	Percent infinitive	Percent present participle	Percent past participle	Percent gerund
Austen	1127	49%	12%	9%	30%
Brontë	837	35	22	20	23
Eliot	1527	44	18	12	26
Dickens	1211	43	24	14	19

4A. VERBALS

	Total verbals	Number infinitive	Number present participle	Number past participle	Number gerund
Defoe	251	156	24	28	43
Richardson	241	138	28	38	37
Fielding	466	187	87	60	132
Burney	250	114	58	32	46
Scott	162	77	25	27	33
E. Brontë	344	106	63	58	117
A. Brontë	354	175	65	67	47
Thackeray	215	103	51	36	25
Trollope	149	83	36	12	18
Hardy	225	112	52	25	36
Lawrence	233	73	67	35	58
Greene	71	29	36	5	1
Joyce	46	21	23	0	2

5. VERBS–ACTIVE, PASSIVE, COPULATIVE, IN NARRATIVE AND DIALOGUE

	Narrative				*Dialogue*			
	Active	Passive	Copulative	Total	Active	Passive	Copulative	Total
Austen	835	120	357	1312	571	29	287	887
	64%	9%	27%	100%	65%	3%	32%	100%
Brontë	757	44	208	1009	460	18	151	629
	75%	4%	21%	100%	73%	3%	24%	100%
Eliot	1210	146	442	1798	812	33	247	1092
	67%	8%	25%	100%	74%	3%	23%	100%
Dickens	1115	79	331	1525	559	22	214	795
	73%	5%	22%	100%	70%	3%	27%	100%

5A. VERBS–ACTIVE, PASSIVE, COPULATIVE, IN NARRATIVE AND DIALOGUE

	Narrative			*Dialogue*		
	Active	Passive	Copulative	Active	Passive	Copulative
Defoe	356	12	126	7	2	3
Richardson	429	27	117	24	2	9
Fielding	413	51	114	50	0	21
Burney	203	29	47	85	2	23
Scott	93	13	25	71	7	18
E. Brontë	301	20	72	167	3	40
A. Brontë	327	34	86	205	9	72
Thackeray	351	48	106	38	2	15
Trollope	270	29	85	113	5	13
Hardy	212	26	84	140	4	49
Lawrence	283	14	67	96	0	20
Greene	145	4	27	40	1	5
Joyce	92	12	5	11	0	2

6. VERBS–PHYSICAL, PSYCHIC, OTHER

	Physical	Psychic	Other	Ratio of psychic to physical	Ratio of other to psychic and physical
Austen	699	324	1032	.46	1.00
Brontë	933	290	555	.31	.45
Eliot	1158	523	1246	.45	.74
Dickens	1611	448	982	.28	.48

6A. VERBS–PHYSICAL, PSYCHIC, OTHER

	Physical	Psychic	Other	Ratio of psychic to physical	Ratio of other to psychic and physical
Defoe	189	89	472	.47	1.70
Richardson	269	124	297	.46	.76
Fielding	348	243	347	.70	.59
Burney	361	128	192	.35	.39
Scott	44	56	170	1.30	1.70
E. Brontë	373	166	150	.45	.28
A. Brontë	458	187	221	.41	.34
Thackeray	354	96	250	.27	.56
Trollope	232	78	250	.35	.81
Hardy	197	81	309	.41	1.10
Lawrence	450	60	235	.13	.46
Greene	177	28	84	.16	.41
Joyce	77	14	31	.18	.34

7. VERBS—MODALS AND PROGRESSIVES

	Total verbs	Modal verbs	Ratio of modals to total verbs	Multi-word verbs	Progressive verbs	Ratio of progressives to multi-word verbs	Ratio of multi-word verbs to total verbs	Ratio of modals to simple verbs
Austen	2543	401	.16	960	110	.115	.39	.23
Brontë	1983	207	.10	580	90	.155	.29	.14
Eliot	3531	466	.13	1332	185	.140	.38	.20
Dickens	3117	311	.10	827	135	.165	.26	.13

7A. VERBS–MODALS AND PROGRESSIVES

	Total verbs	Modal verbs	Multi-word verbs	Progressive verbs
Defoe	750	109	247	24
Richardson	690	106	262	5
Fielding	938	128	331	21
Burney	681	95	242	43
Scott	320	31	122	10
E. Brontë	689	74	207	41
A. Brontë	866	174	329	49
Thackeray	700	72	245	29
Trollope	560	86	241	49
Hardy	587	62	183	35
Woolf	1130	50		30
Lawrence	745	53	153	52
Greene	289	30	88	31
Joyce	122	18	43	10

8. DESCRIPTIVE ADJECTIVES

	Percent of total adjectives descriptive	Ratio of descriptive adjectives of measure to descriptive adjectives of quality	Ratio of total adverbs to total adjectives	Ratio of total descriptive adverbs to total descriptive adjectives
Austen	38%	.48	.48	.70
Brontë	38%	.30	.38	.67
Eliot	40%	.43	.39	.55
Dickens	35%	.42	.51	.92

8A. DESCRIPTIVE ADJECTIVES

	Ratio of descriptive adjectives to total adjectives	Ratio of descriptive adjectives of measure to descriptive adjectives of quality	Ratio of total adverbs to total adjectives	Ratio of total descriptive adverbs to total descriptive adjectives
Defoe	134/920	53/181	502/920	256/134
Richardson	310/797	66/244	454/797	235/310
Fielding	489/1538	223/266	702/1538	406/489
Burney	138/729	49/89	511/729	388/138
Scott	234/681	31/201	199/681	87/234
E. Brontë	267/892	39/228	408/892	322/267
A. Brontë	486/1365	38/192	625/1365	458/486
Thackeray	418/1354	78/340	379/1354	205/418
Trollope	244/663	86/158	303/663	227/244
Hardy	315/1027	29/286	449/1027	347/315
Woolf	434/1882		607/1882	523/434
Lawrence	273/799	44/229	419/799	294/273
Greene	110/478	7/103	170/478	149/110
Joyce	64/197	18/46	75/197	62/64

9. ADJECTIVES IMMEDIATELY PRECEDING NOUNS

	Percent of total descriptive adjectives which immediately precede nouns	Percent of total articles which immediately precede nouns	Percent of total limiting adjectives which immediately precede nouns
Austen	25%	47%	36%
Brontë	24	55	47
Eliot	23	45	33
Dickens	21	68	48

9A. ADJECTIVES IMMEDIATELY PRECEDING NOUNS

	Ratio of descriptive adjectives which immediately precede nouns to total descriptive adjectives
Defoe	40/134
Richardson	82/310
Fielding	138/489
Burney	57/138
Scott	72/234
E. Brontë	158/267
A. Brontë	121/486
Thackeray	89/418
Trollope	59/244
Hardy	58/315
Lawrence	50/273
Greene	28/110
Joyce	26/64

10. DESCRIPTIVE ADJECTIVES—GROUPING

*Percent of total descriptive adjectives separated
from another descriptive adjective by:*

	0 words	1 word	2 words	0, 1, and 2 words
Austen	8.5%	5.6%	6.1%	20.2%
Brontë	12.0	7.5	8.1	27.6
Eliot	7.5	5.0	6.3	18.8
Dickens	7.0	6.4	4.2	17.6

10A. DESCRIPTIVE ADJECTIVES—GROUPING

*Number of total descriptive adjectives separated
from another descriptive adjective by:*

	0 words	1 word	2 words	0, 1, and 2 words	Total descriptive adjectives
Defoe	4	10	4	18	134
Richardson	20	10	15	45	310
Fielding	25	24	15	64	489
Burney	9	14	10	33	138
Scott	14	16	9	39	234
E. Brontë	16	15	15	46	267
A. Bronte	52	22	32	106	486
Thackeray	34	23	26	83	418
Trollope	14	10	14	38	244
Hardy	25	12	14	57	315
Woolf	49	45	33	127	434
Lawrence	39	27	20	86	273
Greene	18	2	2	22	110
Joyce	4	5	3	12	64

11. COMPARISON OF ADJECTIVES

	Percent of total adjectives comparative	Percent of total adjectives superlative	Percent of total adjectives comparative and superlative
Austen	6.2%	5.7%	11.9%
Brontë	4.0	2.8	6.8
Eliot	6.3	4.3	10.6
Dickens	6.5	3.3	9.8

11A. COMPARISON OF ADJECTIVES

	Number of positive adjectives	Number of comparative adjectives	Number of superlative adjectives	Number comparative and superlative adjectives
Defoe	192	6	11	17
Richardson	175	8	8	16
Fielding	285	20	16	36
Burney	179	0	13	13
Scott	109	13	5	18
E. Brontë	172	17	7	24
A. Brontë	341	43	16	59
Thackeray	214	14	7	21
Trollope	135	6	4	10
Hardy	246	13	5	18
Lawrence	185	7	2	9
Greene	71	6	2	8
Joyce	43	2	0	2

12. ADVERBS

	Percent of total adverbs descriptive	Percent of total adverbs which are intensifiers
Austen	54%	15%
Brontë	67	7
Eliot	56	8
Dickens	68	8

12A. ADVERBS

	Total adverbs	Number of descriptive adverbs	Number of adverbs which are intensifiers
Defoe	502	256	60
Richardson	454	235	94
Fielding	702	406	78
Burney	511	388	28
Scott	199	87	35
E. Brontë	408	322	8
A. Brontë	625	458	22
Thackeray	379	205	66
Trollope	303	227	24
Hardy	449	347	39
Woolf	607	523	30
Lawrence	419	294	10
Greene	170	149	14
Joyce	75	62	1

13. RATIO OF SUBORDINATING CONJUNCTIONS TO CONNECTING CONJUNCTIONS

	In narrative sentences	In dialogue sentences
Austen	.48	.59
Brontë	.57	.55
Eliot	.64	.66
Dickens	.73	.71

14. CLAUSES—MAIN, SUBORDINATE, AND INTERRUPTED

	Number of main clauses	Number of subordinate clauses	Ratio of subordinate clauses to main clauses	Number of main clauses interrupted	Number of subordinate clauses interrupted
Austen	1684	937	.56	249	67
Brontë	1429	499	.35	168	20
Eliot	2160	1521	.71	187	101
Dickens	2012	1078	.54	218	45

14A. CLAUSES–MAIN, SUBORDINATE, AND INTERRUPTED

	Number of main clauses	Number of subordinate clauses	Ratio of subordinate clauses to main clauses	Number of main clauses interrupted	Number of subordinate clauses interrupted
Defoe	437	328	.75	72	1
Richardson	389	392	1.00	92	104
Fielding	498	465	.94	144	34
Burney	453	254	.56	48	23
Scott	182	155	.85	32	17
E. Brontë	482	189	.39	30	8
A. Brontë	509	325	.64	41	19
Thackeray	539	349	.65	102	84
Trollope	362	188	.52	22	7
Hardy	341	231	.68	19	9
Lawrence	584	106	.18	21	2
Greene	212	56	.26	12	1
Joyce	81	33	.41	6	1

15. SUBORDINATE CLAUSES

	Total clauses analyzed	Total noun clauses	Restrictive adjective clauses	Nonrestrictive adjective clauses	Total adjective clauses	Total adverb clauses	Adverb clauses of time	Adverb clauses of cause
Austen	890	359	135	113	248	283	139	61
Brontë	458	150	89	33	122	186	75	43
Eliot	1466	512	312	139	451	503	218	130
Dickens	1012	341	149	90	239	432	196	91

15A. SUBORDINATE CLAUSES

	Total noun clauses	Restrictive adjective clauses	Nonrestrictive adjective clauses	Total adjective clauses	Total adverb clauses	Adverb clauses of time	Adverb clauses of cause
Defoe	148	44	17	61	90	21	15
Richardson	141	44	48	92	118	50	4
Fielding	139	99	64	163	143	38	41
Burney	90	23	44	67	97	30	7
Scott	55	33	27	60	38	20	0
E. Brontë	66	31	16	47	61	29	8
A. Brontë	118	25	28	53	122	42	37
Thackeray	110	54	60	114	117	77	0
Trollope	64	6	27	33	56	27	26
Hardy	74	26	35	61	85	45	35
Lawrence	34	16	4	20	50	24	12
Greene	13	7	13	20	19	9	8
Joyce	15	1	1	2	14	1	2

16. CLAUSE STRUCTURE OF NARRATIVE AND DIALOGUE SENTENCES

	Narrative				*Dialogue*			
	Total narrative sentences	Simple sentences	Compound sentences	Compound-complex and complex sentences	Simple sentences	Compound sentences	Compound-complex and complex sentences	Total dialogue sentences
Austen	430	115	52	263	187	47	179	413
Brontë	285	96	70	119	87	53	99	239
Eliot	391	93	28	270	128	66	224	418
Dickens	394	97	47	250	191	40	138	369

16A. CLAUSE STRUCTURE OF NARRATIVE AND DIALOGUE SENTENCES

	Narrative				*Dialogue*			
	Simple sentences	Compound sentences	Complex sentences	Compound-complex and complex sentences	Simple sentences	Compound sentences	Complex sentences	Compound-complex and complex sentences
Defoe	3	7	10	44	2	0	1	1
Richardson	27	10	65	43	3	2	3	3
Fielding	16	9	74	48	6	1	5	10
Burney	16	7	0	24	12	4	7	1
Scott	9	3	15	10	8	0	14	11
E. Brontë	30	28	21	43	58	16	22	11
A. Brontë	27	13	31	40	22	15	19	30
Thackeray	92	17	90	70	9	5	15	3
Trollope	75	21	64	14	41	6	30	3
Hardy	34	12	54	17	38	11	21	15
Woolf	224	47	70	60	30	0	15	3
Lawrence	162	21	41	2	53	3	14	1
Greene	24	18	14	11	21	1	7	2
Joyce	8	10	40	68	16	9	19	10

17. PERCENT MAJOR PARTS OF SPEECH

	Nouns	Verbs	Descriptive adjectives	Descriptive adverbs
Austen	43%	28%	17%	12%
Brontë	42	30	17	11
Eliot	44	28	19	9
Dickens	41	31	14	14

17A. PERCENT OF MAJOR PARTS OF SPEECH

	Nouns	Verbs	Descriptive adjectives	Descriptive adverbs
Defoe	38%	37%	12%	13%
Richardson	35	36	16	13
Fielding	47	27	14	12
Burney	40	34	7	19
Scott	53	24	17	6
E. Brontë	40	33	13	14
A. Brontë	41	28	16	15
Thackeray	51	26	16	7
Trollope	44	30	13	13
Hardy	43	27	14	16
Lawrence	38	35	13	14
Greene	45	29	11	15
Joyce	48	22	16	14

18. NARRATIVE, DIALOGUE, AND MIXED SENTENCES

	Total words	Total sentences	Number of narrative sentences	Total non-dialogue and non-mixed sentences	Number dialogue sentences	Number of mixed sentences	Ratio of narrative to all non-dialogue	Ratio of mixed to dialogue
Austen	46,161	1858	701	934	764	160	.75	.21
Brontë	24,981	1216	487	609	492	115	.80	.23
Eliot	41,124	1599	529	779	575	245	.68	.43
Dickens	23,733	1240	415	493	476	271	.84	.57

18A. NARRATIVE, DIALOGUE, AND MIXED SENTENCES

	Total words	Total sentences	Number of narrative sentences	Total non-dialogue and non-mixed sentences	Number dialogue sentences	Number of mixed sentences	Ratio of narrative to all non-dialogue	Ratio of mixed to dialogue
Defoe	5611	140	54	88	5	47	.61	9.40
Richardson	5070	186	90	156	13	17	.58	1.30
Fielding	8163	224	69	162	25	37	.43	1.40
Burney	4970	206	64	88	45	73	.73	1.60
Scott	3281	107	31	49	34	24	.63	.71
E. Brontë	4987	285	111	135	117	33	.82	.28
A. Brontë	7532	252	97	118	101	33	.82	.33
Thackeray	6088	258	158	194	25	39	.82	1.60
Trollope	4180	291	128	181	90	20	.71	.22
Hardy	5042	248	94	124	102	22	.76	.22
Woolf	9006	561	97	416	62	83	.23	1.30
Lawrence	4405	439	207	228	85	126	.91	1.50
Greene	2161	136	52	68	44	24	.77	.55
Joyce	2569	180	162	172	8	0	.94	0

19. SUBORDINATION IN NARRATIVE, DIALOGUE, AND MIXED SENTENCES

	Narrative		*Dialogue*		*Mixed*	
	Number main–subordinate clauses	Ratio of subordinate to main clauses	Number main–subordinate clauses	Ratio of subordinate to main clauses	Number main–subordinate clauses	Ratio of subordinate to main clauses
Joseph Andrews	179–192	1.07	85–55	0.65	231–134	0.58
Northanger Abbey and Emma	314–175	0.56	249–154	0.62	94–58	0.62
Jane Eyre	308–161	0.52	319–146	0.46	123–51	0.41
Middlemarch	170–199	1.17	165–109	0.66	92–39	0.42
Jacob's Room	372–132	0.35	53–22	0.42	167–31	0.19

20. SUBORDINATION IN COMPLEX AND COMPOUND-COMPLEX SENTENCES

	Complex			Compound-Complex		
	Number of main clauses	Number of subordinate clauses	Ratio of subordinate to main clauses	Number of main clauses	Number of subordinate clauses	Ratio of subordinate to main clauses
Joseph Andrews	**73**	126	1.73	367	346	.94
Northanger Abbey and Emma	105	141	1.34	450	396	.88
Jane Eyre	104	144	1.38	383	260	.68
Middlemarch	155	251	1.62	190	159	.84
Jacob's Room	150	135	0.90	244	157	.64

21. NUMBER AND PERCENTAGES OF PARTS OF SPEECH BY SENTENCE TYPE AND STRUCTURE

	Joseph Andrews	Northanger Abbey *and* Emma	Jane Eyre	Middlemarch	Jacob's Room
Narrative					
Nouns	681	1047	873	849	1049
	35%	35%	32%	35%	37%
Verbs	367	506	488	395	499
	19%	17%	18%	16%	18%
Adjectives	732	1087	1081	912	1005
	37%	36%	39%	38%	36%
Adverbs	194	379	328	266	269
	10%	13%	12%	11%	9%
Dialogue					
Nouns	167	493	581	336	118
	29%	29%	30%	30%	41%
Verbs	138	406	487	277	67
	24%	24%	25%	25%	23%
Adjectives	185	496	543	382	68
	33%	29%	28%	34%	23%
Adverbs	79	292	305	137	38
	14%	17%	16%	12%	13%
Simple					
Nouns	75	289	237	191	632
	34%	36%	34%	34%	39%
Verbs	32	142	147	105	281
	15%	17%	21%	19%	17%
Adjectives	82	279	210	175	545
	37%	35%	30%	31%	34%
Adverbs	32	104	98	92	157
	15%	13%	14%	16%	10%

TABLE 21. (continued)

	Joseph Andrews	Northanger Abbey *and* Emma	Jane Eyre	Middlemarch	Jacob's Room
Compound-Complex					
Nouns	1052	1455	761	616	730
	32%	32%	28%	34%	37%
Verbs	717	869	681	355	400
	22%	19%	25%	20%	20%
Adjectives	1130	1524	883	657	635
	35%	34%	33%	36%	32%
Adverbs	369	643	369	178	216
	11%	14%	14%	10%	11%

(Rounding-off can produce totals not exactly 100%.)

22. RATIO OF PRONOUNS TO NOUNS AND CONJUNCTIONS TO VERBS

	Narrative		*Dialogue*	
	Ratio of pronouns	Ratio of conjunctions	Ratio of pronouns	Ratio of conjunctions
Joseph Andrews	.49	.76	1.00	.71
Northanger Abbey and Emma	.41	.82	.95	.61
Jane Eyre	.51	.62	.94	.49
Middlemarch	.41	.73	.93	.52
Jacob's Room	.29	.65	.64	.27

INDEX

audience and point of view, 43-
48, 50-51, 59-60, 63, 136, 176
Austen, Jane: adjectives and adverbs, 14-15; and readers, 44-
46, 59-60; and Wordsworth,
83-84; as storyteller, 63; characterization, 29-30, 33-36; characters, individual and representative, 34-36, 71-72, 75,
126-28; character movement,
146-47, 157-59; characters,
number, 145-46; conventionality, 125; dialogue, 144-45, 177;
dialogue sentences, 169-70,
178-79; disappointed lover
scenes, 64-84; emotions, 65, 69,
72-74, 77-80, 82-83; emphasis
on meaning, 174; form, superficial and concealed, 23-26,
182-84; formality of presentation, 67, 69; irony, 51-53, 61-
63, 76-77; love, contrast with
Brontë, 129-33; minor characters, 42, 145-48; mixed sentences, 170-77, 179-80; names,
20n; narrative action, 144-45;
narrative sentences, 167-68,
178; nouns, 11-13; omniscience,
contrasted with Eliot's, 59-60;
plot structure, 147-48, 163;
point of view, 44-46; pronouns,
16; proper names, 16, 188-89;
protagonists and secondary figures, 73n; realism compared to
Eliot's, 118; relation to Brontë,
Eliot, 6-8; satire, 49; settings,
143-44; society, acceptance of,
109; style, 151-80 passim; style
as clarification, 68; style described, 182-83, 186-89; style
development as nonmetaphoric,
64-84; style transpicuous, 79,
186-89; subject focus, 163; temporal perspective, 81-84; time
structure, 21, 142-43, 160;
verbs, 13-14, 26n

works:
  Emma, 15-23, 62-63, 75-79,
  151-80 passim, 185-89; chapter
  beginnings, 19-21; chapter
  structure, 159; characterization,
  29-30, 154-56; character movement, 157-59; conscious processes, 155-56; contrasted with
  Middlemarch, Villette, 151-80
  passim; conversation, 151, 155-
  56; dialogue contrasted with
  Middlemarch, 177; dialogue
  sentences, 169-70; form, superficial and concealed, 23-26,
  182-84; generation gap, 186n;
  images, 85; mixed sentences,
  170-77; narrative and dialogue,
  174-75; narrative and dialogue
  sentences, 167-68; resolution
  of, 22; sentence lengths, 167-
  68; settings, 159-60; subject
  focus, 163; time structure, 21,
  160; verbs, 26n
  Mansfield Park, 72-75; and
  Jane Eyre, 87-88; and Felix
  Holt, 138-39; and Shirley, 129-
  31, 133; resolution of, 124-28
  Northanger Abbey, 34, 44-
  45, 49, 64-65
  Persuasion, 79-84, 110, 144
  Pride and Prejudice, 10n, 61-
  62, 68-72
  Sense and Sensibility, 51-53,
  65-68

Babb, Howard S., 45n
Beaty, Jerome, 98n
Beebe, Maurice, 99n
Booth, Wayne, 43
Bradbrook, Frank, 45n, 187n
Bradley, A. C., 45n
Briggs, Asa, 36n
Brontë, Charlotte: adjectives and
adverbs, 14-15; and Austen on
love, 129-33; and convention-
ality, 87, 176; and Dickens,
192n; and Eliot's characteriza-

289